Tribal Education

ABOUT THE EDITOR

S.N. Chaudhary, Professor of Sociology and former Dean, Faculty of Social Science is currently Rajiv Gandhi Chair Professor at Barkatullah University Bhopal, Madhya Pradesh. He has also been a fellow of the A.N. Sinha Institute of Social Studies, Patna, Indian Institute of Advanced Study, Shimla and SMH Paris. He has also conducted field work among Red Indians in British Columbia (Canada). Dr. Chaudhary produced 30 Ph.Ds., completed 27 research projects and published 27 books and 57 research articles. Currently Professor Chaudhary is working on Tribal Indebtedness, Impact of Technology on Society, Suicide among Tribal Farmers and Tribal Development.

TRIBAL EDUCATION

Implications for Development

Edited by

S.N. Chaudhary

CONCEPT PUBLISHING COMPANY PVT. LTD.,
NEW DELHI-110059

ISBN-13: 978-81-8069-904-7

First Published 2012

Published and Printed by

Concept
Since 1974

Concept Publishing Company Pvt. Ltd.
A/15-16, Commercial Block, Mohan Garden
New Delhi-110059 (India)
T: 25351460, 25351794, *F*: 091-11-25357109
E: publishing@conceptpub.com, W: www.conceptpub.com
Editorial Office: H-13, Bali Nagar, New Delhi-110 015, India.

Cataloging in Publication Data–*Courtesy:* D.K. Agencies (P) Ltd. <docinfo@dkagencies.com>

Tribal education : implications for development / edited by S.N. Chaudhary.
p. cm.
Includes bibliographical references and index.
ISBN 9788180699047

1. Tribes—Education—India—Congresses. 2. Tribes—Education—Government policy—India—Congresses.I. Chaudhary, S. N. (Shyam Nandan),1954-

DDC 371.826940954 23

Foreword

It does not require any deep corroboration to mention that tribes are among the socially and educationally most disadvantaged groups in India. There is an obvious historical underpinning behind this situation. For centuries, tribes lived in relatively isolated regions of the country and in closer proximity to forests and natural resources. This has afforded them a measure of cultural autonomy and economic independence. Their education thus was characteristically marked by skill development in recognizing and optimally utilizing natural resources available in the vicinity of their habitat, mostly for daily sustenance. This was the kind of informal education that was passed on from parents to children. Education for the tribes was, therefore, for subsistence rather than for market and employment.

The nature of education is always commensurate with its place and method. Since the nature of education was informal, the place was always either within the settlement or deep inside the forest. Example may be cited of youth dormitories like the Gond *ghotul* or Oraon *dhumkuria* or Juang *majang*, which were traditionally centers of education and learning, besides acquainting the tribal youth about the customary practices. The teachers invariably were the tribal elders and experienced persons, most informally imparting moral education and soft skills in their own mother-tongue. By the time the tribal children were ready to get married and settle in life, their essential training in morality, religion and subsistence skills was almost complete. This rendered them no more eligible as a member of these dormitories with a social sanction to live as a householder.

Situations have changed considerably in recent times. There is a heightened eagerness by the government and others to bring the tribes to the 'mainstream' by formally educating them. This is certainly a laudable effort. But for some obvious reasons, many problems are encountered and many experiments are undertaken in the field of tribal education. Problems relating to relevance of curricula, quality of education, infrastructure, enrolment and dropout rates, school timings, quality of teachers and teacher training etc. are abound in the area of tribal education, which have made the tribes disenchanted to the system of modern school education by chewing everything unfamiliar and alien. As a result, the literacy rate among the Scheduled Tribes could not teach even 50 per cent by 2001.

The most vexed problem in tribal schools is the medium of instruction. Even in pre-primary and primary stages, there is an attempt to impose all kinds of language training on the tribal child than its own mother-tongue. To contravene this dodgy trend, there have been several attempts. I am familiar with such an endeavour in tribal Odisha, which began in 2007 in 200 tribal schools, where children were taught through their mother tongues in the first grades, with materials collected from children, parents and teachers. Prior to this in the year 2004, the Government of Andhra Pradesh introduced similar education from the Grade 1 in 100 schools on an experimental basis. In both the states, experts say, class room performance of the tribal students taught in their mother tongue is better than those studying in the media of the state languages, Odiya and Telugu respectively, despite huge pedagogic problems involved in these experiments. The question, then, is why to impose alien concepts, ideologies and practices, when the tribes can still do well with their own.

The great social scientist of our times, Professor Amartya Sen asserts that poverty is 'capability deprivation' and 'unfreedom'. He adds further that education is a major capability input, while illiteracy a lack of freedom that restricts economic opportunities. School education directly enhances opportunities through easier access to jobs and income and, equally importantly, it adds to social and cultural freedom and empowers persons for adequate participation is exercise of political rights. Therefore, it is imperative to closely monitor the educational system in tribal India, so that they are free from poverty, and are not deprived of economic opportunities, social and cultural freedom, and political rights. I think, this is the right way to ensure development of the tribes in India.

I am extremely delighted that Professor Chaudhary has edited this volume with 20 brilliant and thought provoking essays by very distinguished scholars. All these essays are pregnant with rich empirical information and their deep analysis. I am sure the volume will be of immense interest to educationists, psychologists, anthropologists, sociologists, development administrators, NGOs and students of tribal studies. I congratulate Professor Chaudhary for this excellently edited and presented volume.

Bhopal
9th March 2012

Professor Kamal K. Misra
Director
IGRMS, Bhopal &
AnSI, Kolkata

Preface

The history of informal education among scheduled tribes is very old. Long back it existed orally and its prime function was to capacitate young generation to control and adjust with the local environment. The nature of education was practical and need based. Youth organizations played crucial role in the transmission of cultural heritage from old to the new generation. However, with the passage of time amount of acculturation between tribals and non-tribals increased. And with this the so-called isolationistic approach of tribal development, adopted by the alien administration, was replaced by the so-called integrative approach. There are many functions and dysfunctions of this approach of development and its management. One of the dysfunctional consequences of the so-called integrative approach of tribal development is socio-cultural assimilation and rampant loss of tribal identity. Without any meaningful gain from sustainable development and empowerment perspective. Today tribals are the serious victim of civilizational loss.

In the field of education, in contrary to the ongoing traditional system of informal education, the new experiment was made in the tribal world by the state and civil societies through the introduction of what may be called "Methodical education". Role of Christian Missionaries, Ramakrishna Mission and such other organizations and individuals are very vital in this context. A new definition of literacy and education was planted in the tribal world. The nature of education was formal and alien which completely ignored the local features while formulating its course content. Number of experiments have been made among tribals during the last 65 years in order to popularize literacy and primary education among them. Attempts have also been made to associate tribals with secondary and higher level education.

But in spite of these interventions, right from literacy level to higher education level, the trend of improvement is not upto the mark. Tribals are lagging behind even from scheduled castes in the field of literacy and also all types of education at all the levels. What are the factors and conditions responsible for this state of affair? What efforts have been made to popularize formal education among tribals? What are the levels of development in both qualitative and quantitative terms? How fruits of education and education based opportunity may be made available to tribal masses especially in an era of globalization? These are some of the broad issues in the light of which two days national seminar was organized by Rajiv Gandhi Chair, Barkatullah University, Bhopal in August 2011 in collaboration with Anthropological Survey of India (ASI), Kolkata. We received massive support and guidance from the Director of ASI Professor K.K. Mishra. He was also kind enough to write foreword of this volume. I am extremely obliged and thankful to him.

I am thankful to Prof. Virginius Xaxa, and Prof. Ramjee Singh, who delivered keynote address and valedictory address in the seminar respectively. Prof. Yogesh Atal was kind enough to deliver special lecture on this occasion. Vice-Chancellor Prof. Nisha Dube was also kind enough to grace the inaugural and valedictory function of the seminar by her precious presence and valuable comments. I am thankful to her. I extent my sincere thanks to chair persons and paper-presents for their kind cooperation. Dr. Amithab Sarkar of ASI and his colleague Dr. N.K. Dauray was kind enough to provide logistic support. They also contributed by their physical presence in the seminar. I am obliged to both of them. I am also thankful to Prof. H.V. Tiwary, Prof. P.K. Verma and Shri R.N. Berwa for their gracious presence in the inaugural and valedictory function of the seminar as chief guest and guest of honour.

Last but not the least I am thankful to all the research scholars and field assistants working under the chair for their day and night work to ensure success of the seminar. Dr. Manish Mishra, Research Associate, helped from the very beginning to organize the seminar in a successful manner. He constantly worked to approach the participants and others to ensure success of the seminar. I am thankful to him. I am also thankful to all employees of the university who directly or indirectly helped in the organization of the seminar.

There are 20 articles in this volume. I am thankful to all those, who on my request took pain to provide revised version of their articles for publication. Towards the end I am thankful to Shri Ashok Kumar Mittal for publishing the book within the stipulated time frame.

Bhopal
3rd March 2012 **Prof. S.N. Chaudhary**

Contents

Contributors

Chaturbhuj Sahu, Head, Dept. of Anthropology, VBU, Hazaribagh, Jharkhand.

Debashis Debnath, Associate Professor, IIFM, Bhopal, Madhya Pradesh.

J.J. Roy Burman, Professor, TISS, Mumbai, Maharashtra

K.P. Pothen, Professor (Retd.), DAVV, Indore, Madhya Pradesh

K.R. Sharma, Prof. (Retd.), Regional Education Centre, Bhopal, Madhya Pradesh

Kashnug Zingran Kengoo, Research Scholar, TISS, Mumbai, Maharashtra

Palash C. Coomar, Joint Director, Census Operation, GoI , New Delhi

R.D. Singh, HOD, RPEG, BU, Bhopal, Madhya Pradesh

R.S. Shrivastava, Dy. Director (Retd.), Tribal Welfare Department, GoMP, Bhopal, Madhya Pradesh

Ramjee Singh, Ex M.P., Patna, Bihar

Ratnawali Sinha, Assistant Professor, Centre for Social Studies, Surat, Gujarat

S.K. Biswas, Associate Professor, JNR College, Port Blair, Andaman and Nicobar Islands

S.N. Tripathy, Professor, Gokhale Institute of Economics and Politics, Pune, Maharashtra

S. Prabhakar, Joint Director, Lok Sabha, New Delhi

S.N. Chaudhary, Professor, RGC, BU, Bhopal, Madhya Pradesh

Soubhagya Ranjan Padhi, Assistant Professor, Aeronautics College, Sunabeda, Koraput, Orissa

Swapan Kumar Kolay, Head, Deptt. of Anthropology, Bastar University, Jagdalpur, Chhattisgarh

Tapan Mohanty, Associate Professor, NLIU, Bhopal, Madhya Pradesh

V.K. Shrivastava, Director (Retd.), National SC & ST Commission, Bhopal, Madhya Pradesh

Virginius Xaxa, Dy. Director, TISS, Guwahati, Assam

Yogesh Atal, Ex Director UNESCO, Gurgaon, Haryana

Introduction

I

The history of education among tribes, no matter at what level of modernization and development they are, is very old. However, its nature was highly informal in the past. It was demand ridden. Therefore, it was largely localized with having legitimacy from local ecology, culture and physical environment. The content of education was based on both perceived and felt experience. This education was neither supposed to introduce new and alien world view nor it was supposed to promote only conservatism. The main purpose was to equip children with those set of knowledge and mechanism for its effective functioning which was highly logical, behavioural and, therefore, practical in day-to-day life with reference to both social control and social change. Locals, who were by and large homogeneous in terms of their social and economic status, were not only involved in the establishment and functioning of such institutions to ensure its educational and non-educational functions but also they were involved in the formulation of the so-called content of education which was seldom written. Hence, the nature of education was totally informal but completely functional and, therefore, practical and socially relevant. One can take the institution of *Ghotul* historically found among Gonds of Bastar, as an example of informal educational institution. *Ghotul* type institutions were also found in many more tribes such as *Dekachang* in Garo, *Chang* in Khasi, *Morung* in Abor, *Dhumkuria* in Oraon, *Gitiora* in Munda, *Akhara* in Ho and so on. Needless to mention that these youth organizations stood for complete practical education, worked as an agent of anticipatory socialization and promoter of cooperation, harmony with both animate and inanimate objects and collectivism. It necessarily encouraged core value of tribal society, i.e., collectivism, brotherhood and we-feeling. The following description of youth organization made by Elwin among Munda (reprint 1991) may be taken as an example:

> "These *Gitiora* are in their own humble way seminaries for moral and intellectual training. When young bachelors and young maidens are assembled in their respective *gitiora* after their evening meals, riddles are propounded and solved, folk-tales, traditions and fables are narrated and memorized and songs sung and learnt until bed time" (pp. 296-97).

But as the process of acculturation between tribes and outside forces increased, particularly with the introduction of the British *Raj*, gradually the traditional education system lost its importance. A new education system was half heartedly introduced by both the so-called states and some of the individuals/social organizations. This education was methodical and largely alien to their culture and tradition. Both in terms of objectives and course content it had nothing to do with the local culture, ecology and environment. Rather the foremost aim of this education was to improve quality of life of tribal masses in a limited and material sense by increasing their dependence on outside forces. In many parts of the country inhabited by tribes primary education was introduced by Christian Missionaries. And it is claimed that for this benefit significant number of tribes had to bear cultural cost. They were encouraged to embrace Christianity. It was assumed that the methodical education will contribute to their integration with the rest of the society, as a result of which they will be able to reap benefits of protective benefits of the state which will ultimately lead to improvement in their physical and social quality of life. One of the objectives of the seminar was to examine whether the new education system introduced during British and post-British period have contributed to either assimilation, isolation or integration of tribal masses with the so-called mainstream or non-tribal society. Attempt was also made to examine impact of formal education on their development, empowerment and fulfilment of human rights. Needless to mention that Article 46 of the Constitution of India stressed that "the state shall promote with special care the educational and economic interests of the weaker sections of the people, and in particular, of the SCs and STs, and shall protect them from social injustice and all forms of exploitation".

Today the history of protective discrimination and promotional schemes is about 60 years old and therefore, it is high time to take stock of interface between education and the state induced process of development in different aspects of life such as benefit in admission, employment, promotion and so on. More specifically, the seminar aimed to examine how the so-called popularization of education by different agencies have empowered them in different spheres? It also aimed to trace both inhibiting and enabling factors responsible for the current state of affair among tribal masses.

Needless to mention that the new education system is neither the construct of the local culture or influenced by local culture nor practically controlled at the local level in the true sense of the term, in spite of number of state induced experiments in the recent past such as Panchayati Raj institution, Education Guarantee Scheme, Sarva Shiksha Abhiyan, Mid-Day Meal, Parents-Teachers Associations, free books and uniform, modern infrastructural facilities in schools and so on. Today there are eight Central Government schemes to popularize literacy and education among tribes. These are: Scheme for Construction of Hostels for ST Girls and Boys, Scheme for the establishment of *Ashram* schools in Tribal Sub-Plan areas, Post-Matric Scholarship Scheme (PMS), Book Bank, Upgradation of Merit, National Overseas Scholarship scheme for Higher Studies Abroad, Rajiv Gandhi National Fellowship (RGNF), Scheme for Top Class Education for ST students and Vocational Training in Tribal Areas (VTC) [*Annual Report 2009-10*, Ministry of Tribal Affairs]. But critically speaking there is only limited scope and space for the local requirements and features in the course content of the on-going education system. It is rightly said that today in many schools tribal students at the primary and middle level knows the name of Mahatma Gandhi and such other big leaders and major national and political events like Independence Day and Republic Day because such issues are included in school syllabus and they are taught about all these national issues and events, but hardly any of the student knows about local traditional healers, local reformers, local level tribal freedom fighters and locally available ecological heritage primarily because these issues and items are neither in their syllabus nor taught in the class room (Chaudhary, 2012). Earlier the informal education system used to take care of the local issues and concerns but today even possibility to include these issues in the syallbus is a distant dream. How, to what extent and up to what level of education local features shall be included in their syllabus? This question needs to be debated in order to have an integration between local and the global culture in their syllabus in the wider interest of the society. Also, there is need to debate on medium of education imparted to tribal children in the current globalized situation. There is a point of view that at least at the primary level tribal children should be taught through their mother tongue. Article 350-A of the Constitution of India makes every State responsible for providing sufficient facilities for instruction in the mother tongue at the primary stage of education to children belonging to linguistic minority groups. Instructions in their own language will help the tribal children not only to pick up their subjects quickly but also save them from much frustration, which in many cases, leads to discontinuation of studies in the early stages of education (Dube and Bahadur, 1966). But what about those, and their number is very big, who drop out after just completing primary education due to other reasons? How they will learn languages which are instrumental and in demand outside the tribal territory? All these issues have been covered in different chapters included in this volume.

Earlier door of informal education was practically opened for all the households in a tribal village. All the boys and girls of a specific age group used to attend education. It was both time and cost effective. Seasonal variations had nothing to do with such process. But today we have different types of schools even in the villages. Not only these schools are alien but also these are governed by alien set of procedure with having meaningless interventions by the locals. Earlier tribes were economically to a great extent, homogeneous. Hence, most of them were dependent on *ghotul* type of institution for learning. But today among many of the tribes of central India the process of class formation, although slowly, is taking place. The affluent and occupationally mobile tribals who still live in the villages do not like to send their children in government run relatively poorly equipped schools at the local level primarily because it is generally perceived that the type and quality of education imparted in these schools are extremely poor. Parents of relatively better economic background prefer to send their children in the so-called english schools. And if their children are not enroled in these so-called inferior schools they do not take interest in the functioning of these schools. Usually they become indifferent on school matters. More or less similar steps are followed by those who have migrated from rural areas. Increasing process of individualism among them contributes to this thinking. The issue of quality of education received by tribal children in these schools is alarming. Needless to mention that today there is significant improvement in the literacy and enrolment rate at the primary level due to increasing interventions. Literacy rate was only 8.5 per cent among them in 1961 as compared to 28.3 per cent among non-tribal groups but it increased to 47 per cent among tribes and 64.8 per cent among other social groups in 2001. This data reflect the positive sign of literacy but comparatively it is still alarming among them. Similarly between 1990-91 and 2007-08, Gross Enrolment Ratio at primary level for the total population of the country has increased from 100.1 to 114.6. During the same period the GER for STs have marked a sharp increment, increasing from 103.4 during 1990-91 to 129.3 in 2007-08. A gender-wise comparison, however, indicates that tribal boys have witnessed a moderate increase of GER at primary level, i.e., from 126.8 in 1990-91 to 134.4 in 2007-08, while the GER of ST girls experienced a steep increase, i.e., from 78.6 in 1990-91 to 124 in 2007-08 (Tripathy, 2011).

But the case of dropout is still alarming among them. For instance during 2005-06 it was 39.79 per cent in class I-V, 62.87 per cent in class I-VIII and 78.52 per cent in class I-X among tribal students but it was only 25.67 per cent, 48.80 per cent and 61.62 per cent among non-ST students in the respective classes during 2005-06 (Ministry of HRD, *Annual Report 2007-08*). Number of economic and non-economic factors are held responsible for this state of affair. Also, there is no teaching and learning environment either at the school or at the home or neighbourhood level to popularize education among poor tribals. And those who are enrolled quality of learning received by them is poor. Findings of three studies in Madhya Pradesh, for example, presented below, support the thesis that quality of teaching and learning at primary level education is very low.

Leclercq (2003) conducted study on EGS schools in Betul and Dewas district. He observed: "Achievement was measured through simple tests aimed at checking whether class 5 children—about to complete the primary curriculum—master basic literacy and numeracy. Children were asked to read a few sentences of Hindi texts taken from story books or the *Khushi-Khushi* class 5 textbooks, published by Eklavya. Few children could not read at all, but hardly any could read fluently with few mistakes and correct intonation, understanding the text. Most would either decipher each syllable separately, or read words in one go but pause between them. They would try to read as fast as possible without respecting sentence construction (e.g., pausing at full stops). In fact, children are taught to decipher characters rather than understand sentences and texts. A fraction of the children mastered enough to be able to use literacy for basic activities, but full access to the Hindi written world is still far from sight. Children were asked to write answers to a few questions on their family. The answer sheets show that many children are unable to write up the questions—which were written on the blackboard and read aloud—without making mistakes. Many as well are unable to write correct and meaningful sentences; besides spelling mistakes, sentence construction is often absurd, and the basic sentence structure of the Hindi language (subject/complement/verb) not mastered. Answers are often not understandable. These children are not able to answer simple questions even when they know the answers.

NCERT (quoted in MP *HDR*: 2007, 122) carried out a learning achievement test throughout the country in 2004-05. The test was carried out in classes III, V, VII and VIII. Madhya Pradesh has not been included for class VII but results are available for rest of the classes. In class III the State's performance had been the worst among all States. The mean score in this class were 36.94 per cent in maths. (mathematics), and 42.21 per cent in languages compared to all India figures of 58.25 and 63.12 per cent respectively. In class V mean scores in EVS, maths. and languages were 54.09, 49.03 and 58.25 per cent respectively. In this case also MP lagged far behind the national scenario. In short, as per NCERT report quality of education provided by Government run primary schools in rural M.P. (Madhya Pradesh) is poor.

Chaudhary and Chaudhary (2007) in course of field study in the district of Sehore also observed that students of class V and VI do not know most of the basics of G.K. (General Knowledge), Maths., English, Physics and Chemistry. Only 44 and 48 per cent could correctly name the capital of India and the capital of Madhya Pradesh. Not even a single student know the name of a neighbouring district (Hosangabad) where national poet Makhan Lal Chaturvedi was born.

It is apprehended that how after completing such poor and inferior quality education tribal youth will compete with even those tribal children who are from relatively well-to-do families and who have received quality education in good schools? Needless to mention that due to constitutional provisions seats are reserved for tribal in the Lok Sabha, State Assemblies and at all the three levels of Panchayat Institution. Most of these seats are filled up. How tribal boys and girls who are rapidly losing interest in traditional occupations like farm and wage work will get birth in modern education based occupations? Who will ensure their entry in white collar jobs? According to Annual Report, UPSC (2005 to 2009) of the total candidates 2,190 recommended by UPSC in civil services examinations, only 168 (8.30%) candidates from ST category was recommended. These are some of the pertinent questions which have been covered in articles included in this volume.

More specifically these were the broad objectives of the seminar :

- To examine the nature of interface between tribes and education in the historical perspective;
- To analyse the role of State, Civil Societies, Local Traditional Institutions, Panchayati Raj and new experiments in the expansion of education among tribes;
- To find out challenges before Tribal Education in terms of quality and quantity, economic and non-economic, and macro and micro;
- To map the nature of tribal education tomorrow due to decentralized governance, public-private partnership, new educational experiments and modern information technology; and
- To underline and suggest agenda for action to ensure role of education in tribal development in future.

Articles included in the volume are as under.

II

The paper of Virginius Xaxa examines the system of traditional education found among tribes, introduction of modern education and its status today, historical roots of lower educational status of tribes in general, status of education among Christian and non-Christian tribes, the state of tribal education at the higher classes and so on. Finally, his paper raised some of the pertinent questions pertaining to popularization and expansion of education which needs to be analysed while discussing the state of tribal education in India.

Ramjee Singh examines the changing status of tribes with special reference to the tribes of North-East States. He feels that tribals, with the help of local level resources, have immensely contributed to our society. But today due to deforestation and unregulated acculturation they are constantly losing identity and heritage. The type of education, which they are receiving today, is beyond their reach. Many of them perceive it in an unfriendly manner. They have significantly forgotten the individual and social values popularized by the informal methods of teaching and learning. The modern education, which many of them are receiving today, is alien to their culture and tradition.

The paper of Yogesh Atal entitled "Tribal Studies: Need for Reorientation" deals with trends of tribal studies, concept of tribe and different aspects of tribal development which have drawn attention of cross-section of social scientists in the last couple of decades. About tribal education the paper has positive note. The increasing literacy rate is a testimony to such conclusion. But the author laments that for tribes the situation is not praiseworthy in the field of higher and technical education. Also, many of the most primitive tribes are still far away from the fruits of educational development even today.

According to the paper of R.D. Singh there is a serious policy conflicts in tribal education in particular and traditional societies in general. There is social, economic and ecologic conflict in stakes and access to education. It also unravels the contradiction of exclusive economic policies which is eroding the very existence of tribal societies. The paper identifies the causal factors of problems of stakes and access of tribes to education in India and emerging conflicts of identity, stakes and access identified in naxal problems. The anthropocentric conflicts of identity, stakes and access is increasingly emerging not only in tribal regions but also in agrarian societies. The paper also reviews the education policies of inclusion (social and regional) and excellence and community's form and pattern of access (religious missionary, opportunity costs and subsidies, etc.) and pattern of impacts of education policies on tribal and non-tribal communities, linkages between education and economic well-being etc. Towards the end, some suggestions have been made to store difference in the situation.

Paper of T.R. Mohanty is an attempt to examine rather critically the convergence of State, market and civil society in combating challenge to the human rights of marginalised groups in India. The onset of globalization has only exacerbated the problem and it is in this context, his paper argues for creating a network that will enhance and sustain the human capital of tribal India by providing them technical and professional education to meet, rather successfully, the challenges of globalization. Unless we are serious about the projects promoting to all kinds of education among the marginalised groups, there would be no light at the end of the tunnel.

S. Prabhakar in his paper entitled "parliamentary Initiatives towards tribal education" observed that in spite of various initiatives educational status of tribes is not up to the mark. However, some of recent initiatives may be a mile stone in this matter. He discussed these initiatives in detail. He also gave some suggestions to make parliamentary debates and interventions more effective and fruitful.

S.N. Tripathy made an attempt to focus the problems of tribal literacy, the problem of dropout, tribal female literacy and the related problems in two tribal States of Madhya Pradesh and Maharashtra. Mostly, the secondary sources of data have been used for analysis and interpretation so as to get the final inferences. The paper emphasizes the quality of education for the tribal women as an instrument of socio-economic and political empowerment and its role in the achievement of a wide range of individual and development goals—from better health to higher incomes and stronger economic potential. The primary education obstructed due to certain crucial problem such as inadequate admission of girls, dropouts, stagnation, defective curriculum, irregular attendance, lack of study materials, poor nutrition of children and so on.

The paper of S.N. Chaudhary deals with the state of literacy and education in a tribal village of M.P. It examines the level of literacy, functioning of primary and middle schools and the issues of enrolment, absenteeism, villagers and teacher's perception, quality of teaching and learning, functioning of Mid Day Meal (MDM) as perceived by different stakeholders and other State initiatives, infrastructural facilities in school, attitudinal change in favour of girls education, state of college education among tribal boys and girls, difficulties experienced by students and parents at different levels of education and agenda of action for all the concerned. The paper concludes that there is a positive change in the field of education especially at the primary and middle level. There is massive improvement in enrolment at the primary level. But gradually there is an increase in the rate of non-enrolment and dropout at the higher classes. Also, the quality of teaching and learning at the primary and middle level is poor. Both the villagers and change agents are indifferent on these issues. No efforts are made to address such problems. Finally the paper underlines some action agenda in favour of quality education at the primary level.

The paper of Chaturbhuj Sahu examines the state of affairs in the field of tribal education, especially in the light of number of institutional interventions. To him the subject matter of the book taught to tribal children is mainly related to angels, gods, pilgrims, male Hindu gods, fairy tales, magic, *aswamegh yagya* and so on. The tribal heroes were kept aside. In these circumstances how the tribal students can ever be expected to respect the very course book. Many tribal people get repelled and prohibit their children from such education. Passing of traditional society to modernity demands the introduction of new set of institutional behaviour patterns through inculcation of required set of values and attitudes which is possible through the spread of sensitive model of education. The paper has attempted to discuss about the educational situation among the tribal children of the study area. Emphasis has also been given on the governmental initiatives and its impact on the education of tribal children.

D. Debnath examined the educational status of two primitive tribes of Madhya Pradesh namely Sahariya and Baiga. To him among tribal children in the age group 5-14 years, half of the total tribal children are still out of schools. The status of girl literacy is worse in tribal community in comparison to total tribal literacy, particularly among Primarily Vulnerable Tribal Groups (erstwhile Primitive Tribal Groups, PTGs) like Sahariya and Baiga. Even among the scheduled tribes, the education level is very low among these two tribes. The paper also underlined different dimensions of literacy and education among them. Finally the paper warned that unless we respect and make necessary alterations in the content and curriculum in accordance with their culture, languages and social practices, it would be a difficult task to continuously retain the interest of tribal children in education and preventing their early dropouts.

Paper of J.J. Roy Burman deals with the status of education among Thankul Nagas. To him the Thankul Nagas are one of the dominant ethnic groups residing in the Ukhrul district of Manipur who are leading an upsurge against the Indian State. They were converted into Christianity by the missionaries during the colonial days and basic western education was imparted to them. But higher education has not made any significant inroad into the community. Even after independence, government apathy and resource crunch has not enabled the Thankuls to make much educational progress. But the youth have urge to go for higher education and many of them land up in distant cities of the country. In this paper some of the practical problems relating to the attainment of education by the tribesmen have been briefly discussed.

Kashung Zingran Kengoo analysed education system among Meiteis and tribal minorities of Manipur. To him education systems that remain under the dominant administration undermine the rights to equality to the tribal people. Efforts made by the State in order to improve educational status of tribes is highly unsatisfactory. It is not made available to the tribal and non-tribal population in an equitable manner.

According to the paper of K.P. Pothan the Constitution of India has made special provisions for the all-round development of tribal communities in India including education. The population of scheduled tribes in India is more than seven crore, which is slightly more than 8 per cent of the Indian population. The literacy rate of scheduled tribe (men and women) is very poor. The paper also deals with social and demographic profile of tribal students studying in colleges/University. To him, of 300 studied students majority of them are males. The tribal population in Madhya

Pradesh is substantial especially in districts like Jhabua, Dhar, Mandla, Chhindwara and Khargone. Out of 300 students, 219 (73%) are males and 81 (27%) are females. These students make sincere efforts to study with the help of scholarship and hostel facility received from the government. They speak different tribal language/dialects, but all the students have Hindi medium in their study. These students have high ambitions. But most of them prefer government jobs. They are in favour of government reservation for higher studies and jobs. Most of them follow Hindu faith. Arts and commerce are the subjects chosen by majority of the tribal students for their higher education.

The paper of K.R. Sharma examines educational attitude of tribal students. He found that all the independent variables namely, sex, family size, family education and parental income and occupation exercise a powerful influence in developing favourable educational attitude among the students. These variables play an important role in the development of attitude towards education both among tribal and non-tribal students. The educational attitude scores show that there is not much difference between the tribal and non-tribal students. The educational attitude of the tribal students is an important factor in determining the education of the tribal students and it also interacts with various independent variables, i.e., sex, caste, family size, family education, parental occupation and family income.

R.S. Shrivastava made a comparative study of tribal and non-tribal population in terms of literacy, retention and so on. To him the comparison of growth in literacy in general population to Scheduled Tribe population during the last forty years (1961-2001) shows that the growth of literacy among scheduled tribes has been more as compared to the growth of literacy amongst general population. The growth of female literacy in scheduled tribes is quite high during the decade of 1981-1991, as it is 198.06 per cent as compared to general female literacy of 85.17 per cent. This may be due to special efforts and various types of incentives given to boost education among the scheduled tribe girls. Despite effective efforts both from governmental and non-governmental organizations to boost education amongst the scheduled tribes and retain them in the Primary Schools, the dropout rates among them are high. The reasons for dropouts are: working in field, agricultural labour or other labour work, sibling care, cattle grazing, weak financial condition, lack of educational facilities, social beliefs due to which parents are reluctant to educate girls, handicapped or prolonged illness, school environment not conducive to education, and migration. Towards the end some suggestions have been made to bring meaningful improvement in the situation.

Paper of V.K. Shrivastava covered state of tribal education in Madhya Pradesh in the historical perspective on the basis of certain parameters, viz., approach to tribal education, policies formulated, conceptualization of education and literacy in the tribal context, pros and cons of the present approach, development of educational infrastructure/institutions, method of imparting the education programme, level of awareness, management of educational system, preparation of teaching and learning materials and so on. Finally the paper ended with different suggestions for the overall educational development of tribes.

For Palash C. Coomar and S.K. Biswas also education is the key catalyst to the development of human resources. It is a crucial part of legitimate entry in the national level participation of development as well as social stream of the nation. In the past education was one of the main considerations for hierarchical classification in Indian Hindu society. Education was out of reach to the poor and backward people and also to tribals. Lack of it is largely responsible for the exploitation and pitiable plight of the tribal masses. For them, education is the pivot on which their success depends. The paper is an attempt to underline different dimensions of tribal education. Also, some suggestions have been made to improve state of tribal education from both human rights and empowerment perspective.

The paper of Ratnawali Sinha explains that with the increasing attention on the schooling of the tribal children in recent decade, there has been a rising trend in the enrolment and decline in the dropout rate among these children. However, quality or outcome of learning still remains a major issue which has wide ramification on the development of the tribe. Despite the policy proclamation in the successive plan documents, it is not uncommon to find tribal people in the lowest rung of development. Gujarat is the home to 15 per cent tribal population. Economic development in Gujarat has resulted in per capita increase in GDP but it has not translated an equal development in its social indicators. Such indicators are poorer for the marginalised community to which scheduled tribes are one of the major constituents. The paper is an attempt to present the status of education and its economic implications in the lives of the tribal people of the State. While there is substantial improvement in the access to school and rise in the proportion of educated youth, underemployment and limited opportunity to diversify the economic base remains one of the barriers in the upward mobility of the tribe. It thus argues that not only the quantitative but qualitative aspects of education also needs to be improved to achieve the objectives of development.

The paper of Swapan Kumar Kolay aims to investigate state of child education among Santal, Mahali and Lodha/Savar tribes of Midnapur, Bankura and Purulia districts of West Bengal. To examine the significance of child education among these tribal groups, existing and expected role of tribal parents as well as contributions from government and community was examined. Sample comprised 437 parents and 18 teachers/educational workers. The data was collected through structured interview schedule. The findings were the parents' positive perceptions toward their child education but at the same time severe scarcity of human and physical infrastructure for child education was also present in the study area. The paper recommends several steps to overcome these problems including provision of new school locations and ensuring the availability of school buildings, supporting infrastructure and sufficient number of teachers for effective functioning of schools.

The paper of S.R. Padhi is an attempt to analyze the educational status of tribes in Orissa. He has explored various constraints in enhancing the educational levels of this marginalized section. Opening part of the paper spells out the relationship between education and tribal development. The paper has covered the relevance of education for the emancipation and empowerment of tribes. In the context of inclusive growth, the author found "Education" as the best input that can open up opportunity for individual empowerment of the marginalized section, ignite social change and catalyze economic growth. It also covers issues like nature and extent of education among STs in Orissa. It highlights the gap between the literacy rates of the general population and STs, disparity in education in the tribal dominated district of Orissa, findings of the field study reveals the dismal picture of educational scenario of a tribal village. The significant barriers of educational development have also been discussed.

On the basis of overview of all these twenty articles, most of which are empirical and field based, it can be concluded that in spite of various interventions since long the level of literacy and education and quality of education received by tribal children is not up to the level. Only few of them have really availed education and its fruits in different realms. However, all of them have paid socio-cultural cost of educational development. Tribals have totally lost their traditional educational arrangement. The modern education system do not respect their identity. It works like an alien institution. Scholars have given, some suggestions. But none of the contributors are sure about the meaningful functioning and impact of these suggestions under the given socio-economic and political environment. However, if implemented, some difference can definitely be achieved.

REFERENCES

Chaudhary, S.N. and Chaudhary P. (2007): *Primary Education through Sarva Shiksha Abhiyan: A Study of its Status and Functions with reference to Sehore district,* (Mimeo), Bhopal: Rajya Shiksha Kendra.

Chaudhary, S.N. (2012): *In Search of Sustainable Development: Scenario in a Tribal Village of Madhya Pradesh,* New Delhi: Serials Publications.

Dube, B.K. and F. Bahadur (1966): *A Study of the Tribal People and Tribal Areas of Madhya Pradesh,* Bhopal: Tribal Research and Development Institute.

Elwin, V. (reprint 1991): *The Muria and their Ghotul,* New Delhi: Oxford University Press.

Government of India (2009-10): *Annual Report,* Ministry of Tribal Affairs, New Delhi, pp. 106-117.

Government of Madhya Pradesh (2007): *Fourth Human Development Report,* Delhi: Oxford University Press.

Leclercq, F. (2003): "Education Guarantee Scheme and Primary Schooling in Madhya Pradesh", *EPW,* Vol. XXXVIII, No. 19, May 10-16.

Tripathy, S.N. (2011): "Empowering Tribes through Education: A Study of Female Literacy in Orissa", in *Educational Scenario of Tribes in India: Current Issues and Concerns* (ed.) S.R. Padhi, New Delhi: Manglam Publishers and Distributors.

1

Tribes and their Education in India

Virginius Xaxa

Raising the socio-economic conditions of tribes has been one of the major concerns of the State in India after it attained independence. To this in mind various kinds of provisions have been laid down in the Constitution of India. As a part of the fulfilment of this obligation, India has taken up various kinds of programmes with a view to improve their socio-economic conditions. Among these programmes, educational development of the tribes has remained one of the most critical. In this address, I shall merely touch upon some of the critical issues and would like to place them in a comparative perspective but again in very general way.

Traditional System of Education

An important criterion in terms of which the tribal society has been marked off from others is that they lack the tradition of reading and writing. It is also conceptualized as a society characterized by homogeneity. This meant that everyone was engaged in the same mode of making a living and shared knowledge, ideas, emotions and values that were identical. It represented a society what in Durkheimian sense is characterized by a mechanical solidarity. In such a society there was no specialized or differentiated institution that engaged or concerned with what we generally associate with education today. Tasks associated with education such as imparting knowledge, skills, values and norms were normally carried out by the families themselves. In some societies there were institutions of youth dormitories, which in addition to imparting knowledge about values and norms passed on customs and traditions especially its dance and music forms to the younger generation. Knowledge, skills were mainly concerned with modes of their making a livelihood and culture, norms and values with the way they were to conduct themselves in society. In tribal societies, task that we associate with education were primarily if not exclusively concerned with in maintaining its social order unlike in modern societies where tasks are also oriented towards change and transformation. This was natural as there was no design or plan to bring about change of a certain kinds that we tend to associate with modern education. There was no radical economic transformation in the society. Hence, demand for a kind of knowledge and skills required to man the new economic system did not arise as was the case under transition from pre-capitalistic social formation to capitalistic social formation.

Introduction of Modern Education

Since the tribal society did not have the tradition of reading and writing, knowledge and values were passed from one generation to another orally. It was the Christian missions, to begin with, who introduced the tradition of reading and writing among them. The missionaries expected converts to be able to read and write. Thus with the coming of the Christian Missionaries a distinct and specialized institution emerged in tribal society, which took upon itself the role of imparting knowledge, values and skills that were alien to tribal society. It was directed primarily towards change and transformation in the society. Its emergence to a certain degree undermined the place of traditional institution but did not replace it. Thus both traditional institution and institution introduced by the Christian Missionaries existed side by side. One was oriented to change and the other to traditional social order giving rise to much stress and strain in the society.

The educational institutions introduced by the Christian Missionaries cannot be understood independent of their agenda and objectives. They were historically tied to the larger objective of evangelization. The two have now become autonomous but interlinkage and interconnection still prevails. The Christian missions and their educational institutions gave rise to new associational life which was marked by its absence in the traditional social setting. Such associational life moved from village to tribe, tribe to inter-tribe giving rise thereby to a larger identity. Such associational life were religious (different tribes becoming a part of one single religious community) to begin with. Non-religious associational life too emerged in course of time and the role of education imparted by Christian missions was critical. After all, it was education, which gave rise to emergence of middle class, new and old in tribal society and it was middle class which brought non-religious associational life in tribal society.

The educational institution introduced by the Christian Missionaries touched upon only some tribal pockets and some tribes in different parts of the country. A very large chunk of the tribal region and population had as such no such exposure under the colonial rule. Though the colonial government extracted the enormous revenue by exploiting resources in the tribal region, it did little to improve their lives through extension of modern education and modern health services. They remained one of the most exploited. After India became independent serious concerns were shown to improve the life situation of the tribal population. In keeping with this, various provisions were laid down for them in the Constitution of India. It is within this backdrop that the State's agenda towards tribe have to be understood. The different measures taken for their upliftment can be thus divided into three categories. The protective measures include constitutional and legislative rights that safeguard the interests of the tribal population. Reservation aims to provide them fair share of representation in the fields of education, State employment and political institutions such as parliament and State legislatures and thereby acts a mobilization process. Development points to policies and programmes oriented to the upliftment of the tribal people and education constitutes a critical component of it.

Status of Education

As a first step to developmental initiatives, special multipurpose development projects as a supplement to the community development projects were introduced in the tribal areas in 1950s. This strategy was continued with some modifications here and there until the Fifth Plan period. Education formed an important part of this strategy. The Fifth Plan (1974-79) is taken as a landmark in the sphere of tribal development. Not only it made shift in policy perspective from welfare to development but also introduced new concept of tribal sub-plan and integrated tribal development projects. The plan entailed a separate budgetary head for the purpose. The immediate objective of this strategy was to eliminate the forms of exploitation that existed in the tribal areas and accelerate the process of development education and health being an integral component of it. The tribal sub-plan itself has been at work for about thirty-seven years. It is important that we make an assessment of what gain has been made in course of over sixty years after independence.

Literacy is taken as an important indicator of development status in education. In 1991, the literacy rate of the scheduled tribes was 29.60 per cent as compared to 52.21 per cent for the general population. The gap between the two was as high as 28.09 per cent. By 2001, the literacy rate for the general population had jumped to 65.38 per cent as compared to 47.1 per cent for tribal population. The gap between the two has been somewhat bridged but the difference of 21.71 per cent is still very large (Government of India, 2007). There is no doubt that there has been steady increase in the rate of literacy but it is still very low and the gap between tribes and non-tribes is quite wide. Why is such a status of education among tribes? What accounts for this? How do we understand and explain this phenomenon? I shall try to look into this aspect at a later stage of my address.

The steady increase in literacy among tribes in last one decade has been due to factors. One is the better enrolment of children to school which could be due to new initiatives such as scheme of mid-day meal taken up by the governments. The other could be campaign such as *sarva siksha abhiyan*. Interestingly, enrolment of tribal children since last one decade has shown increase faster than the enrolment of other categories in primary, upper primary and even in other categories. Gross Enrolment Ratio (GER), defined as percentage of enrolment in primary (I-V) and upper primary (VI-VIII) to the estimated child population in the age group (6-11) and 11-14) respectively, indicates 10 per cent points gaps in the case of boys, 15 per cent in case of girls and about 12 per cent for both boys and girls as per 2001-02 data. (*ibid.*) Gross enrolment ratio is taken to bolster claim for progress made in expanding school education in India. But enrolment is a very unreliable basis for assessing the degree of access to education (Dubey, 2009). What is important to assessing the progress of expanding education is figures for attendance and dropout rather than enrolment. Now the enrolment of tribal children in school is not that low but dropout rates are exorbitantly high.

It is the dropouts that constitute the most serious problem as far tribal children's education is concerned. Dropouts at primary, upper primary and secondary was as high as 52.3, 69.5 and 81.2 respectively as compared to 39.0, 54.6 and 66.0 for the general population in 2001-02. In 2002-03 dropouts had declined by mere 1 per cent at all three levels. The data on dropouts rates for the period 1996-97 to 2002-03 indicate decreasing trend and hence an improvement for tribal children at all levels of school education. All India dropout rates fell during 1996-97 to 2002-03 by 5.3 per cent for all children in classes I-V and by 5.2 per cent for tribal children. For classes I-X, dropout rates for all children at all India fell by 7.37 during 1996-97 to 2002-03. The figure for the same period was 3.92 in case of tribal children (Government of India, 2007).

Explanation

The explanation given for such sorry state of affairs is diverse. Lack of infrastructure such as schools as well as personnel are one set of critical factors in terms of which the poor social development indicators among tribal communities have been discussed and studied. This argument is often linked with the argument of inadequate resource allocation for tribal development. However, even with an increase in resource allocations since the Fifth Five-Year Plan beginning in 1974, the material conditions of tribals have failed to improve proportionally. In fact, resources earmarked for various educational programmes in many States have gone unutilized years after years.

The ineffective implementation of the programmes is seen as another line of argument by which the issue of social development among tribals could be meaningfully explained. In this discourse, the thrust of the solution lies in accelerated and effective implementation of State-sponsored development programmes and schemes, whether these pertain to livelihood/income-generation activities or education or health or communication facilities.

While there is no denying the truth that certain aspects of traditional social structure and culture do constraint development programme, it is equally pertinent to ask as to why even after over sixty years of national reconstruction process there has still been a large tribal population, which has not been connected with development projects or why there has still been poor implementation programme or delivery mechanism in tribal areas. This is a question which needs to be problematized and explained. Much of the answer to this lies in the relation between tribes and the larger society especially in the regional context. The larger society has always viewed tribes as those who are alien to their society and, hence, there is overall indifference towards their cause and development. Rather the relation between the two historically and even today is one of domination of the tribal society by the larger society. This has not been adequately factored in addressing the question of tribal development by policy makers and administrators. This is an argument which needs merit.

The third set of argument is built around traditional socio-cultural aspects of tribal life. The low literacy among tribes is generally attributed to indifference or lack of interest in education by tribal population. This is further attributed to socio-economic condition and socio-cultural values of the tribal society. While the lack of interest in education or the role of socio-economic condition cannot be denied, there is a need for more nuanced understanding of the phenomenon. At the outset it is important to problematize the issue. Is the low rate of literacy among tribes mainly due to factors inherent in socio-economic and cultural aspects of the tribal society? Are educational facilities really accessible in tribal areas? If it is not, does the onus of low level of literacy lie with tribes or with someone else? It is important to explore the extent to which the low literacy rate is to do with socio-cultural features and the extent of unavailability of educational facilities. The onus of low literacy need not solely rest on tribes as has generally been the case in the existing literature.

Even in case of aspects of education other than literacy such as high dropout rates or stagnation or absence of tribal students in the institution of higher learning, the onus is put on tribes and their socio-economic condition and socio-cultural lives. The point is made that they need to change their ideas, values and ethos to be able to take the modern education. This is basically a modernization perspective, which has been in currency world over in discussion of modernization of traditional societies. This is an argument, which is applicable for the whole of the Indian society. However, this has been sharply problematized in the context of the tribal society as if the rest of the Indian society has already become modernized. While there is some relationship between the lack of development and traditional social structure and culture, this aspects needs to be further probed and carefully examined. After all, lack of development may not be so much due to their social structure as to overall cultural and value framework of State development process. The framework of development is after all not so alien in case of the larger society, as it is so in case of tribes. For example, language and curriculum of education imparted to the larger population including scheduled castes is not alien in case of wider society but this is so in case of tribal society. The same is the case in respect of personnel involved in development and administration of tribal people. Groups other than tribes do not suffer such constraint and ethos and hence social development process in their case is relatively smooth. In this case observation made by Dubey may be pertinent. Dubey attributes the problem such as dropout rates in the context of general population to poor curriculum and syllabus, deficient pedagogy, negligent teachers. Parents too are held accountable for dropout and poor quality (Dubey, 2009). Now, if this is the case with the larger population in whose language and ethos, school education is imparted, whose history and culture, the school curriculum and syllabus represents, even teachers belong to same cultural group as the students, then imagine the state of tribal children for whom education at imparted all levels is alien to their life, history and experience. That partly explains as to why the impact of development programmes initiated by the state or external agencies has been slow and protracted. Hence, either there is a need for reorienting development in tune with tribal ethos and tradition or for more humane dimension in the approach to tribal development if it is to cast in a perspective, which is alien to them.

Differentiation in Educational Status

While the general status of education among tribal communities is poor, this is not so across regions and communities. Rather, there is striking variation in regard to educational status of tribes across regions and States. The educational status of tribes is much better in North-East Region than the rest of India. This can be seen at all levels of education so much so that each State has a university now though the population size of most of the States would be many time lower than the population of Gonds or Bhils. Not only that there has been strong movement of students from the region for higher education in other parts of India. There is not only State and regional variation but there is variation along tribes as well. Some tribes within the region have done much better than the others. This is so in North-East India and so is the case in rest of India. How do we explain the better educational status of the tribes in North-eastern region? There is no doubt they had longer history of exposure to modern education. This partly explains as to why there has been better educational status. It is to be noted that literacy level of the tribes in the North-East till 1970s was no way better. It began to pick up since 1980s and became fairly visible in 1990s. Today literacy levels of tribes in most of the States approximate the national average and some have even higher than the national average. How do we explain development? It is to do with self-governance which came with the autonomous district council (limited though in its power) but more importantly with the formation of the tribal States. With this tribal issues and questions came to be manned by tribal themselves. The differences in educational status are not only across regions but also tribes. Some tribes even in the North-Eastern Region have better educational achievement than other tribes. For example, in Nagaland, Ao and Angamis has much better educational status than other tribes and so is the case let say with Khasis in comparison to Jaintias but more importantly with the Garos. Such scenario one can see in mainland tribal region as well. Mennas in Rajasthan, Oraons in Jharkhand and Chhattisgarh, Kharias in Jharkhand are some stray examples in the region.

The differences in educational status can also be seen across their religious affiliation. The educational status for example, is much better at all levels of education among tribal Christians than non-tribal Christians. Over and above, the differences in educational status are highly marked across gender. In fact in every State the educational status of women in tribal society falls far short of educational status of men. Even in matrilineal societies of

Meghalaya, the status of women is lower than those of men. In fact the gap between the education of men and women in tribal society is larger than those of the non-tribal societies. The status of women in tribal society is considered better than those in non-tribal societies. How to explain this paradox in tribal societies? The fact of the matter is that though women in tribal societies enjoy better status in comparison to non-tribal societies, the burden of work load is much more in respect of women as they have to manage aspects of agricultural operations as well as the domestic work. This burden of work comes as hindrance to their schooling. Further, there is invariably bias in favour of boys against girls and that explains the status of lower literacy among tribal women whether it concerns the north-eastern region or Christian tribal population or any particular tribal community.

As far as the higher education is concerned, the position is even worse. The enrolment remains poor. In institutions of higher education especially those run by central government is difficult to find tribal boys and girls from regions other than North-East and to some extent Jharkhand region. Further in case of higher education, the presence of tribals in science and technical education is indeed extremely poor.

Some of the questions that emerges and that needs to be addressed are as follows:

- What is the present status of literacy and enrolment? Has there been marked or notional improvement? In case there is marked movement what has come to account for it?
- What is the status of dropout rates in general and at different educational level in particular? How to account for high or low dropout rates?
- What is the status of education across States and within State across districts and different tribes? In fact, it is advisable to examine the problem of enrolment and dropout rates across States and within State across districts and tribes.
- Equally important is to explore the gender question within the tribal society in view of wide disparity between boys and girls across States, religion and tribes.
- How to address the poor share/representation of tribal

boys and girls of the region other than North-East India in higher education?

NOTE

Keynote address delivered in the inaugural function of the national seminar.

REFERENCE

Dubey, Muchkund. (2010): "The Right of Children to Free and Compulsory Education Act 2009: The Story of a Missed Opportunity," *Social Change,* 40 (1), pp. 1-13.

Government of India (Planning Commission) (2007): *Report of the Working Group on Empowerment of Scheduled Tribes for the Eleventh Five Year Plan* (2007-12).

2
Educational Roots in the Tribal World*

Ramjee Singh

Literacy is neither the beginning nor the end of education. The Sage philosophers of Africa, the primitive Greeks or the early Vedi Upanisadic seers did not compile any Encyclopaedia but it would be foolish to deny that they were devoid of wisdom. The Great Prophet of Islam was 'Unlettered'. The medieval Indian Martin Luther and revolutionary saint of India like Kabir himself acknowledges that he did not ever touched pen or used ink or paper. This does not mean that I plead for illiteracy but we must recognize its limitation. After all education aims at the all-round development of the individual as well as the society. Hence, it must aim at the unfolding of the threefold faculties, i.e., head, hand and heart. This is no utopia or simply Gandhian fad but it is total scientific pedagogy. We must add into it the socio-cultural dimensions.

Coming to the question of the state of education in the tribal world. We must not ignore their overall conditions. If we want to prescribe the same wasteful liberal general education, this is hardly relevant for their life and livelihood. Even after spending 60 precious years, they are neither fit for a robust healthy view of life, nor they become self-reliant to earn a livelihood.

At best, they are uselessly waiting for a job in the longest que. On the other hand, they become unfit to cooperate and help their family members in their domestic work. In fact, they become a burden and an unwanted partner. This compels them to join any gang of anti-social group and they lose their sense of simplicity,

* Edited version of the valedictory address delivered in the seminar.

innocence, truthfulness and on the other hand learn to waste their time in idle-gossip, drinking usually local wine or smoking vicious things. This is a loss to the entire society. They forget the individual and social values of the tribal culture, which is much more valuable than the present formal western education.

Firstly, they gradually become averse to hard physical and manual work necessary in the field of agriculture, cattle keeping or any type of hand work. Manual work does not provide some livelihood only, it imparts skill to become self-reliant. The cult of dignity of labour is a great cultural and moral value. The *Vedas* gives the moral and spiritual values of human labour. It has a great social value. An individual or a society, which depends upon others labour, are like parasites. The Bible advocates "Bread labour", so the *Gita* also says that those who do not work for bread-labour are like thieves. Today, we have been gradually adopting machine-culture. We have neglected our necessary natural and physical culture. And we devise physical exercises or sports which are not only costly but also unproductive. We should remember that if we can correlate knowledge with work, work becomes less boresome and knowledge becomes more sound. A great Russian educationist Makrenko had pointed out the lack of work-element in Soviet educational system. Madam Montessari has, therefore, combined "Learning by doing". Mao-Tse-tung had also given a revolutionary slogan for "Half Work and Half Learning". In ancient India, the pupils were required to live with their teachers participating in all types of work of the household. The names of famous *Ashram* disciples are Aruni, Upamanyu, Veda, etc. There was no division between work and learning. Gandhi, getting inspiration from the ancient system of combining work with learning has developed a theory of correlation on scientific basis. Our tribal people have learnt about agriculture, animal husbandry, weaving, bee-keeping etc. as a part of their life. True, an input of new ideas, etc., can be introduced along with their work. Even we can introduce literacy through their mother tongue. Imposing any other medium other than ones own mother-tongue is a crime against the child as well against the science of pedagogy.

Secondly, our tribal people have developed a very high sense of community life, which has been highly eroded in our social and cultural life. Perhaps Gandhiji might have borrowed both dignity of labour as well as the community living from the tribal people along with others. The modern culture has made us extremely individualistic, self-cultured and to some extent unsocial: Modern Indian life has become more materialistic than the west. The tribal people have a positive and strong sense of "we-feeling". They play together, they work together, they drink or dance together. Ruskin has advocated a great truth that "our individual welfare is contained in the welfare of all" To me the tribal culture is nearer to the *Sarvodaya* culture of universal welfare.

Thirdly, though the tribal people have been pushed back to the uninhabitable forests and mountains, this has proved a blessing in disguise. Of course, this is a crime on the part of the so-called 'civilized world' to push them into the forest areas and later on, they are being dispossessed from their abode for exploitation of natural and universal resources. But they are in the lap of nature with healthy and unpolluted environment. They are true children of nature. Their life-style is simple and close to nature. They enjoy the sight of 'tongues in trees, books in running brooks and sermons in stones". They get enough of oxygen, free air and fruits and roots from nature. In such natural surroundings, they develop poetic imaginations and love. Today, we have only 16 per cent of forests with the result, we have been facing ecological disasters. According to the scientists, there should be at least one-fourth of green space, but we have hardly 16 per cent. This is very dangerous. The tribal people are the true protectors of the forests and its life. They are the true children of nature.

Fourthly, tribal life and culture have provided inspiration to the writers and poets. For example, the *Vedic* hymns are attributed to nature which symbolize life and vitality. It seems that the objects of nature have physical frame but they are also personified, moralized and spiritualized. This symbolism from the physical to moral and the spiritual is a unique feature in God-making. The great poet Valmiki got inspiration from the tragedy of a pair of birds for his *Ramayan*, so also Kalidas has shown his great imagination by making the clouds as the messengers of love. Through these we have works, we know about the very intimate relation between man and nature. We have references about Ram and his devotee Sabri who was an illiterate tribal woman, and Ram's love and respect for tribal chief Nisad Raj. Even during medieval period, there has been a very patriotic role of the tribal chiefs by helping Maharana Pratap and offer safer shelter to his family in the forest. Even the Cavalier patriot Shivaji Maharaj had received ample support from the tribal heroes while fighting the Mughal imperialism. In modern times, the tribal chiefs and soldiers have shown exemplary valour and heroic martyrdom in fighting the British rulers. The Santhal Revolt, the martyrdom of Birsa Munda, Tilka Manjhi and the absolute dedication of the Tana Bhagats on purely Gandhian lives are well known. The tribal people always stood for unity and integrity of India.

A unique feature in the tribal people that though they are not very much educated and sophisticated in our sense of the terms, they are dedicated to their mission during the service to the people. They are mainly of non-party temperament and non-violent in nature. By nature, they are a truth-loving and truth speaking people. They are very straight-forward. They would not give any false evidence against anybody.

Conclusion

India is a land of many religions and many tribes. There are many distinct ethnic tribes. Similarly, there are many castes, races and sects. In short, it is a land of variety. But there is also a perennial quest of unity in variety. This is an old legacy. However, the tribal communities in the North-East are basically different from rest of India. The percentage of literacy is very high in most of the tribal groups. Even the exploitation of the tribal people by the non-tribal outside people is non-existent. The ownership of the land is with the tribal people themselves. It rests with the individual village or the clan. No land in the village can be sold to the outsiders. The traditional form of village local-self government is found in many groups. In Nagaland, a new progressive measure has been introduced. Every village has a development board, which is responsible for development, and for which they get funds directly from the State govternment. It is a statutory body. Any change in the rules are done only by the village boards. Such systems exist in four States—Nagaland, Mizoram, Meghalaya and Arunachal. The village Boards are elected by the people. This has constitutional validity as it place finds in the Sixth Schedule of the Constitution. The remaining three States like Assam, Manipur and Tripura have different system as there are mixed population of the tribals and non-tribals in those States. There is the same system in the villages.

They manage everything concerning food, shelter, etc. Thus, they are the self-governed and self-sustained villages of Gandhi's dream. Though, village Boards receive ample funds from the State Government but there is corruption like elsewhere. The spread of violence by different groups is the most dangerous phenomenon which needs sustained and organized peace work. Gandhiji had established *All India Harijan Sevak Sangh* all over India to serve them. So also *Adm Jati Seva Sangh* was established under the leadership of Thakkar Bapa to serve the tribal people which needs to be strengthened on non-party and non-violent basis.

3

Tribal Studies : Need for Reorientation*

Yogesh Atal

I have been privileged to attend almost all the annual seminars on the Indian tribal scene organized by the Rajiv Gandhi Chair at this University in the past few years. I presume this to be the last in the Series as most of the aspects of Tribal India have been covered. This Special Lecture offers me an opportunity to consolidate my views and provide a perspective for Tribal Studies to be carried out in future. For this, I am grateful to Professor S.N. Chaudhary who did not accept "no" from me for his kind and friendly invitation although I feel that I am over-exposing myself. Not without an escape route I am rendered helpless; and I apologize for inflicting yet another Lecture on this august audience.

I shall dwell upon three issues in this Lecture:

- Anthropology and Tribal Studies.
- Need for a definition of the Tribe.
- How do we approach Development?

Anthropology and Tribal Studies

There exists a general image that anthropology is the study of the tribes. On questions related to tribes, the government agencies and the informed public look at the anthropologist for knowledge-

* Edited version of special lecture delivered in the seminar.

based answers. However, the situation in this regard has considerably changed over the years.

If one were to visit the University departments of Anthropology one would get the impression that anthropology is getting redefined as "Physical" anthropology and is coming closer to biological sciences. This is a trend significantly different than the one prevalent when people of my generation joined the anthropology departments. At that time, anthropology was almost coterminous with tribal studies. An anthropologist was the one who studied the primitive groups; physical anthropology focused on the past prehistory and paleontology. Concerned with the origin of Man, and the evolution of cultures and civilizations, anthropology was then defined as the study of the "primitive" and the "past"; the anthropologist was trained to handle both these aspects. Since the "past" of human culture was seen to be partly present in the so-called tribal communities that were vastly different, and distantly located from the so-called civilized societies, anthropologists of that era focused on them to trace the missing links in human history. They contributed to the emerging science of ethnology—used almost as a synonym of Anthropology. Genetics, Racial studies, Eugenics, Prehistoric Archeology, and Paleontology were treated as subsets of this discipline. However, the public image of the discipline remained that of tribal studies. The names of Verrier Elwin, von-F?rer Haimendorf, S.C. Roy, N.K. Bose, D.N. Majumdar, S.C. Dube, Sachchidananda, L.P. Vidyarthi—to name a few pioneers of Indian anthropology—had all worked on Indian tribes. None of them was known as a physical anthropologist although Majumdar did some work in that area; so did Irawati Karve (who had a doctoral degree from Germany in that speciality). Even those who chose to specialize in physical anthropology at that time carried out their initial field researches in tribal communities; for example, P.C. Biswas and Inder Paul Singh—both of Delhi University have to their credit work in the area of social anthropology in the beginning of their career. Today's leading anthropologists in India, barring exception, are specialists in physical anthropology working in the area of human genomics, anthropometry, serology, and dermatoglyphics. The scope of the discipline has been considerably redefined. Work in the tribal areas is carried out mostly by the Anthropological Survey of

India; however, even then one notices a gradual shift towards physical anthropology and human biology.

Today, 37 years later, the scenario has vastly changed. University departments of Anthropology are no longer the departments of an integrated and interdisciplinary study of Man. It is Physical Anthropology that dominates; social anthropology has become not only secondary or marginalized but is neglected to the extent that some of the departments do not even have permanent lecturers in that speciality. The fact that the Rajiv Gandhi Chair for Tribal Studies is located here at this University in the Department of Sociology which is indicative of the trend. I recall an incident when I was invited to deliver a lecture in my former department—that too at the instance of the Vice Chancellor who heard me speak in a different Seminar in the town and learnt of my old association with that University. After the lecture, I was informed that the Lecture was boycotted by all the physical anthropologists in the faculty barring the Head (as she was the one who invited me and thus was obliged to attend). It was chaired by my colleague and friend of long standing—who incidentally joined the department as physical anthropologist with me in 1960. He had to suffer me for one full hour; later in private he told me that he did not understand what I said. Incidentally, I spoke on Changing Orientation to Change and began with evolutionary theories that have been the forte of anthropology of our times.

In 1973-74, as Research Director at the Indian Council of Social Science Research, I was engaged in the task of establishing afresh a set of priorities for research in various social science disciplines. For this task, ICSSR involved noted scholars from various universities and also sought inputs through a mailed questionnaire from the working social scientists. The priorities recommended for the tribal studies by the expert team headed by Professor S.C. Dube included restudies of those tribes which had been studied previously—and mostly—by foreign anthropologists as the monographs produced by them have become dated and the communities studied have been undergoing substantial changes. Along with it the Committee also recommended new ethnographic studies of the tribes that were not covered, by encouraging younger teachers and anthropology students to carry out field work in them.

That exercise has also not yielded good results.

Recently, I had an opportunity to visit Shillong. At the library of the regional station of the Anthropological Survey of India I looked for any new books—particularly ethnographies—on the tribes of the North-East, I did not find any restudies of the Khasis or the Garos, or any other tribes that were studied earlier by the British anthropologists and read by us as students. Of course, more specialized works are being produced; for example, there is an excellent study of the Angami Nagas done by N.K. Das under the auspices of the AnSI titled *Kinship, Politics and Law in Naga Society* (1993). There is also a first rate monograph by Vinay K. Srivastava on the Raikas of Rajasthan that earned him a Ph.D. from Cambridge in the 1990s, but it focused on the religious aspects of this semi-nomadic tribe. However, these are exceptions. In general, it can be said that there are few restudies of the tribes, and very few new studies of the tribes in a holistic framework have been undertaken that has been the hallmark of anthropology in our student days. A review of tribal studies for the fourth round of ICSSR Survey of Research in Sociology and Social Anthropology, carried out by Vinay Srivastava, brought out the fact that there is decline of interest in the conventional field of anthropology. Of course, during this period some encyclopaedias on tribal societies appeared. Also the People of India Project of the Anthropological Survey of India covered the tribal communities. In addition, some good pictorial, in fact, costly coffee-table books done by professional photographers, in league with anthropologists, who provided the script, have also come to the market. But most research is reported as articles, and communications in professional journals such as *Man in India* and *Eastern Anthropologist.* Even here, the number of articles on social anthropological aspects of tribals is falling. The survey revealed that only 67.11 per cent of the articles published in *Man in India* during (1993-2002) and 18.9 per cent articles published in *Eastern Anthropologist* during the period 1988-2001 related to the tribals.

There is another development in regard to the study of the tribes. While interest amongst the social anthropologists is generally declining, people from other social sciences have begun taking interest in the study of specific aspects of tribes, particularly those related to development. Papers presented at this Seminar give evidence of this trend. Additionally, there is now emergence of what is called "auto-anthropology"—studies carried out by indigenous scholars of their own society. Such scholars have brought in not only the "insider view" but also challenged the very definition of the discipline of anthropology—as "the study of other cultures".

As an important growth point, what we must take note of is the fact that both insiders and outsiders, and scholars from various disciplines—and not only the anthropologists—are now getting involved in tribal studies. This is a definite change in orientation towards tribal studies, which would hopefully enrich our understanding of the changing tribal India. The changing demographic profile of researchers doing tribal studies is also reflected in the themes covered. There are relatively few studies on tribal family and kinship, and social structure, and religion. There is growing interest in tribal demography, tribal economy in the context of national economy, tribal ecology, tribal languages, tribal women, politics in tribal areas, and on indigenous knowledge. But the knowledge produced by these efforts needs to be properly consolidated and systematised.

I must hasten to add that in the 1950s there began a new trend of village studies in social anthropology, particularly in India. It is through this route that Srinivas came to social anthropology from sociology. Dube also established himself as a pioneer in village studies with his study of Shamirpet in Andhra Pradesh. He came to anthropology via political science and qualified as an anthropologist by studying the Kamars of Chhattisgarh. The village studies by these scholars distinguished from other such efforts by following the ethnographic techniques of investigation and presentation. Their work gave spurt to village studies; in the process tribal studies also received a certain setback. Today, even village studies of that genre are also on the decline. No new villages are studied in that paradigm, and no restudies are being carried out. I have recently paid visit to the famed Shamirpet village which earned Dube a worldwide recognition. The village that is portrayed in the *Indian Village* represents the past of the present day Shamirpet which is highly urbanized with a few vestiges of the old order. Village of today in India, like the tribes of today, demands a fresh set of studies. The stereotype of the tribe does not match with the actually existing and rapidly changing social structures of these communities. The same is true of the village communities.

It should also be noted that while ethnographic studies of the tribes somehow became less attractive, several new actors entered the scene to carry out studies of specific aspects of tribes using techniques other than participant observation that required longer duration of stay, learning of the native language, and living away from the comforts of the towns. Also, technology has provided new means to collect and preserve data. In an unpublished article on the field work among the Raikas, written by Vinay Srivastava—that I had the pleasure of reading, there is an excellent recounting of the hazards of field work in the 1990s. Compared to the 1960s, these are less painful, but nevertheless indicative of the disincentives for the young researcher. A camera, a tape recorder, facility for postage that helped the researcher to mail his notes to his supervisor or to a safer place for storage, and receipt of instructions and comments on the notes from the supervisor were definitely the new facilitators that were not available to a researcher some 50-60 years back. But today, many more are added—a laptop, internet connection in the remote areas, even mobile connections are now there for speedy dispatch and receipt of messages. Additionally, with the spread of literacy and education, educated locals are available for support; these are the new potentates. Vinay Srivastava has recounted some of the hazards associated with such available manpower.

To sum up, the profile of tribal studies has considerably changed over time. No longer is the anthropologist the only outsider collecting all sorts of data. Tribal studies are no longer the monopoly of the anthropologist. People from different disciplines, and even belonging to governmental and non-governmental agencies, are carrying out specific studies amongst the tribes. Different kinds of statistics are available regarding the individual tribes. The discipline of Anthropology is changing because of the inner dynamics and academic politics. Practitioners of sociology in India who resisted the so-called "intrusion" or "encroachment" of anthropology in their domain are now providing a space for tribal studies while anthropology departments are virtually giving up their claim and concentrating on the biological aspects of the study of Man. On top of all this, our tribal communities are in the throes of change. These developments require a change in the paradigm for the study of tribes.

The Concept of Tribe

While investigating tribes, it must be remembered that there is no uniformity in the use of the concept of Tribe. Ethnographies written in the idiom of 'eternal present' regarded these population groups as non-changing. Since they attracted the attention of the pioneering anthropologists visiting remote areas as being very different and perhaps representing the earlier stage of their society's own evolution they just dubbed them as "primitive" and "preliterate" without bothering to furnish a definition. As a consequence, anthropology became a study of "other cultures"—cultures other than one's own. When Indian anthropologists started studying Indian tribes and villages they somehow challenged that definition of the discipline because they were, in a way, studying their own culture—a multi-cultural outfit called *indigenous civilization*. Unstated, they regarded those as tribes which were studied by alien anthropologists, and those that were listed in earlier censuses as tribes. During those times it was convenient to classify India into urban, rural, and tribal as three distinct population groups based on residence. Tribes were regarded as those that were isolated and distantly located in relatively non-accessible geographical areas.

When independent India adopted its new Constitution that made provision for the listing of tribes in a special Schedule the officialdom took recourse to the Census and listed all the tribes registered therein. In doing so, they ignored the finer distinction made by the Census Commissioners by classifying them on the basis of their religion which excluded all converts—*Hindus, Christians, Muslims, Jains*, etc.—and listed only the non-converts (or the animists) into the category of the tribals. Hutton (1931) went to the extent of saying that tribal religion represents that part which is yet to enter the temple of *Hinduism*! But the official listing included all those that bore the tribal name. Thus, a total of 19,116,498 (19.1 million), divided into 212 tribes, got listed as population of tribal India, constituting 5.36 per cent of the total Indian population in 1951. In undivided India of 1941, this percentage was 7.8 per cent but the deficit of 1951 represented that section which became part of Pakistan (both East and West). Today the number of tribes listed as ST has burgeoned to around 700, and represents a little more than 8 per cent of the total population. The increase in the number of tribes is attributable to separate State-wise listing of the same tribe and inclusion of several other groups which claimed a tribal status. In the process, a group bearing the same name, and claiming the same origin, has become a non-tribe in some States. But we lack anthropological evidence to justify such exclusions.

It is for the latter purpose, that of granting a tribal status to a claimant group, that the question of defining a tribe became significant. Unfortunately, anthropology did not provide an answer, as it did not bother to fashion one. Dube listed six features as descriptors of a tribe, but that was hardly a definition in the real sense of the term. The Government took note of Dube's formulation and came up with the following criteria to judge the candidature of a group for the tribal status:

- Primitive traits;
- Distinctive Culture;
- Geographical isolation;
- Shyness of contact; and
- Backwardness.

These are too vague to judge the candidature of any group. Moreover, if these are applied to those groups that are already included in the ST category, many of them will have to be de-scheduled. In effect, a tribe, in the Indian context, is the one that is included in the official Schedule. There are cases where a tribe bearing the same name belongs to the ST category, but is not included in that category in another State. And many new ones are included in specific States but denied that privilege in another. A case in point is that of the Gujars who were included in the tribal category in the State of Jammu and Kashmir, but not in Rajasthan where there is a mass movement pressing for its inclusion in the ST category. Students of tribal studies take up those groups which enjoy government recognition without bothering about a scientific definition that would be universally applicable. The implication is clear: academic research is carried out along political lines without raising crucial issues. It is, in my opinion, the task of the researcher to point out flaws in the policy and offer guidelines rather than toe the official line.

We need to remind ourselves that while early anthropologists studied tribes as non-changing phenomena, there was an underlying assumption that these are already a part of the evolutionary ladder and are likely to move away to a different destination like the developed societies. A tribal status is, thus, a transitional status in the same manner as, for example, youth is. In due course of time, a group has to give up the tribal status and assume the status waiting for it at another destination. In other words, we need to ask the pertinent question: *When does a Tribe cease to be a tribe?* If we took recourse to history, each one of us can claim to have belonged to one tribe or the other just as the Gujars are doing today, even after enjoying the status of a Hindu or a Muslim caste for several generations. We need to insist that there cannot be a path-reversal, of moving backward. It is the government policy that is putting breaks to halt the process of status change. Today's India cannot be classed into the neat categories of Urban, Rural and Tribal. While the first two are residential categories, the third one is an ethnic or a racial category. That is why tribes can also be classified into urban and rural; certainly sections of them that still remain less mobile—socially or spatially—may need special assistance to move out of their insulation, but this cannot be the case for the entire community.

It is in this sense, that the clubbing together of all statistics for the 8 per cent of the population designated as tribal serves little purpose.

In the late 1950s and early 1960s when I carried out field work in the villages of Rajasthan and Madhya Pradesh, I found presence of the tribal groups in the multi-caste villages—the Bhil in Mewar and the Gond in Madhya Pradesh. They were part of the village system and their families were treated as representatives of their respective castes. The Gond and the Bhil families spread in a number of contiguous villages in the two regions had structures identical to castes and were part of the interactive system of multi-caste communities. The ethnographic descriptions of Morris Carstairs or of Verrier Elwin were not at all applicable to them. Ajit Jogi, former Chief Minister of Chhattisgarh, claiming a tribal status has failed in his attempt to align with the same name tribal group. But the Gond and the Bhil of the two villages of my study in two different States now enjoy the ST status on empirically invalid premises; there is no *gol gadhedo* among the Bhils, and no *ghotul* among the Gonds, who share the residence with other castes.

A politically desirable continuity of the confusion should, in my view, not become the basis for objective portrayal of the existing reality. It is time that we, as social scientists, propose the definition of tribe as a *transitional* structural unit and also suggest the process of its transformation into a larger society as well as its assimilation as a subset in a larger social system. Indian society provides adequate material for such exercise.

Approach to Developmental Issues

A good deal of social science work in recent years is related to developmental issues. Broadly it can be divided into two types: (1) assisting the agents of development in evaluation; and (2) articulating the concerns of the people affected by development.

Since research money is provided by the governmental agencies, the projects carried out as commissioned studies have performed the role of internal assessment highlighting both the achievements and shortfalls. Such exercises served the purpose of giving praiseworthy certification to developmental agencies and of offering recommendations and suggestions—mostly unsolicited. Detached scholars have raised doubts about such researches as they do not generally question the value premises of the development paradigm and follow the politically or administratively defined protocol.

Those critical of developmental policies have followed the usual path of finding fault with the process of modernization, and now of globalization, and showing concern for the gradual death of traditional cultures. It is the perceived ill-effects of development that provided the needed ammunition to such critics.

To my mind, both the approaches are somewhat lop-sided. Of course, we must acknowledge that the use of social scientists in developmental work, particularly for purposes of evaluation, is a welcome trend. It is also desirable that the civil society takes up the cause of the "down-trodden". But this should not rule out the other role of independent assessment in an objective fashion so as the outcome is compared not only with the expected goals, but with the overall impact in terms of both anticipated and unanticipated consequences. At the same time, it is important to examine the premises on which the development paradigm is built and actions initiated. While working with the agency introduces certain biases, taking a protective stance for the cultures brings the social scientist nearer the NGOs who only see the bleak side of the picture. I must make it clear that I am not denying the importance of these roles; I am only suggesting that they are different roles than that of the researcher who ought to be unbiased and evaluate the process objectively—and not with the tainted glasses.

While lecturing in a Seminar in these very premises and under the same auspices, I had raised the question regarding the manner in which we look at development. Development is criticised for (i) its failure in achieving the ends, (ii) its poor implementation and consequent wastage, and (iii) its adverse effects on culture and tradition. In seminars like this, we generally tend to adopt the advocacy role for saving the culture. Such a stance taken earlier by anthropologists earned them an allegation that they are conspiring "to keep the tribals in a zoo". Verrier Elwin, who vociferously advocated the cause of the tribals, was equally eloquent in denying such an allegation. But the undercurrent of such ambivalence still persists. When we want to do something to take the people out of their backwardness we are obliged to initiate programmes of change. And change involves departure from the present state to another one—higher or lower, depending on how we rate the States. It requires no particular skills to identify the areas that get affected by the processes of change—be they planned or self-evolving. Change—whether orthogenetic or planned—does result in the death or disappearance of certain cultural traits. This is inevitable. It is important to record all this, but not to repent. Should we endorse the plea for a halt to development? Are we favouring the cry for retaining anthropological zoos?

Criticism is also laid for the non-effects of change. A good instance is poverty. All these years of planning, since India attained its independence in 1947 have focussed on the alleviation of poverty, and yet this task is on the top of the agenda. How do we view this trend? Should we rest with raising our voices to convey our dissatisfaction and ask for more or for further acceleration of the pace? Or do we challenge the very premises on which the programmes are mounted?

Poor planning, bad administration leading to faulty execution, waste of resources, and continuing plight of the target population are known talking points of any reviews of development exercises.

The message that is generally conveyed is "more of the same" or "different of the same" is needed. For all this, sociological imagination is not needed. What it is that we, as social scientists, can do that is distinct and useful?

For the weaker sections of the society, defined in terms of ascriptive status, the Government enunciated the policy of special treatment by according them a "policy of reservation", and offering them a host of privileges. Originally divided into ST and SC, the weaker sections were given yet another category of the OBC. Hoping that special packages for them would bring them at par with the rest of the society in about 10 to 15 years, the policy and programmes were devised and implemented with considerable publicity and fanfare. More than 64 years have passed and yet we are nowhere near the intended goal. The number of entries in the three categories is constantly rising, and there is clamour for more inclusions. Such demands are raised not only by those who are really poor, but also by the rich and the powerful, and numerically preponderant agricultural groups. What the policy has done is (i) to reinforce a vested interest in backwardness amongst those that are already in one of these lists, and (ii) to encourage those who once hated being dubbed as "lower" or "backward" to gladly assume the designation of "*Dalit*". As long as there are categories of *Adivasis, Dalits,* and of *Pichhada Varg* their assimilation into wider society will remain somewhat suspended. The policy favouring them has initiated the process of moving backward—some sort of *reverse Sanskritization*. It is difficult to say whether this is the intended consequence or an unintended one. Since it was not part of the manifest objective, one would believe this to be the Latent Function of the Policy. Rather than highlighting this, we tend to examine the policy and its effectiveness in terms of the official "givens", and even join the chorus in support of other groups, and even non-Hindu communities, who are seeking relocation in these "privileged categories".

There is yet another anomaly to which regretfully social scientists have not paid adequate attention. SC and ST categories are based on the principle of ascribed status—now also known as *Janma-pradhan*. When a new category was invented to accommodate the newer groups in the privileged section, it was named as Backward *Classes*—classes and not class. Sociologically, class is distinct from caste and tribe, as it represents *achieved* status (*Karma-pradhan)* and allows mobility of its constituents upwards or downwards. But what were listed into this category were *castes,* using basically the criterion of backwardness conceived in terms of poverty and other attributes as resultant of poverty. This subtle distinction is nowhere properly highlighted, and we have also willy-nilly allowed ourselves to fall in this trap.

I have elsewhere indicated that poverty exists at several levels.

At the level of the country or the region it expresses differently and is generally measured in terms of natural endowment or GNP/ GDP. Strategies needed for removal of such poverty require a different orientation: creation of suitable infrastructure, better connectivity, rational use of the available resources, and proper distribution mechanism.

At the level of the family and the individual we need a different strategy. Such poverty ought to be delinked from group-based or region-based poverty. A single community-ethnic or religious—has both rich and poor families. Poverty or affluence does not get distributed equally amongst all its members. Perhaps this is the reason for the introduction of the concept of BPL at the level of the family. But, to perpetuate the ambivalence, government is now collecting data both about the castes and the BPL. If the Constitution forbids identification of castes, and the base data about BPL provides all indicators for judging the poverty status of a family why collect data on Caste? How do you abolish caste while using caste as a status-indicator?

I am tempted to elaborate this point, but shall stop here and proceed towards the problem of tribal education which is the theme of the present Seminar.

State of Tribal Education

I have heard speakers lamenting the poor state of education amongst the tribals, and following the same style of reasoning to which I have alluded earlier in this Lecture, they lament over the deficit. I found the argument along the expected lines. It is true that aggregated data on tribal education paint an unfavourable picture compared to the overall data for the entire Indian population. But there is another way of looking at these figures. Compare these figures with those of 1951 Census figures. At that time, our literacy rate for the country as a whole was dismally low—around 18 per cent, and most of it amongst the male and the young populace. Since the tribals reside mostly—as much as 93 per cent—in rural areas, they were part of the share of country's huge illiterate rural population.

When the country got its independence from the British, the overall literacy rate was low and most of this percentage came from Men, with women, in general, having a really very low—in fact dismal—literacy rate. Surely, the situation must have been pathetic in our tribal belt, and in rural India as a whole which constituted nearly 88 per cent of the total. Literacy then, was typically an urban trait. In our tribal population, literacy rate in 1961 was as low as 9.51 per cent compared to overall literacy percentage of 28.30 per cent. Female literacy amongst the tribals jumped from 1961 average of as low as 3.16 per cent to 34.76 per cent in 2001. This means that Tribal female literacy in 2001 was close to overall Indian literacy rate in 1971 Census. And the literacy rate among tribal males in 2001 was more than the 1981 average for the country as a whole. In the year 2001, our literacy rate further improved to reach 64.83 per cent level, and in 2011, it now stands at 74 per cent. Today our literacy rate in the rural areas is as high as 68.91 per cent, more than the overall literacy rate for the year 2001. Even the female literacy today has gone up from a meagre 8.66 per cent in 1951 to 65.46 per cent in 2011. Literacy data for the tribals for the years 1961 through 2001 tell a revealing story. From a mere 8.54 per cent in 1961 it reached 47.1 per cent in 2001. One would expect that this figure is overtaken by the 2011 Census—the figures for which we will have to wait for some time.

Table 3.1: Tribal Literacy—1961-2001

Year	*Male*	*Female*	*Total*
1961	13.83	3.16	8.54
1971	17.63	4.85	11.39
1981	24.52	8.05	16.35
1991	40.65	18.19	29.60
2001	59.16	34.76	47.10

One can rejoice the literacy climb of the tribal component of our population. It is not a small achievement that female literacy amongst the tribals jumped from 1961 average of as low as 3.16 per cent to 34.76 per cent in 2001. This means that Tribal female literacy in 2001 was close to overall Indian literacy rate in 1971

Census. And the literacy rate among tribal males in 2001 was more than the 1981 average for the country as a whole. What is more satisfying is the fact that amongst tribal children (of the age group 6-14) the enrolment ratio is as high as 86.06 per cent (90.58% for boys and 81.10% for girls)—this ratio ranges from 60.90 in Nagaland to more than 108 in Kerala, Manipur, and Tamilnadu, and as high as 114 in Sikkim. Recent statistics also indicate that as many as 539 ST girls are enrolled for their Ph.D.s. The total number of tribal girls in Higher Education, including the Polytechniques, is as high as 1,42,280. These figures definitely indicate a rising percentage of literates, particularly among the young population of tribal women. Of course, this must be acknowledged that the overall average does not suggest the precarious condition in some tribal groups or in sections of particular tribes that still lead an isolated existence. But more than 80 per cent enrolment of girls leaves out only less than 20 per cent of them in the category of non-school going population.

Given my limitations of time, I have dwelt only on all-India figures for the tribal population. They prove the point that literacy is spreading in our tribal belts. More important than this is the point that we have reached at a stage where we need disaggregated data for individual tribes in different States; and regions within the States. Since tribal areas in certain States are also classified as urban and rural, it is important to locate not only the percentage of the literates but also of the educated in them. I suspect the profile of literacy and education to be substantially different amongst the tribal groups of our North-Eastern region. Given such heterogeneous profile of our tribal communities it would be unwise to suggest a panacea—a common cure for all the tribes; this is time to think of community specific strategies. For this, we need systematic investigation of individual regions that would enable us to draw dependable profiles and to prepare noteworthy research papers in place of those that fall into the category of journalism or NGO type advocacies. No doubt, they are equally important, but they cannot be substitutes for an in-depth enquiry.

Then, there is a need for giving up over-emphasis to literacy and to primary education. Having attained 74 per cent literacy, using whatever yardstick, we are left only with 26 per cent of our population that need to move in the realm of literacy. In the 1950s, literacy in the entire Third World was at low ebb, and the world community, under the aegis of the United Nations, particularly UNESCO, assigned eradication of illiteracy a well-deserved priority. It is in that format that the countries devised their own programmes and action plans. The challenge was so huge that the government budgets allocated for education were largely diverted to literacy and adult education programmes, virtually to the neglect of higher education. In the changed circumstances of today where countries are recording high percentages of literacy it is necessary to rethink our priorities in the field of education. In saying so, I am not undermining the huge challenge that still bothers us with regard to removal of illiteracy. While percentage-wise there is a fall in our illiteracy rate, but in terms of numbers, our 26 per cent illiterates account for around 240 million people—close to the population of India at the time of partition!! But with so many literates around, the task of spreading literacy has become a bit easier. There are some scholars who believe that the IT revolution has opened new windows through which people can be educated without being literate. Even the literates are rendered illiterate because of *computeracy*—this is a new indicator and requires adequate attention to save people from remaining *incomputerates.*

In our enthusiasm to promote literacy and universalise Primary Education, we have continually undermined secondary and tertiary education. Despite mushrooming growth of our schools and colleges, and universities, we are not able to accommodate the burgeoning number of students knocking the doors of these institutions. That is why the sub-culture of coaching centres and other surrogate structures has developed. That is why the cut-out line for admissions to colleges is reaching 99 per cent. All those who have passed the examinations conducted by competent bodies do not get automatically admitted to higher classes. And in such a competing milieu, we have brought in the additional factor of reservation of seats for special categories of people for whom the cut-out line is also lowered.

The question is that of denying admission to the deserving irrespective of one's ascribed status. An educational status is an *achieved* status. One ascends the educational ladder through one's performance. At the point of initial entry—that is, at the nursery or kindergarten level—admissions can be made on the basis of the child's *ascribed* status; but once it enters the educational domain, it is the child's performance which should matter irrespective of one's caste or tribe. To carry the culture of partiality in a system that is built on the premise of performance is to render the education system defunct.

When we examine the situation of education among the tribals, we need to address to this anomaly in our policy. Surely, this cannot be the politician's cup of tea; and the bureaucrat, who is expected to execute the orders of his master, has no choice but to fall in line. Sadly, actors in the academe have also not properly articulated this concern.

I also notice a trend that supports the idea of reviving traditional system of education among the tribals on the ground that the modern ways of teaching are alien to them. This argument makes education synonymous with socialization and enculturation. It implies, in a way, denial of access to the world of knowledge that is larger than the knowledge sphere of a tribe. We must carefully examine such a recipe. The tribals themselves may see in it a conspiracy of the elite to deprive the tribals from the fruits of modernity.

For instance, witness the trend of reintroducing English at the primary level in many of the Indian States. In view of the fact that many of the IT related companies are hiring people who have command over English leaders are seeking such a revision to facilitate the poor sections of the society who go to government schools and are not taught that language until they reach Grade VI. The fear that a foreign language would earn supremacy over the native language is part of cultural awakening, but the attendant disadvantages are the concern of the families that are struggling to move out of deprivation.

There is no time to elaborate the argument here. I have used this platform to only raise certain issues that I regard crucial and need careful examination. I conclude with the hope that in the ensuing sessions you will have occasion to launch an assault on my line of reasoning or to further sharpen it.

4

Paradoxes of Anthropocentric and Globalisation with reference to Tribal Education in India

R.D. Singh

Introduction

The traditional communities like tribes and non-tribal agricultural communities have seriously suffered due to denial of education to preserve socio-political dominance and preservation of rigid caste system in India in Sanskritic and English medium education. The impact of pursuance of the elitist policies have resulted in isolated caste, cultures and regions which paved the ways to exogenous political economic dominance during Muslims and British periods.

The stagnation of tribal communities in exclusive elitist socio-political policies has created anthropocentric conflicts due to dominance and succession process primarily under the condition of exclusive economic policies during colonial and post-colonial periods. The social reform policies of reservation to tribes in education and employment could not create much impact because of non-recognition of their social structure, economic base and impact of exclusive economic policies on their existence, identity, stakes and access to the common property resources. Due to serious environmental and ecological economic conflicts resulting from deforestation, environmental economic impacts, increasing population and dominance and succession process has serious implications on extinction and impoverishment of tribes.

The resulting anthropocentric conflicts have created serious problems of caste and community conflict and social attitudes of rejection of education and incapacities of nomadic and pastoral tribal economic base creating social and economic inaccess to education. The access to education, in that sense, needs to be viewed in terms of identity, freedom, stakes and access, as identifiable in the education policies.

The increasing anthropocentric conflicts and regionalism have created conflicts of cultural identity and linguistic regionalism in education. The elites have rejected it and moved to English dominated private and exclusive education, a rejection of social coexistence and with an intent on retaining the political and economic dominance in globalization and privatization policy regime.

Contradiction between Inclusive Education and Exclusive Economic Policy

The education policy being promoted for social inclusion has been constrained by exclusive economic policies of modernization, globalization and privatization. The sustainable development policies for ensuring economic sustenance to tribes has failed because of denial of stakes and impacts of monopolistic markets fast accessing forest, land, mineral and water resources. The resources of tribal regions are flowing to market regions in globalization-privatization mode marginalizing the tribes to be unorganized labour force to outmigrate for livelihood.

The monopolistic market is now controlling the resources which is flowing outside the tribal regions and the compensation in decentralized planning is denied in Myrdal's (1957) core-periphery contradictions.

The tribes facing serious problems of losing stakes over resources are conflicting over identity, freedom, stakes and access. The tribal sub-plan and tribal regional plans pursue preservationist and conservationist policies rather the inclusive policies and non-integrated sectoral economic policies focused on community and regional development.

The serious community and regional level development conflicts in market economies pose serious tribal ecological and the habitat conflicts. The long term policies of restructuring and readjustment in globalization and privatization have created further problem of unemployment, livelihood insecurity in drought affected tribal regions. That is why tribal habitats are fast vanishing in forest and grazing regions in most of the States as reported by various census reports.

The education policies of inclusion and access is treated on a sectoral policy framework in total disregard of social structure, economic base and geographic conditions as well as anthropological conditions in nomadic, pastoral and agricultural ecologic relations, thus fragmented and social and geographical isolation (Kavoori, 2007). The dominating problems of tribes is extinction of primitive tribes, serious ecological and economic conflicts of pastoral tribes and serious poverty and unemployment among tribes dependent upon agriculture. Thus, the major problem of tribes is economic and ecologic, which is threatening their stakes over resources. Under this situation, supply of education as sectoral policy with subsidies to the children though has increased access, it has touched the fringe population which have adapted to modernizational mode of economy and society. In majority, the peripheral (Socially, economically and geographically) tribal population still faces problems of access as in most of the traditional communities there is supply based centralized decentralization programmes.

The exclusive economic policy under globalization and privatization has resulted in increasing market control of common property resources such as minerals, forests, land and water for the exogenous global market, creating a vicious circle of circular and cumulative causation of Myrdal type. The flow of resources outside the region though has induced production due to privatization, it has created serious substitution of employment and poverty and the conflict over stakes has increased in the form of community revolt against the private interests being promoted by the government. Sen termed "Collective Choices" and "identity and freedom" as the sole purpose of development of societies or communities.

The sustainable development approach in globalization and privatization led restructuring policy has largely failed to readjust the tribal communities as all other traditional communities. The alarming call for inclusive growth is being promoted in which ecologic and economic resources are being monopolized as in case of Posco in Orissa.

The micro and regional planning in programming framework has two serious problems. The feudal and now capitalist market structure is creating serious problem of stakes and access to common property resources, on the other hand, limitation of planning due to experience, lack of resources (due to economic backwardness) and feudal and market economic policies have created inter-regional political conflicts leading to cultural fundamentalism rather than adaptation to alien globalization, privatization and modernizational mode under the condition urban-rural dualism (Jandhyala, 2007).

Social Response to Education

Missionary education with religious and political ideological frame is influencing education. Promotion of *madarsa* and Christian missionary education among traditional communities increased in socio-political dominance. Other Hindu cultural outfits are also influencing tribal education in different manners resulting in social and cultural stratification and resulting in socio-political conflicts (Mishra, 2007).

Missionary schools imparting English medium education have been accepted by elites in globalization and privatization policies. Privatization of education has a growing tendencies of moving away of social and economic elites from public education institution. This has serious implications of increasing opportunity costs and inaccess to tribes.

Public education infrastructure as inclusive policy is posing problem of social and cultural isolationism and acting against multi-culturism with emerging influence of market led globalization. This poses a problem of integration of education with economic policies in which tribal regions face a serious challenge.

The level of literacy has an increasing trend among tribes. This is not translated much in economic capacity building but rather increased social and economic insecurities due to lack of employment opportunity.

The structural changes in regional economies which are being influenced by exogenous policy implications on the principles of maximization of production and profits is alien to tribal societies. The government's effort of bringing social change and access has limited and short-run impact causing serious socio-political conflicts. The attempts of social stratification and social sector approach in political and economic policies has created serious and widespread social conflicts, but acting against the social capacities for adaptation and development.

Implications of Planned Interventions to Tribal Education

The goal and objectives of education have for long been debated and discussed from cultural, economic and social standpoints. However, in modernization approach in globalization and privatization process, many developing countries including India, emphasized maximization of economic growth to keep pace with western economies. The social objectivity to education during colonial period was related to legal protection of society, health, administration, etc., along with freedom and independence. After independence, creation of administrative superstructure and specialized sectoral demands motivated education. The education as a service to society as a public and social policy led to creation of a foundation for education in India, which has created public superstructure and infrastructure. Privatization of education in liberalization policy has serious profit motives which has led to social vulnerability and deterioration in quality of both private and public education system. Increasing cost of education and problem of opportunity cost has rendered an economic criteria to education, rather than education as medium of social and human development to attain identity and freedom, rather than part of the emerging market forces which have limited employment opportunities. The lack of infrastructure and quality in education is resulting in spurious education as quantitative measure having limited economic impacts and bringing in social and economic inefficiencies. Though education infrastructure is increasing in tribal regions, access to tribes is a serious problem in horizontal and vertical dimension. There is also increasing problem in differentiation of education on the basis of infrastructure, quality and contents of education. Thus, the dichotomous and dysfunctional education system prevails in public-private mode. The educational infrastructure in tribal regions are poorly developed and supply of education has a feudal mind set in fragmentations of educational policies.

The problems of social adjustments and social change to adapt to modernization mode of education is constrained because social change are forced through displacement for education and access to employment.

Concluding Remarks

Inclusive education policies in differentiated formal education system, vocationalisation, distance learning programmes, etc., do not have much impact in most of the rural areas and tribal regions. Majority of the traditional societies and regions are facing serious economic problem due to losing traditional rights to resources and serious environmental, economic and socio-cultural economic problems. The educational planning in regional framework needs to be developed in view of social and economic needs and demands based upon social organizations, community needs and aspiration to evolve a regenerative education policy to make it inclusive, participatory rather than supply based homogeneous educational policies. Even in the globalization policy framework, creation of local capacity and access in need based, demand based policy framework is required. This would require making the education and economic policies really inclusive in developmental planning process, rather than political inclusion in programme framework.

REFERENCES

Jandhyala, B.G.Tilak (2007): "Inclusive growth and education: On the approach to Eleventh Plan" *EPW*, Vol. XLII, No. 38, pp. 3872-3877.

Kavoori, Purnendu S. (2007): "Reservation for Gujjars: A Pastoral Perspectives, *EPW*, Vol. XLII, No. 38.

Mishra, Udayon (2007): "Adivasi Struggle in Assam", *EPW*, Vol.XLII, No, 51, pp. 11-14.

Myrdal, General (1957): "Economics of Underdeveloped Regions", Duckworth.

5

Globalisation and Expansion of Education with reference to Indigenous Population in India

Tapan Mohanty

Background

A cursory glance at the history is enough to ensure the role of globalization as a process of macro sociological change in setting the agenda and restructuring the conditions of existence. After the industrial revolution and colonialism, globalization is the most influential event that has set the course of history. Of late, there has been a virtual flooding of literature on globalization examining its various dimensions and directions across the world especially on its social, cultural and economic facets (Robertson 1992; Giddens 1994, 1996; Waters 1995; Marginson 1998; Mundy 2000; etc.). Therefore, it would be both redundant and revisionist to review the vast amount of literature on globalization and trace its meaning, nature and scope or highlight is origin, growth and development. Therefore, in this essay I would limit myself focusing on the impact of globalization on legal education in general and delineate it further in the context of India. The reason behind my effort lies on my own experience of working in the area of legal education and obviously my involvement in the study of globalization. My current location in Europe and consequent participation in a global educational programme offers me the unique opportunity of mapping the meaning and magnitude of globalization as well as its impact, systematically and substantially. Finally, it may be added that this significant amalgamation of anthropological methods of emic and etic research enables me in developing a perspective that is both pragmatic and paradigmatic.

Before delving into the dynamics of the topic it is essential and imperative to provide a brief conceptualization of globalization particularly in the form mapping a perspective that would entail the essay in developing a structure and allow us to follow a definite format. This means the narrative has to be both minimalistic and macrocosmic. Therefore, I have to follow the discourses on globalization like a painting with rapid strokes of brush rather than an encore meant for connoisseurs. Purely for the description and analysis a sociological perspective on globalization has been emphasized upon and essentially a cultural and sociological analytical framework has been used following the writings of leading sociologists. Consequently, the parameters of globalization defined and developed by Giddens, Waters, Bauman, Beck, Mundy, Castelles, Stromquiest are used in the essay. Subsequently, globalization has been defined both as a 'process of integration and differentiation', a process of time-space compression and an awareness about so', and 'essentially a phenomenon of 90s'. Based on thematic synchronization of globalization a certain number of parameters has been developed thus making it easy for systematic analysis. The parameters are following:

- Information and knowledge intensive.
- Global competitiveness.
- Structural and functional flexibility.
- Market Driven.
- Transnationalism.

At the analytical level the impacts of globalization on education in general and legal education in particular have been examined and arguments are substantiated from the events from India. Therefore, it is not difficult to understand that people living in the era of 'liquid modernity' (Buaman, 2000) are fast restructuring the conditions of their existence including the norm of interaction in the 'legitimate community of practice'. Consequently the production, distribution and exchange of knowledge are largely determined by the formal instructions and structures, viz., schools, universities and centres of learning are undergoing perceptible transformations in response to the challenges of 'risk society' (Beck, 1992).

Investment in education has long been accepted as an important dimension of development, particularly in democratic nation-states. In fact, the increasing emphasis on 'social capital' and 'good governance' as *sine qua non* of human development, have reinforced the importance of education making educational studies both interesting and imperative. This is more so in case of secondary education which the main link between primary and higher education. Secondary education becomes an important instrument of analysis for a variety of reasons that includes its position in the educational structure, its linkage with other sectors of education, its relevance to the educational context as well as its contribution towards supply of manpower in a growing economy.

Secondary education becomes its acts as a conveyor belt between the primary education at the one end and the higher education at the other. First, as creating opportunities for students by enabling them to accrue higher, technical and professional education and subsequently to gain the benefits of such education in their personal and professional life. Similarly, it also supplies manpower for primary education that in turn uses their expertise in elevating the standards of primary education. As an important point of transition secondary education offers a significant point for understanding and analysis of prevailing educational scenario in the country. Research evidences show that secondary education is the fastest growing sector in most of the countries further emphasizing the need of universalization of secondary education. No country in the world could achieve sustainable development without being providing opportunities for secondary education. Due to various reasons primary education remained the focus of state sponsorship. Literacy movements and opening of primary schools become a favourite state engagement. Similarly, the need for industrial development and technological requirements coupled with administrative necessity ensured the growth and popularization of higher education. Needless to add that in our flight towards high literacy, fancy for technical and professional education and regard for higher education somewhere secondary education could not get due attention. However, it would be wrong to assume that secondary education in India was entirely left to fend for itself primarily because sporadically efforts were made to look into the problems of secondary education even if in relation to either primary or higher education.

A proper perspective on the development of secondary education can be evolved only when we critically look at the secondary education scenario in India. In that direction this chapter intends to examine the extent of access to and expansion of secondary education facilities on the one hand and the demand for secondary education at the other. The access part examines the spatial availability in terms of distance and the population coverage. It also examines the demand for secondary education in terms of enrolment besides capturing the overall national scenario. It is essential to examine the pattern of the growth of secondary education in different States to highlight the diversity vis-à-vis their levels of socio-economic development. In order to compare and contrast the development of secondary education in different States based on diversity and disparities the indicators, viz., access, extent of growth and expansion of institutions, rate of participation, extent of enrolment and types of delivery mechanism have been analyzed and explained. Besides these, rural-urban, gender and ethnic disparities too have been examined.

In order to arrive at a comprehensive understanding of the system we have tried to examine these issues from national, State level (sample States) and further down to the district level. The data from four sample States provide information on size, structure and particularities of the access scenario. Same is the case with our analysis of growth, demand and delivery mechanisms. This helps us in solving the queries relating to the extent and dimension of growth of secondary schools at the all India level, in the particular State as well at micro level.

In India though government is the main provider of school education at various points of time there have been other players engaged in delivering education to students. Based on the funding, management and administration schools in India can be classified into three broad categories namely, (i) Government (funded and managed), Private aided (established and managed by private agencies but funded by government) and private schools (both funded and managed by private bodies). Apart from these three there are many unrecognized and unorganized schools at the lower level of school education spread across the country.

Since education comes under the Concurrent List, the responsibility of catering to the educational needs becomes the joint responsibility of the central and respective State governments. Therefore, the term government has a wider connotation here and needs further clarification. Government here includes State and local bodies and many schools in India are funded and managed by either of them. While State governments are largely responsible in providing schools, Central Government under the special scheme for transferable central government employees has opened and managed a few schools commonly known as *Kendriya Vidyalaya* (central schools). Similarly, in order to take care of rural talented students the Central Government has opened and run pace setting schools. There are a total number of 508 such schools known as *Jawahar Navodaya Vidyalayas* (JNVs) spread over 508 districts of the country.

In the context of India it is difficult to have a universal picture simply because there are so much diversity and differences. National pictures do not reflect the correct situations and micro data have little relevance for macro policies. More often than not macro data either conceal or inflate local contexts thus negating the very methodology of studies. Therefore, in this paper an emphasis is given in depicting national, major States, sample States and local societies to provide more realistic picture.

This chapter is an overview of overall educational scenario in the country and expansion of schools. It also examines the extent of access (in terms of distance and coverage of rural population) to secondary education, equity in access and number of schools per 10,000 populations. The trends and pattern of growth of schools at the national, inter-State, rural-urban areas, sample States, intra-State (regional levels) have also been comprehended in this chapter. This chapter also concentrates on trends of demand for secondary education measured in terms of growth of enrolment at different levels, viz., increase in the number of institutions. It also deals with average class size rather section size in order to primarily assess and identify the extent of the demand in terms of participation in educational institutions and the supply in terms of the provision of institutions. Towards the end of the chapter an attempt has been made to examine the gross enrolment ratio in secondary education given the extent of growth of institutions and enrolment in its various dimensions and by different providers.

Educational Scenario : An Overview

India has taken up the challenge of providing educational access and opportunities to its vast segments of population rather boldly. The post-independent India inherited a poor educational infrastructure from its colonial masters and had to begin from the scratch the massive agenda of educational development. In fact, the Constitution of India guarantees education to its future citizens. According to the Article 45 of the Constitution the state shall provide free and compulsory education to the children below fourteen years of age. Similarly, Article 46 empowers the state to specially take care of the educational needs of the weaker sections of the country namely the scheduled castes and tribes. In order to fulfil these Constitutional mandates and obligation the Indian State has taken considerable steps to step up educational provisions in general and school education in particular. Substantive efforts have been made in translating the Constitutional mandate to reality even norms and principles have been made flexible to expand the base of education particularly for disadvantaged sections and in unserved areas. A brief glance at the Table 5.1 shows the magnitude

Table 5.1 : Education in India at a Glance: Total Number of Institutions, Size of Enrolment and Number of Teachers, 2001-02

Educational Institutions	*Number of Institutes (In '000)*	*Size of Enrolment (In Millions)*	*Number of Teachers (In '000)*
Primary	664.04	113.88	1928.08
Upper Primary	219.62	44.83	1467.92
Secondary	91.43	20.05	1018.80
Higher Secondary	42.05	10.45	758.70
Tech./Indus./Arts and Crafts Institutes	4.3	0.06	n.a.
Polytechnic Institutes	1.2	0.04	n.a.
Teacher Training Institutes	1.2	0.01	n.a.
Higher Education Institutions	13.15	8.85	426.80
Universities#	0.27	*	*
	1037.26	198.17	5600.3**

* Included in Higher Education Institutions.

** Figure does not include teachers in Technical/Industrial/Arts and Crafts Institutes, Polytechnic Institutes and Teacher Training Institutes.

\# Includes deemed Universities and Institutions of National Importance.

Source: Selected Education Statistics, 2001-2002, MHRD, GoI, 2003.

of educational system in India. The network of the educational system in the second highest populous country like India is its vast size comprising of 1037.26 thousand educational institutions having 198.17 million students with 5600.3 thousand teachers covering different levels of education.

The educational facilities include 0.66 million of primary schools, 0.21 million upper primary schools and 0.09 million lower secondary schools, 0.042 million higher secondary schools, 0.013 million higher educational institutions and 270 universities including deemed universities and institutions of national importance in the country. During 2001-02, these educational institutions enrolled 113.88 million students in primary, 44.83 million in upper primary, and 20.04 million in lower secondary and 10.45 million students in higher secondary and 8.85 million in higher education. Such network of institutions had been developed over a long period of time. India has one of the largest networks of educational institutions in the world.

Institutional Expansion : Trends and Perspectives

At the backdrop of this huge Indian educational network, it is important to underscore to what extent the facilities are able to provide access both in terms of distance and coverage of population. The following section examines in detail the access condition. The phenomenal growth of education in India can be gauged from the fact that in 1950-51 there were only 209 thousand primary schools, 13.6 thousand upper primary schools and 7.4 secondary and higher secondary schools. Compared to the existing situation mentioned earlier it pales into insignificance. However, it needs to be emphasized that the current educational development profile reflects the improvement of access conditions in a broader perspective. There had been phenomenal expansion of educational facilities at all levels of school education and more so in case of secondary education (Table 5.2).

The expansion of secondary schools cannot be seen in isolation as it has both forward and backward linkages with other sectors of education especially the lower levels of school education. More importantly, achievement in elementary education is a pre-requisite for the growth of secondary education besides various other factors such as accessibility, availability, affordability and

Table 5.2: Number of Institutions by Levels of Education in India

(Figures are in '000)

Year	Institutions (Figures are in '000)				
	Primary	Upper Primary	Secondary	Hr. Secondary	Secondary and Hr. Secondary together
1950-51	209.7	13.6	7.4*	–	7.4
1960-61	330.4	49.7	17.3*	–	17.3
1970-71	408.4	90.6	37.1*	–	37.1
1980-81	494.5	118.6	39.3	12.3	51.6
1990-91	560.9	151.5	59.5	19.2	79.8
2000-01	638.7	206.3	87.7	38.4	126.1
2001-02	664.0	219.6	91.4	42.1	133.5
2002-03	651.3	245.3	90.7	46.4	137.2

* Includes Secondary and Higher Secondary/Intermediate/Pre-University/Jr. College/Pre-Degree Institutions.

Source: Selected Educational Statistics, various issues, MHRD, GoI, New Delhi.

social demand, etc. At primary level expansion of educational institutions made in last few decades is quite commendable. From the decade of 1950s to 2002-03 there has been 3-fold increase in the number of primary schools. Similarly at upper primary and secondary levels the schools have grown by around 19 and 18 times between the periods of 1951 to 2002-03. While increased number of schools reflects importance attributed to education but it does not reveal the extent of facilities available in terms of distance and coverage of population. Towards this we need to examine access conditions.

Secondary Education: Access and Coverage

Access to educational facilities is a pre-condition for educational development although it is not a sufficient condition. Access is usually defined as the absence of barriers (economic, physical, etc.) that keeps an eligible student away from the school—the education service delivery point. The numbers of factors which affect access to the education system include primarily, the distance from the school, travel cost, etc. The lesser (more) the distance from the school the easier (more difficult) is the access for children to participate in schools. The indicators on access such as the proportion of population served with schools by distance is important in the sense that the availability of schools does not automatically improve the access. This is because the real physical distance from home to schools as well as the equity in distribution of schools spread over territories is of critical importance while ensuring access. According to Sixth All India Educational Survey (1993) only 18.9 per cent of rural population in India had lower secondary schools within the habitation while 27.16 per cent of people were served by lower secondary schools located within the radius of two kilometres. Nearly 78 per cent of rural populations were having secondary schools within 5 kilometres of radius of their habitations whereas 10 per cent of people had to travel more than 8 kilometres to access the lower secondary school.

Further at higher secondary level only a small proportion of populations had school facilities within the habitation while 15.36 per cent of population had access to higher secondary schools within the distance of 4-6 kilometres from their habitations. However, a majority of rural populations had access to higher secondary schools within a radius of 8 kilometres of their habitation. Comparatively, there was better access condition for primary and upper primary levels. This shows that with the increase in the level of education there had been a corresponding increase in distance between the home and school at least in rural areas.

The extent of physical access to secondary schools in rural areas varies across the States and among the social groups, based on the geographical and socio-economic context besides the policy of the State. Out of 17 major States in 15 States more than three-fourth of the rural population was provided with the lower secondary school service within the radius of five kilometres.

In case of Rajasthan and Uttar Pradesh two of India's backward States around two-third of population had access to lower secondary schools. In fact, except Madhya Pradesh, all other major States had provided lower secondary school facilities to more than 80 per cent of their population within the radius of 8 kilometres. There were of course, some States, viz., Punjab, Kerala, Haryana and West Bengal who had provided lower secondary schools to more than 90 per cent of its rural population within five kilometres of their habitation. Similar disparities had also been found at higher secondary level in the form of coverage and distance. Among the major States Maharashtra tops in terms of providing higher secondary schools to a large number of population within the habitation (11.12%) and is closely followed by Gujarat (10.25%) and Haryana (9.75%). Bihar with (1.21%) occupies the bottom while a few other States were pegged at 2 to 3 per cent. In 12 States more than 70 per cent of population had access to higher secondary schools within the distance of 8 kilometres from their habitations. In many States one-third of their population and in other States more than half the rural population had to cover more than 8 kilometres to seek higher secondary education.

Among the four sample States Maharashtra had the highest percentage of population (35.08) covered with facility of lower secondary school within the habitation, while Uttar Pradesh had the lowest average. In Kerala and Andhra Pradesh less than one-third of population were served by lower secondary schools within the habitation. In case of Kerala and Maharashtra except a negligible percentage of population, the rest had access to lower secondary schools within the radius of five kilometres. However, 15 and 9 per cent of the population in case of Uttar Pradesh and Andhra Pradesh, respectively had to travel more than 8 kilometres to approach the lower secondary school.

Maharashtra though had the highest percentage of rural population covered with higher secondary schools within the habitation, yet 43 per cent of them had to travel more than 8 kilometres for a higher secondary school. A high majority of rural population in Uttar Pradesh and Kerala had access to higher secondary schools within the radius of 8 kilometres. In case of Andhra Pradesh, more than half of the rural population had to travel more than 8 kilometres in order to approach a higher secondary school. This pattern of access to lower secondary education, for rural children definitely constrained their participation in school, especially for girl students, where physical distances are really difficult to overcome.

Equity in Access

In a country like India with different types of disparities, the important question is whether access to education is equitably distributed among different social groups. In fact, S.C. and S.T. are the disadvantaged sections of the Indian society who lags far behind the other communities in terms of social and economic development. Furthermore, it may be added that scheduled castes (16%) and scheduled tribes (9%) constitute one-fourth of India's total population. The Scheduled Tribes largely live in exclusive areas, which correspond geographically difficult terrain of forest and hilly areas. The tribal habitations are characterized by low density of population and are scattered. These geographical features and density of population play an important role in ensuring access to schools as norms regarding access to schools are based on population. Although in last few decades the norms regarding opening of schools have been relaxed for tribal areas but it is largely confined to primary schools only. The SCs despite living in the plain areas along with other castes, have their separate habitations which are normally away from the upper caste dwellings. In view of their segregated habitation patterns and socio-economic disadvantages it is essential to look into the issue of equity of access so that real Indian perspective on access can be generated.

During 1993, at all India level 8.5 per cent of scheduled caste and 7.8 per cent of Scheduled Tribe population were served by lower secondary school within their habitation while one-third of SC and one-fifth of ST population have the access to lower secondary schools within the distance of two kilometres. One-fourth of SC and one-fifth of tribal population needed to travel 2-4 km. to avail the lower secondary schooling facilities. Compared to the general population as well as SC which has a higher access to lower secondary education roughly 78 per cent, the ST are poorly placed at only 59 per cent. One-fourth of tribal populations are unable to access lower secondary education unless they travel more than 8 kilometres.

The distance in tribal areas need to be understood in terms of barriers that makes really difficult to overcome as they are filled with hills, mountain, forests, wildlife, waterbodies, etc. In effect, the 8-kilometre barrier cuts the chance for one-fourth of tribal population the access to lower secondary education. In case of higher secondary education a large segment of tribal population (56.62%) have little or no access to education in view of their isolated existence and social discrimination. However, this national level picture does not necessarily reflect the real extent of access in different States.

Among the 17 major States there are variations in provision of schools in predominantly SC and ST habitations. In order to ascertain the degree and depth of these variations, we have undertaken the study of sample States. Among the four sample States, a small segment of SC and ST population had access to secondary and higher secondary schools within their habitation. Only 2.6 per cent of SC population in Uttar Pradesh had access to secondary schools within the habitation, though the State has a sizeable SC population in the country. Maharashtra shows a better picture as one-fifth of SC population in the State are provided with secondary schools within their habitation. In case of tribals, Kerala had higher percentage coverage with secondary schools within the habitation. However, in Kerala tribals are very small segment compared to Maharashtra and Andhra Pradesh. While educationally developed States like Maharashtra and Kerala have relatively better access opportunities for SC and ST, the State of Uttar Pradesh did not show concern in providing access to secondary education for disadvantaged groups which typically characterizes the backwardness. Although Andhra Pradesh has lesser percentage of SC and ST population, but they are served with secondary schools within the habitations, this State has distinction of providing hostel facilities to SC and ST students in large number to facilitate participation in secondary education which is not the case in fact it is surprising that despite Dalit (SC) political party called BSP being in power in Uttar Pradesh, there has been no improvement in access conditions for SC population. However, the States with higher socio-economic development standard had better access for SC and ST communities for secondary schools, i.e., within the habitation, than backward States. But backward States with higher concentration of SC and ST population had poor access condition for these communities.

The data of sixth all India Educational Survey was more than a decade old and since then there has been significant expansion of schools at all levels, including secondary education as per the prescribed norms. With concerted efforts, India has been successful in providing primary schools to a large majority of rural habitation in close proximity. This is true in most of the States and also among four sample States. As a part of DPEP and *Sarva Siksha Abhiyan*, the norms for establishing primary schools had been relaxed and also alternative schools were established for providing access to primary education within the habitation. According to a rough estimate more than 98 per cent rural habitation are having either formal or alternative primary schools within the habitation and remaining of them have within one kilometer distance.

Further, large number of schools was upgraded from primary and upper primary levels thereby increasing access at higher levels of school education. This has been viewed as an important strategy for achieving universalization of elementary education and improving the transition rates. As a result, in most of the states, secondary schools have been provided within 8 kilometres distance as per the prescribed norm. The provisional data of seventh All India Education Survey of sample states shows that in Maharashtra and Kerala all most all the rural habitations are provided with secondary schools within the distance of 8 km, while in case of Andhra Pradesh 87 per cent of rural habitations have access to secondary schools within 8 km distance. Further, the micro level data from the case studies of sample schools in rural areas show that the catchment area of the schools covered less than 8 km.

Affirmative Action in Education

Affirmative action remains one of the most controversial political philosophies throughout the world. Conservatives and liberals alike recognize that injustices inherent to many political systems have affected the economic and social progress of discriminated groups. However, the debate remains whether the State should employ policies that attempt to redress the wrongs of the past, even if these policies may be inherently discriminatory. Even supporters of affirmative action disagree over the most effective way to implement policy.

Affirmative Action is defined as the employment programmes required by federal statutes and regulations designed to remedy discriminatory practices in hiring minority group members; i.e., steps designed to eliminate existing and continuing discrimination, to remedy lingering effects of past discrimination, and to create systems and procedures to prevent future discrimination; commonly based on population percentages of minority groups in a particular area. Factors considered are race, colour, sex, creed, and age.

There are currently two dominating policy models that persist in governments throughout the world. The first and most controversial model is a direct quota system. Governments that have adopted these policies, for example in India, Malaysia, and Sri Lanka, have imposed aggressive quantized reservation system, requiring a set number of positions to be reserved for members of a disadvantaged class. Often these reservations have expanded beyond the public sector, affecting private enterprise. The second model calls for more subversive policies. The affirmative action policies of the United States and Great Britain fall within this model. US law prohibits the use of quotas or reservations. Instead affirmative action policies encourage a holistic approach when analyzing an individual's candidacy for a position. The theory is that candidates will increase diversity while also maintaining the same quality of work.

The case for affirmative action for Blacks in the USA and the former untouchables, or *dalits*, in India can be made both on account of historical deprivation as well as on grounds of persistent disparity and continuing discrimination. Thus, despite the differences between race and caste as institutions, the end result for Blacks and *dalits* are very similar. Affirmative action can be, and is, viewed as a programme of compensation for historical injustices and very few would argue with the contention that historically, dalits and Blacks suffered deep injustices, disparity, deprivation and discrimination. However, the case for affirmative action on grounds of *contemporary* disparities and discrimination is highly contentious. In what follows, it will be argued that both in India and the USA, the current economic and social systems perpetuate patterns of caste-based or race-based disparities in all spheres of life: education, occupation/work, income/consumption, health indicators. The continued presence of social and economic discrimination aggravates these disparities.

In addition to the caste system, more than 50 million Indians belong to tribal communities, that are often distinct from the Hindu religious fold. These are the *adivasis,* (literally, original inhabitants) who have origins that precede the Aryans and even the Dravidians of the South. Many have lifestyles and religious practices that are distinct from any of the known religions in India and languages distinct from the official languages of India and their dialects. Most live on the margins of existence, excluded from the mainstream of development process. These tribes are also targets of affirmative action, similarly notified in a government schedule and hence referred to as Scheduled Tribes or STs.

Implementation of Affirmative Action

In India there is no national enforcement mechanism for the reservation system, even though there is a Ministry for Social Justice in the Central Government. While civil action is not an available remedy for denial of due benefits, the alternative is in the form of a writ jurisdiction under Article 32 and 226 of the Constitution of India. However, given the dominance of upper castes in the judiciary, there is an upper caste/elite bias in the redressal mechanism. A formal writ application and subsequent appearances by lawyers in a court are too expensive for most potential petitioners. The Central Government does have a National SC/ST Commission, but so far it has played a little active role in ensuring implementation of quotas.

In the evaluation of how many members of the target groups have been benefited from the quotas, the following must be kept in mind. The quota-based scheme in India is similar to a guaranteed minimum scheme, in that quotas are supposed to be filled first and the rest of the seats are allocated on "merit". Thus, the total number of SC-ST individuals in a job or educational institution will overestimate the actual amount of preference, if some members of the target groups get in without availing themselves of affirmative action. The one area where caste based quotas are completely fulfilled is the electoral sphere. Thus, constituencies that are designated "reserved" can only elect SC/ST candidates as the case may be. However, given the enormity of this change, a few generalized comments are offered here. The reserved constituencies have led to a noticeable change in the caste composition of the elected representatives that even 40 years ago were dominated totally by upper castes. There are major *dalit* political parties as well as key political players, ensuring that dalit issues remain in the foreground in some fashion. However, it would be wrong to assume that this represents a fundamental betterment in the material and/or social conditions of the majority of the *dalits*. Several of those elected from reserved seats are members of mainstream political parties and thus, are committed to the overall agenda of their parties, which may or may not include the reduction of caste disparity. Also, even in reserved constituencies, the voters are both SC/ST and upper caste, and in order to appeal to the latter, the candidates often have to tone down their pro-*dalit* agenda. Of course, along the political spectrum, there is a strong tendency to be opportunistic and self seeking, thus *dalit* or not, often those elected work primarily to consolidate their own power rather than transfer any real benefits to the people that they seek to represent.

R. Pande looks political reservations explicitly and finds that political reservation has increased redistribution of resources in favour of the beneficiary groups. Pande found that reservations at the village level local self government improve targetting of low spill over public goods towards members of beneficiary groups.

Coming to the two other spheres of affirmative action, government jobs and education, the picture is more complex. Xaxa attempts an assessment of reservations in the University of Delhi, one of the premier institutions in the country.

- In 1999-2000, of all the undergraduate students, only 8.6 per cent were SC (with a quota of 15%) and 1.8 ST (quota of 7%). Of the post-graduate students, 5.5 per cent were SC and 2 per cent ST (with actual quotas the same as that at the under-graduate level). Thus, quotas are grossly underfulfilled and if this could happen in the capital city, things might be worse in other parts of the country. The situation in the teaching posts is even worse. Teachers in Delhi University have bitterly opposed the introduction of affirmative action, even though it is a constitutional provision. As a result, reservations were introduced as late as 1996. At that time, out of the 700 teachers in post-graduate departments, 7 were SCs and 2 STs. Out of the 4,512 teachers in university affiliated undergraduate colleges, 11 were SCs and none ST.
- The picture in the non-teaching posts conforms to the overall pattern in other government jobs: the higher the representation of SC/ST, the lower paying the job. Xaxa's figures for 1998-99 show that whereas only 3 per cent of Group A jobs were filled by SC/ST combined, the corresponding proportions for Groups B, C and D were 7.4, 13 and 29 per cent respectively. The menial jobs

(cleaners, sweepers and so on) often are performed almost exclusively by *dalits*, in particular those *jatis* whose traditional occupation was cleaning/scavenging.

In all the opposition to affirmative action, there is never any protest against *over representation* of low castes in low paying jobs. In other words, as long as *dalits* do not compete in traditional upper caste bastions or "stay where they belong", it is acceptable.

Coming to government jobs, between 1953-75, on the whole about 75 to 80 per cent posts in lower levels were filled. However, in the higher categories of officers (called Class I and II), quotas remain unfulfilled, revealing a picture quite like Delhi University above. This can be attributed to *"indifference/hostility on the part of the appointing authorities, insufficient publicisation of vacancies and the sheer expense of application"*. At the higher levels or promotion stages, formal and informal procedures had operated to keep out the SCs, such as *ad hoc* and temporary positions, elimination through personal evaluation procedures like interviews, personality tests and unfair adverse entries in confidential records.

Galanter (1993) has attempted one of the most comprehensive explorations of the Indian affirmative action programme. A monetary cost-benefit evaluation is not possible because of the manner in which the Indian programme is formulated. However, he undertakes a crude assessment of the SC/ST affirmative action programme and some of his major findings are as follows:

- The programme has shown substantial redistributive effects in that access to education and jobs is spread wider in the caste spectrum than earlier, although redistribution is not spread evenly throughout the beneficiary groups. There is evidence of clustering, but Galanter believes that these reflect structural factors, since the better situated enjoy a disproportionate share of the benefits in any government programme, not just in affirmative action programmes.
- The vast majority of *dalits* are not directly affected by affirmative action, but reserved jobs bring a manifold increase in the number of families liberated from subservient roles.
- In the short run, beneficiaries might get singled out and

experience social rejection in offices, colleges, hostels and other setups where they are introduced through affirmative action. However, in the long run, education and jobs weaken the stigmatising association of *dalits* with ignorance and incompetence. Moreover, "resentment of preferences may magnify hostility to these groups, but rejection of them exists independently of affirmative action programmes".

- Affirmative action has kept the beneficiary groups and their problems visible to the educated public, but it has not motivated widespread concern for their inclusion beyond what is mandated by government policy.

Thus, Galanter concludes that affirmative action has been a partial success. It has accelerated the growth of a middle class and SC/ST members have been brought into central roles considered unimaginable a few decades ago.

Conclusion

In the light of the above discussion it can be said that globalization has tremendously affected education and more so legal education. Globalization has ushered the knowledge economy and universities as centres of production and distribution of knowledge have been the most affected institutions. The transformation of knowledge from inner realization and enlightenment to a service and consequently its collapse into a structure of industry has both altered and accentuated the domains and dimensions of education. This understanding becomes crystal clear from the above presentation. In order to conclude, let us sum up in the lines of Loyotard: "Knowledge is and will be produced in order to be sold, it is and will be consumed in order to be valourized in a new production: in both cases, the goal is exchanged (Loyotard, 1984:4)". In the vortex of exchange and exploration globalization will remain the ultimate process of transformation and the parameter further dynamics.

In order to create a level playing field for the deprived and disadvantaged minority of India under the hegemony of globalization need a safety net. It is believed that an effective affirmative action policy must account for all of the complex social, institutional, and economic interactions that have resulted in limited opportunities for discriminated groups. To be effective these policies must be based on an understanding that the discrimination that has led to the disadvantaged position of minority groups is systemic. Therefore, any ramifications made must account for the disparities that exist on many levels and not just provide equality at the top. A conscious and deliberate effort is necessary to insure that these individuals may one day be elevated from their current conditions. However, there needs to be awareness that the discrimination faced by these groups is deeply entrenched within the current social and political framework, therefore, overcoming them will take several generations of change. To be truly effective affirmative action in any place in the world can no longer be seen as a temporary initiative, but instead should be made apart of a more lasting social movement. It is unfair to expect that centuries of oppression will be overcome with decades of preferential treatment.

REFERENCES

Department of Education (1968). *National Policy on Education.* Ministry of Human Resource Development, New Delhi: Government of India.

——(1986): *National Policy on Education.* Ministry of Human Resource Development, New Delhi: Government of India.

Dev Nathan, Govind Kelkar and Pierre Walter (2004): *Globalization and Indigenous Peoples in Asia: Changing the Local-Global Interface,* New Delhi: Sage Publication.

Dreze, Jean and P.V. Srinivasan (1996): *Poverty in India: Regional Estimates, 1987-88,* Working Paper, New Delhi: Institute of Economic Growth.

Galanter, M. (1993): *Law and Society in Modern India,* New Delhi: Oxford University Press.

Govinda, R. (ed.) (2002): *India Education Report: A Profile of Basic Education,* New Delhi: Oxford University Press.

International Fund for Agricultural Development (IFAD). (1996): *India: Country Strategic Opportunity Paper,* Rome.

Kaldor, Mary. (2001): *New and Old Wars: Organized Violence in a Global Era,* Stanford: Stanford University Press.

Kaul, Inge, Isabelle Grunberg and Marc Stern, (eds.) (1999): *Global Public Goods,* New York: Oxford University Press.

Saksena, H.S., V.K. Srivastava and S.K. Chaudhury (eds.) (2006): *Scheduled Tribes and Development,* New Delhi: Serials Publications.

Singh, A. and M. Jabbi (1996): *Status of Tribals in India,* New Delhi: Har-Anand Publications.

Singh, Chhatrapati (1986): *Common Property and Common Poverty: India's Forest, Forest Dwellers and the Law,* New Delhi: Oxford University Press.

United Nations Development Programme (UNDP) (1998): *Human Development Report,* New Delhi: Oxford University Press.

UN Working Group on Indigenous Populations. (1993): *Draft Declaration,* Geneva

World Bank (2000): *World Development Report,* Washington D.C.

6

Parliamentary Initiatives towards Tribal Education

S. Prabhakar

Parliament of India is the highest legislative body representing the people in implementing the provisions of Constitution and its goals. Indian Parliament has earned the glory of being the largest working parliamentary democracy in the world.

Our Constitution provides for abolition of untouchability, prohibition of discrimination on grounds of religion, race, caste, sex or place of birth; equality of opportunity in matters of public employment, promotion of educational and economic interests of deprived and oppressed strata of society, particularly, STs, SCs, and other weaker sections, reservation of seats for SCs and STs in the House of the People, and Legislative Assemblies of the States, Panchayats and Municipalities. According to Census of 2001, we have 8.43 crore tribal population in the country. It is a well known fact that they are lagging behind in many spheres, particularly, economy and education. They are deprived of basic amenities like drinking water, good healthcare, etc. It is an accepted fact that less than 1 per cent of the Budget allocation of the country is given to the Ministry of Tribal Affairs. To be precise, it was 0.86 per cent for 2010-11. For 2009-10, the Budget allocation for the Ministry was 0.98 per cent and in 2008-09, it was even less, 0.74 per cent. Considering the 8.43 crore tribals spread across the country, it is undoubtedly a meagre sum.

Our Constitution contains various provisions for the development of such marginalized groups. For instance, Article 342 for STs. After the Constitution came into being on 26th January, 1950, Parliament has enacted a number of laws to initiate the process of social justice, which in turn helped the Government agencies to make the laws not only effective but also to implement them in letter and spirit. Article 15(4) deals with special provisions for advancement of other backward classes (which includes STs); Article 330 provides reservation of seats for STs in Lok Sabha.

The paper deals with Constitution in securing social justice and equality, Parliament Initiatives on Tribal Affairs—Parliament and Acts, Ministry of Tribal Affairs, Departmentally-Related Standing Committee, Consultative Committee for the Ministry of Tribal Affairs, Debates on Tribal Affairs in the 15th Lok Sabha, Demands for Grants of the Ministry of Tribal Affairs, Parliament and Media, Limitations, Suggestions and Conclusion.

Parliamentary Initiatives on Tribal Affairs

Parliament and Acts

Various Acts have been passed by Parliament which aim at addressing the issues concerning tribals of the country. For example, the Scheduled Castes and the Scheduled Tribes (Prevention of Atrocities) Act 1989; Forest Rights Act 2006, Protection of Civil Rights 1955, Protection of Civil Rights Rules 1977, SC/ST (Prevention of Atrocities) Rules 1995; the Provisions of the Panchayats (Extension to the Scheduled Areas) Act 1996 (PESA), and the Constitution (Eighty-Ninth Amendment) Act 2003. Responsibility of implementing the Acts concerned the Scheduled Tribes lies primarily with the Ministry of Tribal Affairs. Parliament by way of debating and passing the grants and Parliamentary Committee system has been contributing in its own way in overseeing the various functionings of the Ministry and that of the Government. This process ensures accountability of Executive, that is, the Government, to the Legislature, the Parliament. Under Article 275(1) of the Constitution, funds were released on the basis of approved projects continued during the year 2007-08 and up to 31.12.2007, an amount of Rs. 314.90 crore has been released to various States for the welfare of Scheduled Tribes and raising the level of administration in the Scheduled Areas in these States. Ministry of Tribal Affairs is devoted to ensure that the problems and concerns of the tribals are attended to ensure that their well-being is taken care of.

Ministry of Tribal Affairs

Ministry of Tribal Affairs is the nodal Ministry which takes care of the welfare and development of tribals in the country. Ministry of Tribal Affairs came into being in October 1999. Its objectives were providing more focused attention on the integrated socio-economic development of the most under-privileged sections of the Indian society, namely, the Scheduled Tribes (STs), in a coordinated and planned manner. It also oversees the overall policy, planning and coordination of programmes for development of STs.

Ministry is divided into Divisions of Scheduled Castes Development, Backward Classes Development, Disability and Social Defence. Ministry's annual plan allocation for 2009-10 is Rs. 2,500 crore, of which around 76.9 per cent is for development of SCs; 11.6 per cent for OBCs; 9.3 per cent for Disability and 2.2 per cent for Social Defence sector.[1] It is heartening to note that 98 per cent of the said allocation had been utilized up to 31.3.2010. But the budgetary allocation of the Ministry has substantially increased to Rs. 4,500 crore for 2010-11, which is a marked increase of 80 per cent over the previous year.[2] It is to be noted that the Planning Commission has allocated only Rs. 2,500 for 2009-10 as against the proposed plan outlay of Rs. 5,000 crore.

According to the Ministry, educational development is a stepping stone to economic and social development. Ministry is making maximum efforts to improve their education status. Various plans, schemes, programmes are in place to realize the overall development of the tribals of the country. For example, the flagship scheme of the Ministry is 'Post-Matric Scholarship (PMS), a Centrally sponsored scheme to promote higher education among STs. Under this scheme, an amount of Rs. 140.86 crore was spent up to 31st December, 2007 to benefit more than 10.52 lakh students.

Likewise, the scheme of Hostels for ST Boys and Girls aims at reducing the present dropout rates of the middle/higher level education among STs, by providing a major support service to ST boys and girls. Rs. 35.28 crore has already been incurred up to 31st December, 2007 in constructing 304 hostels across the country.

Ashram Schools is yet another innovative effort which aims at extending educational facilities and conducive educational atmosphere to ST boys and girls through dedicated residential schools. A sum of Rs. 3.74 crore has been released for construction of *Ashram* Schools to the Governments of Madhya Pradesh and Karnataka as on 31st December, 2007.

Up to 31st December, 2007, Ministry has extended a grant of Rs. 8.71 crore to voluntary organizations and autonomous societies of State governments for constructing 59 Educational Complexes under "Educational Complex in Low Literacy Pockets' for development of ST female literacy in tribal areas. This covered 7,775 students. There are similar schemes under the Ministry which aims at the development of primitive tribal groups.

There is also a Standing Committee on Inter-Sectoral Issues relating to Tribal Development headed by Dr. Balchandra Mungekar, Member, Planning Commission, with Secretaries of some key Ministries concerned with tribal development as Members. It submitted its Second Interim Report on 7th May, 2007 entitled "Displacement, Resettlement and Rehabilitation of Scheduled Tribes".

National Commission for Scheduled Tribes (NCST), under the Ministry, was constituted with effect from 19th February, 2004. Its main function are (i) to investigate and monitor matters relating to safeguards provided for STs, (ii) to inquire into specific complaints relating to rights and safeguards of STs, (iii) to participate and advise in the planning process relating to socio-economic development of STs, and (iv) to evaluate the progress of their development under the Union and any State, etc. The Commission has powers to investigate and inquiry and is vested with powers of a civil court.[3] The Commission presented the Third Report for the year 2007-08 to the President on 29th March, 2010.[4]

Ministry of Tribal Affairs is also providing insurance cover through 'Janshree Beema Yojana' to one earning member from all the families of Particularly Vulnerable Tribal Groups (PTGs) in the country. This is an insurance scheme of Life Insurance Corporation of India. Needless to add that the cost of the insurance cover of PTGs is borne by the Ministry of Tribal Affairs.

Most of the schemes of the Ministry are deemed to be demand driven and the States are the implementing agencies for these schemes. States are not able to provide their matching share of 50 per cent for various schemes.

Last year, Home Minister of the Government of India has made a statement to the effect that law for SCs and STs could be strengthened.[5] This shows the reality that laws governing the SCs and STs are not really serving them the way it should be and much more needs to be desired. To highlight as to how much of the funds of the Government of India is allocated to the Tribal Affairs, I would like to state that the total budgetary allocations of all the Ministries and Departments of Government of India put together is Rs. 12,57,728.83 crore, out of which a paltry sum of Rs. 3,740.01 crore is allocated to the Ministry of Tribal Affairs, which is 0.30 per cent. Considering the tribal population of 8.43 crore spread across the country, the allocation for the Ministry of Tribal Affairs should be increased to at least 3 per cent.

A mere sum of Rs. 3 crore was kept for the purpose of generating awareness in 2010-11. This year, 2011-12, it is Rs. 2.89 crore. Awareness is spread primarily through advertisements and publication. For a vast country like ours and for the tribal population that is spread in different States, this meagre amount is a pittance. More funds should be allocated for spreading awareness about various schemes and programmes of the Ministry of Tribal Affairs.

Exchange of Visits by Tribals is a good scheme but funds were not utilized during 2008-09 and 2009-10 as no proposal has come from State and UT governments or proposals which came were incompleted and revised proposals were not sent thereafter to the Ministry. But in 2010-11, Tripura, Assam and Chhattisgarh received Rs. 10.43 lakh for undertaking the exchange of visit.

Under 'Organization of Tribal Festivals' scheme, Gujarat, Orissa and Assam organized tribal festivals during 2008-09 and in 2009-10, Madhya Pradesh, Maharashtra, Tamil Nadu, Tripura and Chhattisgarh received funds to organize a national level Tribal Festival 'PRAKRITI' in Delhi for 3 days.

Under 'Special Central Assistance to Tribal Sub-Plan', in 2008-09, out of Revised Estimates of Rs. 860.50 crore, only Rs. 780.87 crore has been utilized; in 2009-10, it could utilize the funds allocated to the tune of Rs. 481.24 crore. But in 2010-11, out of Rs. 941.96 crore, only Rs. 769.49 (as on 31st January, 2011) has been utilized. There is a need to utilize funds without ascribing reasons of non-receipt of complete proposals in prescribed format and non-submission of utilization certificates but efforts should be made to ensure that State and UT Governments fulfil the required formalities to avail funds.

Under the National Overseas Scholarship Scheme of the

Ministry of Tribal Affairs, Government of India, in 2008-09, out of the budget estimate of Rs. 2 crore, only Rs. 0.0118 crore has been utilized. In 2010-11, out of Rs. 1 crore, only Rs. 0.01 crore has been utilized till 31st January, 2011. From 2004-05 to 2009-10, only 7 out of 29 selected candidates actually got admission to foreign accredited universities. Hence, the amount allocated could not be fully utilized during the said period. Efforts should be made to train people in order to ensure funds allocated during the period is utilized and tribal students benefit out of this National Overseas Scholarship Scheme.

Under another very important scheme for strengthening education among Scheduled Tribes girls in low literacy districts, a sum of Rs. 40 crore has been allocated in 2008-09, and the same has been utilized but in 2010-11, out of Rs. 39.70 crore, only Rs. 22.58 crore up to 31st January, 2011 has been utilized. From the budget estimate stage to revised stage, amount has been reduced drastically due to election process in some States and delay in receipt of recommendations from many State level Committees.

In a startling revelation in a newspaper report in *Indian Express*, Delhi edition, dated January 19, 2011, it was reported that Scheduled Tribes were missing in private sector jobs and corporate employment for Scheduled Tribes has not been proportionate to their population. There is a huge gap in this.[6]

Government of India has been taking steps to strengthen the law governing the Scheduled Tribes. Home Minister, P. Chidambaram, while participating in the debate on increasing atrocities against SCs and STs in Lok Sabha,[7] called for institutionalization of oversight mechanisms at the grassroots level to prevent atrocities against *dalits* and tribals. He gave the data which revealed that the number of cases against SCs and STs had increased in the last three years from 26,665 cases in 2006 to 29,875 cases in 2007 and 33,365 cases in 2009. This is certainly a disturbing trend. He highlighted that this sorry state of affairs of historical injustice against SCs and STs is due to divisions in society.[8]

It has come at the right opportune time for the educational upliftment of the Scheduled Tribes. In August 2009, the Supreme Court asked IIT Delhi to provide SC/ST students with additional coaching facilities so that they could do better.[9] It is shocking to note that 6 *dalit* students had been expelled from IIT-Delhi after performing poorly.[10] Justice P. Sathasivam had stated while delivering this verdict that these communities, socially and economically backward, need to be taken care of even in the specialized institutions like IITs and IIMs. IITs took it further by drawing the assistance of institutions like Centre for Research and Education for Social Transformation in Kozhikode, which since 2002 had already been working with hundreds of SC and ST youths, mostly graduates from professional courses.[11] This is an historical thing.

This is certainly a breakthrough in emancipating the educational aspirations of tribals and efforts should be taken to take this forward to ensure that tribals join the mainstream and compete and succeed in IITs and IIMs.

Another emulating example has been reported in the national Press. Tata Institute of Social Sciences, Mumbai took initiative to highlight the opportunities in educational sphere. Likewise, Bharat Calling, a venture that has been helping rural students, especially those belonging to SC/ST categories to gain access to higher education. This institution held around 30 students from Kesla Block in of Hoshangabad District in Madhya Pradesh, one of the poorest in the country, with 90 per cent of the families in the BPL category, get into Benaras Hindu University, Devi Ahilya Vishwavidyalaya, Indore, Dr. H.S. Gour Central University, Sagar (M.P.) and even TISS. Another redeeming feature in this great attempt is 50 per cent of them are girls. [12]

If we compare the literacy rate of the total population vis-à-vis tribal population, there is a huge gap—in 1971, the literacy rate of the total population was 29.45 per cent and that of tribal population is a mere 11.30 per cent; in 1981, for total population it was 36.23 per cent and for tribal population, 16.35 per cent; in 1991, it was 52.21 and 29.60 and in 2001, it was 65.38 and 47.1 per cent respectively.[13]

Even in the case of dropout rates among STs and total population between 1990-91 and 1998-99, there is a huge gap. The dropout rates concerning total population during the said period was 42.60 per cent and tribal population was 62.52 per cent in 1990-91; in 1998-99, it was 39.74 per cent and 57.36 per cent; in 1990-91, it was 60.90 per cent and 78.57 per cent; in 1998-99, it was 56.82 per cent and 72.80 per cent; in 1990-91, it was 71.34 per cent and 85.01 per cent; and in 1998-99, it was 67.44 per cent and 82.96 per cent respectively.[14]

When it comes to tribal women's literacy, it is abysmal in States like Bihar, Uttar Pradesh, Andhra Pradesh, Madhya Pradesh, Rajasthan and Orissa.[15]

Education in tribal areas is a far cry. There cannot be two opinions on this stark reality. Tribals across the country speak more than 270 languages and maintain exclusive identities.[16] Literacy rate of STs across the country was 8.54 per cent in 1961, 11.29 in 1971, 16.35 in 1981, 29.60 in 1991, 47.1 in 2001 but in the case of female, it has come down to 34.8 in 2001.[17]

There are many aspects that go into the tribal education in the country like fear of losing tribal identity, economic factors, role of teachers, medium of instruction, location and timings, infrastructure, nature of curriculum. I would like to briefly touch on these aspects.

The reasons for low level of literacy among ST population are geographical isolation, inadequate infrastructure and economic backwardness. In this regard, Ministry of Tribal Affairs supplements the efforts of Ministry of HRD through various schemes like Scheme of Hostels for ST girls and boys; Scheme of establishment of *Ashram* Schools in Tribal Sub-Plan Areas, Post-Matric Scholarship for ST students, scheme of strengthening education among ST girls in low literacy districts.

Eklavya Model Residential Schools scheme provides quality education to ST students from Class VI to XII. Under this scheme, utilization of funds by Chhattisgarh, Madhya Pradesh, Karnataka and other States are good.

There is a specific scheme called Strengthening Education among ST girls in Low Literacy Districts which aims at improving literacy among tribal girls. Ministry provides grant in aid to State governments/UT Administrations and NGOs for setting up and running of Vocational Training Centres with a view to upgrade the skills of tribal youth in various traditional and modern vocations.

According to 1991 Census, literacy rate for SCs was 37.41 per cent and for STs 29.41 per cent. But in 2011 Census, there has been an increase but it is not considerable by any stretch of imagination.

HRD Ministry's *Saakshar Bharat* (Literate India), an Adult Literacy Programme, launched on 8th September, 2009 focus on illiterate women, SC/ST and other minorities to make them literate in a time bound manner.

If we take the overview of the Annual Report for 2010-11 of Ministry of Tribal Affairs, Government of India, we come out with the following facts :

- There are specially tailored schemes for the economic, educational and social development of tribals of the country.
- Educational development is a stepping stone to economic and social development.
- Maximum efforts should be made to improve the educational status of tribals.
- Flagship scheme of the Ministry—Post Matric Scholarship (PMS) continues to be an important centrally sponsored scheme to promote higher education among STs. Till 30th December, 2010, Rs. 319.91 crore has been spent during 2010-11.
- Hostels for ST Boys and Girls scheme aims at augmenting the availability of educational facilities to ST students with the intention to reduce the dropouts at middle/higher level education. Rs. 74.80 crore had been incurred under the Scheme till 31st December, 2010.
- Vocational Training is imparted to ST youth to increase their employability. A maximum assistance of Rs. 30,000 per annum per ST trained is given. This is provided to the State Governments/UT Administration Institutions or Organisations, State run Vocational Training Centres, NGOs. Rs. 5.63 has been spent till 31st December, 2010.
- During 2010-11, upto 31st December, 2010, Ministry has funded 40 Educational Complexes under the scheme of Strengthening Education among ST Girls in Low Literacy Districts for improvement of ST female literacy in tribal areas covering about 7,089 ST girl students by extending grants of Rs. 7.51 crore to voluntary organizations and autonomous societies of the State governments.
- Under the scheme of Grants-in-aid to Voluntary Organisations working for the welfare of STs, the Ministry during 2010-11 up to 31st December, 2010 has funded about 283 projects covering residential schools, non-residential schools, hostels, libraries, mobile dispensaries, ten or more bedded hospitals, computer training centres,

rural night school, agricultural training, etc., by granting Rs. 32.74 crore benefiting about 6,14,614 STs.

- Under the scheme of Development of Particularly Vulnerable Tribal Groups (PTGs) during 2010-11 up to 31st December, 2010, Rs. 178.86 crore has been released to 10 States for implementation of prioritized activities as per "Conservation-cum-Development Plans for PTGs.
- Under the scheme of "Research Information and Mass Education, Tribal Festivals and Others" grants are provided to 17 Tribal Research Institutes on 50 : 50 sharing basis with the States.

There are STs almost in every State—Andhra Pradesh (35), Arunachal Pradesh (16), Assam (14), Bihar (33), Chhattisgarh (42), Goa (8), Gujarat (32), HP (10) J&K (12), Jharkhand (32), Karnataka (50), Kerala (43), MP (46), Maharashtra (47), Manipur (33), Meghalaya (17), Mizoram (15), Nagaland, (5), Orissa (62), Rajasthan (12), Sikkim (4), TN (36), Tripura (19), Uttranchal (5), UP (15), WB (40), A&N Islands (6), Dadra and Nagar Haveli (7), Daman and Diu (5), and Lakshadweep (1).

Apart from the Ministry, a part of the Executive, that is, Government, which is answerable to Parliament, we also have Departmentally-Related Standing Committee whose main purpose is to scrutinize the functions of the Ministry of Tribal Affairs and the Bills referred to it. It would help make Parliament more effective in exercising control and giving direction to the functioning of the Executive, thereby making the Executive more accountable to Parliament.

Departmentally related Standing Committee

Ministry of Tribal Affairs comes under the Departmentally related Standing Committee on Social Justice and Empowerment which consists of 21 Members from Lok Sabha and 10 Members from Rajya Sabha. In the 15th Lok Sabha, Shri Dara Singh Chauhan is the Chairman of the Committee.

Since the start of 15th Lok Sabha till 30th August, 2010, Committee has taken up the evidence of representatives of the Ministry of Tribal Affairs 4 times. On 20th October, 2010, it took up for consideration and adoption of draft of Tenth Report on the subject "Implementation of Scheduled Tribes and Other Traditional Forest Dwellers (Recognition of Forest Rights) Act 2006 and the Rules made thereunder".

On 18th January, 2011, Committee took evidence of the representatives of the Ministry of Tribal Affairs on the subject "Working of Ashram Schools in Tribal Areas". On 5th January, 2011, it considered and adopted the draft Fourteenth Action Taken Report of the Committee on Demands for Grants (2010-2011) of the Ministry of Tribal Affairs. On 20th October, 2010, it took up for consideration and adoption of draft Tenth Report on the subject "Implementation of Scheduled Tribes and Other Traditional Forest Dwellers (Recognition of Forest Rights) Act 2006 and the Rules made thereunder".

During these meetings, apart from other issues, it has also taken up implementation aspect of Scheduled Tribes and other traditional Forest Dwellers (Recognition of Forest Rights) Act 2006, consideration and adoption of Draft Action Taken Reports on Demands for Grants 2009-10, Demands for Grants for 2010-11, discussed Scholarship Schemes for SCs/OBCs.

From time to time, the Committee has been making recommendations to the Government. As per the 14th Report of the Committee on Demands for Grants 2008-09 of the Ministry of Tribal Affairs (which comes under the Ministry of Social Justice and Empowerment) made a number of recommendations. For example, the Committee pointed out that against the budgetary allocation of Rs. 64 crore, during 2009-10 for construction of hostels the actual expenditure till 31st January, 2010 was only Rs. 32.40 crore and recommended strongly that it may be taken up with the concerned State Chief Secretaries for completion of construction of these hotels within a definite time frame. It further recommended that some penal action be taken against the defaulting States.

Out of 23 recommendations, 14 have been implemented,[18] that is, 60.86 per cent. I would like to briefly elaborate here. Committee had recommended that the Government to facilitate the admission of ST students in the Top Class Institutes and for this purpose, a different criteria for ST students be worked out and some coaching/ training be also imparted to prepare them for entrance examinations. Committee strongly felt that scholarships for poor ST students at pre-Matric stage be vigorously taken up with the

Planning Commission for early clearance of the Pre-Matric Scholarship scheme for ST students.

In this scenario, one cannot brush aside the role of Standing Committee in the implementation of various schemes and programmes of the Ministry. Apart from the Departmentally related Standing Committee, we have a Consultative Committee, which too plays a part in furthering the interests of tribals of the country.

Consultative Committee for the Ministry of Tribal Affairs

In the 15th Lok Sabha, Shri Kantilal Bhuria, Minister of Tribal Affairs was the Chairman of Consultative Committee for the Ministry of Tribal Affairs. Shri Mahadev S. Khandela, Minister of State in the Ministry of Tribal Affairs was also a Member. There are 10 Members from Lok Sabha and 6 from Rajya Sabha with 2 Ministers of State in the Ministry of Parliamentary Affairs, namely, Shri V. Narayanasamy, and Shri Ashwani Kumar as ex-officio Members.[19]

In the 15th Lok Sabha, till August 19, 2010, Consultative Committee met 4 times and discussed various plans, schemes, programmes of the Ministry of Tribal Affairs and Empowerment. For example, on 23rd February, 2011, it discussed the issue concerning boys and girls hostels for ST students, on 12th August, 2010, it discussed for providing training centres for tribal areas, on 19th May, 2010, it took up Post-Matric Scholarship for ST students; and on 17th February, 2010, achievements in the implementation of Forest Rights Act was taken up.

The Consultative Committees in reality have no authority or responsibilities. At best, the Members can suggest and make recommendations to the Minister, who is not obliged to consider their advice or suggestions. But it cannot be said that Consultative Committees serve no purpose. The meetings of the Consultative Committee do, however, serve one useful purpose. Since the proceedings of the meetings are confidential, Ministers can part with details and situations emanating on a certain policy or issue, which cannot be disclosed elsewhere.

The Consultative Committee of Parliament on Tribal Affairs is thus an important institutional link between Parliament and Government.

Debates which take place from time to time in Lok Sabha in different forms, namely, questions, play a major role in highlighting the issues and problems that exist concerning tribal population of the country and the response of the Government.

Debates on Tribal Affairs in 15th Lok Sabha

In the 15th Lok Sabha, up to 16th March, 2011, there were 216 questions, both Starred (oral) and Unstarred (written), on Tribal and Tribal Education. Questions varied from education in tribal areas, committee on tribal people, road connectivity to tribal areas, acquisition of tribal lands, tribal population, funds for scholarships to tribal students, life expectancy of tribals, tribal health, professional education, education to tribal girls, etc., to seek information from the Government.[20]

These interventions in Lok Sabha had brought to the fore the core issues involving women. This debate has helped the Government in evolving a strategy to deal with the issues raised in Lok Sabha. The Government on its part has come out with the factual information on the issues asked by the Members. Debates certainly throws light on the issues in vogue and helps Parliament to know as to what the Government is thinking on an issue and as to how it is going to resolve them. Sometimes, as in 2010-11, Demands for Grants of the Ministry of Tribal Affairs were taken up in Lok Sabha for a detailed discussion.

Demands for Grants of the Ministry of Tribal Affairs for 2010-11

In the 15th Lok Sabha, in spite of over 80 Departments of the Government of India, the Parliament has chosen to debate the Demands for Grants of the Ministry of Tribal Affairs[21] , apart from three-four Ministries, as is the case every year. This shows the importance given by Parliament to the tribal issues.

While initiating the debate, Sushmita Bouri of Communist Party of India (Marxists) highlighted the fact that less than 1 per cent of the Budget of the Government is allocated to the tribal affairs. She pleaded that at least 1 per cent of Budget should be demarcated for implementing various schemes and programmes aimed at tribal welfare and development. She brought out the increase rate of infant mortality and maternal mortality. She demanded that tribals should get the forest rights and their alienation should stop.

Many prominent Members of Parliament participated in the Debate on the Demands for Grants of the Ministry and highlighted various finer points and made suggestions. For example, Hemanand Biswal of Congress suggested that in Indian Army, a Tribal Regiment should be raised on the lines of Dogra Regiment of Himachal Pradesh. Shailendra Kumar of Samajwati Party suggested that a Tribal Advisory Council should be constituted. J.M. Aaron Rashid made a suggestion that a Joint Parliamentary Committee should be set up to go into the problems being faced by the tribal community at the grass root level. Mansukhbhai D. Vasava of Bharatiya Janata Party requested for establishment of hospitals which should be well equipped with all modern facilities for the benefit of tribals. M. Anandan of AIADMK has stated that out of 83 Departments and Ministries under the Government of India, only 18 have allocated funds for the schemes meant for STs, and out of that 8 Departments and Ministries have made allocation below 5 per cent.

While replying to the debate, Minister of Tribal Affairs, (now ex) Kanti Lal Bhurai has stated that the Ministry is continuously making efforts for uplightment of STs. One of its main objectives is to bring the STs into the mainstream. While responding to a suggestion made by the Member in his speech, the Minister too felt that the Tribal Advisory Council should be constituted at the national level. He highlighted that the Special Central Assistance under Tribal Sub-Plan Programme is being implemented in 22 States and 2 Union Territories and went to State that Rs. 442 crore has been provided to the States to implement this project. He stated that Rs. 961 crore is proposed to be given to this scheme during the current year.

He gave the information that so far 100 *Eklavya* Residential Schools have been opened with the grants under Article 275(1) of the Constitution. These schools are at par with quality schools of the country. He enumerated various other steps initiated by his Ministry for the upliftment of STs. He concluded by saying that the Government would endeavour to bring the people living in tribal areas into the mainstream of the country and the separatist forces would be dealt with sternly.

Parliament and Media

There is no doubt, media has highlighted and exposed the issues related to underprivileged, particularly tribal people. Media though has not given the required coverage to the issues related to tribal affairs, and the news items concerning tribal people of the country, there is no denying of the fact that it has brought issues involving them to the limelight issues. For example, it is the print media which has brought to the limelight the abject poverty in which Adivasis are living, even after over 60 years of Indian Independence.[22] More such information should be given wide publicity if we have to bring the plight of tribals to the forefront.

According to the interview given by Kishore Chandra Deo, Minister of Tribal Affairs by establishing quality residential schools educational status of tribes may be improved. The Ministry has disbursed Rs. 12 crore for the creation of infrastructure and once it is completed, it gives over Rs. 40,000 per student per annum Here, the condition is that schools have to show 15 acres of land for this purpose, which was 20 acres earlier, and there should be a minimum of 480 tribal students of which 50 per cent should be girls. [23] One can say that such news reports in the Press would go a long way to bring to the fore and for the knowledge of tribal population the schemes which they can make use to improve their educational standards.

If one is an avid follower of parliamentary debates, one can easily decipher how press plays a role in almost every aspect of the debate. Members keep churning out comments, figures, and the performance of the programmes of the government debate after debate, day after day. It was rightly stated that: "Most of the raw materials, for parliamentary questions, motions, debates and discussions, comes from the daily press and this is an important instrument on which a Member relies."[24]

There cannot be two opinions on the fact that the exposure given by the press to the parliamentary news and debates, to say the least, is minimal. This has been brought out by the then Speaker of the 14th Lok Sabha, Somnath Chatterjee when he remarked in his speech. I quote :

"It pains me to say that the media hardly gives adequate coverage to the Parliament and has failed to protect the institution with the respect and seriousness it deserves."[25] This is not farther from truth.

Sincere efforts should be made by media and press to set right this disturbing trend. This sorry state of affairs can be altered by highlighting many issues and debates that take place in Parliament during the Sessions and take the parliamentary news and parliamentary debates many notches up in standard. Press can make general public and readers more aware of the decisions and debates that take place in Parliament during the Sessions. Secondly, parliamentary debates should be given more prominence in newspapers, which would attract the attention of readers of newspapers, and would ultimately help the public to form an opinion on important issues, including those related to tribal affairs that are being discussed in Parliament.

Another pertinent point to be brought to the notice is that only a miniscule portion of the policy aspect is scrutinized by the committees with the result that majority of the important aspects of different ministries and departments are left out and never come in the domain of discussion and debate in the committees.

The Lok Sabha Speaker, Meira Kumar has expressed her concern and anguish over collapse of question hour as it would dent Parliament's image. In this direction, Lok Sabha Rules Committee has carried out an amendment in the rules to prevent collapse of Question hour. The Committee has also taken a series of decisions to ensure that the proceedings of the House were not stalled for some reason or the other.

Suggestions

Parliament should generate public awareness about its role, powers and functioning, particularly matters concerning social justice. Parliament's role in delivering the social justice is tremendous. Parliament wields enormous power in the governance of the country. The actions of government can be questioned and scrutinized by Parliament in its functioning. This advantage should be taken seriously by bringing more and more issues concerning social justice. There is a need to increase the budgetary allocation to the Ministry as the target group of this Ministry, that is, tribal population, would be increased to over 10 per cent under the current census, which has started. As stated earlier, when we compare the total plan and non-plan allocation of GoI Ministries/ Departments, Rs. 3,200 crore allocated for the Ministry of Tribal

Affairs is a measly sum, considering the 8.5 per cent tribal population according to 2001 Census. More funds should be allocated to the Ministry considering the beneficiaries of its programmes. A general awareness and proper and effective monitoring is lacking with the results we can see funds being not utilized and surrendered. This disturbing trend should change. Publicity of various schemes should be given prominence. Central Government should sensitize the State governments about various schemes. Most of the schemes of the Ministry of Tribal Affairs are implemented by the States but States find it difficult to contribute 50 per cent of their shares, which lead to underutilization and many times non-utilisation and surrender of the funds.

The Members of Parliament Local Area Development (MPLAD) Fund can also be utilized to provide basic amenities to the tribal populace of the country. Recently, from Rs. 2 crore, the fund has been increased to 5 crore. Stakeholders and NGOs in the respective constituencies can also make efforts to avail MPLAD funds for tribal welfare.

Parliament is bestowed by our Constitution with powers to oversee the functioning of the Executive. This very purpose would be defeated if the sittings of Parliament are few and far between. Efforts should be made to evolve a consensus on not only having nearly 100 days of sitting but also to ensure that there will not be any stalling of parliamentary proceedings on one pretext or another.

Conclusion

As we can see, earnest efforts are being made by all concerned—be it the Parliament, the Executive and the Fourth Pillar of Democracy but the bitter fact is that still Tribals are still at the bottom in most indicators as we could come to know about Adivasis of Kerala are still living in abject poverty even after 63 years of Independence. This shows that much needs to be done in bringing in social justice to the less privileged strata of society by providing the basic quintessential requirements of life like two square meal a day, proper clothing and a decent housing facilities, apart from imparting education and giving them health amenities. There is no denying the fact that debates and discussions in Parliament, meetings of the Department related Standing

Committee on Social Justice and Environment, which examines the Ministry of Tribal Affairs, Consultative Committee for the Ministry of Tribal Affairs do have impact on the implementation of the various plans, schemes and programmes of the Government of India concerning tribal education.

On the part of Government of India, there is a thinking that law meant for STs, specifically in enhancing their educational aspirations, should be strengthened and efforts are being made in this direction. There is no doubt, Ministry of Tribal Affairs, Government of India is making every effort with its new initiatives, as we have seen in this chapter, by paying more focused attention on education of Scheduled Tribes. These initiatives would ensure that Scheduled Tribes get their due to join and contribute in the national mainstream. At the same time, renewed efforts should also be made to make parliamentary debates and interventions more effective.

REFERENCES

1. Annual Report of Ministry of Social Justice & Empowerment for 2009-10, p. 19.
2. Fourth Report, Standing Committee on Social Justice and Empowerment (2010-2011), April, 2010.
3. http://ncst.nic.in. dated 21.3.2011.
4. Press Note of the National Commission for Scheduled Tribes, dated 29.3.2010.
5. *The Pioneer*, dated 30th August, 2010.
6. *Indian Express*, Delhi, 19.1.2011.
7. Debates, Lok Sabha, dated August 30, 2010.
8. *Ibid*.
9. *Indian Express*, Delhi, dated 26.7.2011.
10. *Ibid*.
11. *Ibid*.
12. *Ibid*.
13. Education Development of SCs and STs, Department of Education, Ministry of HRD, GoI, Census 2001.
14. Educational Profile of States/UTs, Department of Education, Ministry of HRD, GoI, New Delhi.
15. Census of India, Series-1, Paper-1, Provisional Population Totals 1961, 1971, 1981 and 1991 and Ministry of HRD Annual Report.

16. 'Ignored Citizens: A Study on Tribal Education in India', Raju Narayana Swamy, *Yojana*, June, 2010.
17. Census of India, Series-1, Paper-1, Provisional Population Totals 1961, 1971, 1981 and 1991 and Ministry of HRD Annual Report.
18. Fourteenth Report, Standing Committee on Social Justice & Empowerment (Ministry of Tribal Affairs), 15th Lok Sabha, Lok Sabha Secretariat, January, 2011.
19. http://mns-nic, Accessed on 07.09.2010.
20. http://164.100.47.132/LssNew/psearch/qsearch14.aspx, Accessed on 9.1.2010.
21. Debates, Lok Sabha, Demands for Grants of the Ministry of Tribal Affairs for 2010-11, dated 23.4.2010.
22. *The Pioneer*, dated 4th May, 2011.
23. *The Pioneer*, dated 20th October, 2011.
24. *Ibid*. p. 77.
25. Address on "Media as People's Voice—Pre and Post Independence', in New Delhi on November 16, 2007. http://speakerloksabha.nic.in/Speech/SpeechDetails.asp Accessed on 3.4.2008.

7

Some Reflections on Provision of Literacy and Primary Education for the Tribes

(With Special reference to Madhya Pradesh and Maharashtra)

S.N. Tripathy

Introduction

Education has been considered as a crucial input for economic and social development. This is crucial for building human capabilities and widening the horizon of opportunities. It empowers disadvantaged groups with increased efficiency and ability to protect their interest, raise voice against oppression and make them politically conscious. Education is the prerequisite factor, which improves human capabilities, enhance increased participation of people in production and thus, establish synergic relationship between human development and social development. It goes without saying that education is an essential input to improve peoples' behavioural quality, to modernize their way of life, to trigger reasoning power. Education acts as an agent of socialization and promotes harmony and peace in the society (Tripathy, 2010).

Literacy is the first step of empowerment of an individual; it opens the door to acquire knowledge. Quality education is the biggest solution to poverty as well as means of empowering people; and as such, school environment affects the quality of learning:

when adequate, it can have a positive impact on attendance and success rates.

In the above backdrop, an attempt has been made in this chapter to focus the problems of tribal literacy, the problem of dropout, tribal female literacy and other related problems in two tribal States (Madhya Pradesh and Maharashtra). Mostly, the secondary sources of data collected from the census and other literature have been used for analysis and interpretation of the data so as to get the final inferences. This chapter emphasizes the quality of education for the tribal women as an instrument of socio-economic and political empowerment and it will act as prospects of achieving a wide range of individual and development goals—from better health to higher incomes and stronger economic potential. The primary education obstructed due to certain crucial problem such as inadequate admission of girls, dropouts, stagnation, defective curriculum, irregular attendance, lack of study materials, poor nutrition of children, etc.

There are wide variations in educational attainment and literacy rates across the regions and social classes of India with a tribal population of 8.4 crore as per the 2001 census, which is approximately 8.14 per cent of the total population of India. The States of Madhya Pradesh, Chhattisgarh, Maharashtra, Orissa, Jharkhand and Gujarat have more than half of the total tribal population in India who are the backward, marginalized and poverty stricken population. The State of Madhya Pradesh, situated in central India, is a poor, tribal State with 20.2 per cent of population belonging to tribes has been socially and economically backward, being one of the 'BIMARU' States.

With regard to the State of Maharashtra, about 16.5 per cent of the geographical area is under the Tribal Sub-Plan (TSP). The tribal population constitutes about 9 per cent of the total population, the main tribes being Bhils, Gonds, Mahadeo Kolis, Pawras, Thakurs and Warlis. The tribes are mainly concentrated in the hilly districts of Dhule, Nandurbar, Jalgaon, Nashik and Thane and the eastern forest districts of Chandrapur, Gadchiroli, Bhandara, Gondia, Nagpur and Yavatmal. Maharashtra ranks fourth among the States in India having large tribal populations.

Table 7.1 analyses the literacy rate between general population and tribal population in some of the major States in India. The Table indicates the glaring disparity in the level of literacy among

Table 7.1: Progress of Literacy Rate (per cent)

States	*General*					*Scheduled Tribes*				
	1961	*1971*	*1981*	*1991*	*2001*	*1961*	*1971*	*1981*	*1991*	*2001*
Andhra Pradesh	21.19	24.57	29.94	44.09	60.47	4.41	5.34	7.82	17.16	37.04
Bihar	18.4	19.94	26.2	38.48	47.00	9.16	11.64	16.99	26.78	28.17
Gujarat	30.45	35.79	43.7	61.29	69.14	11.69	14.12	21.14	36.45	47.74
Karnataka	25.03	31.52	38.46	56.04	66.64	8.15	14.85	20.14	36.01	48.27
Madhya Pradesh	17.13	22.14	27.87	44.2	63.74	5.1	7.62	10.68	21.54	41.16
Maharashtra	29.82	39.18	47.18	64.87	76.88	7.12	11.74	22.29	36.79	55.21
Orissa	21.66	26.18	34.23	49.09	63.08	7.36	9.46	13.96	22.31	37.37
Rajasthan	15.21	19.07	24.38	38.55	60.41	3.97	6.47	10.27	19.44	44.66
West Bengal	29.28	33.2	40.94	57.7	68.64	6.55	8.92	13.21	27.28	43.4
India	24.03	29.45	36.23	52.19	64.36	8.54	11.3	16.33	29.6	47.08

Source: (i) Census Reports, Relevant Issues; and (ii) Scheduled Tribes Atlas of India, 2001.

the tribes in our country. It is well evident that while the education level for the country as a whole is grim, the educational status of the tribes is far worse. The scheduled tribe performed worse than their counterpart in educational attainment and as a result in seeking government and teaching jobs. This is not to deny that the literacy rate for STs has gone up from 8.5 per cent in 1961 to 29.6 per cent in 1991 and to 47 per cent in 2001. As per 2001 census, it is found that in terms of literacy of the general people (other than SC and ST) Bihar (47%) has the lowest literacy among the States under review. The State of Orissa with 63.08 per cent and Madhya Pradesh 63.74 per cent of general literacy are legging behind the national level of literacy (64.36%).

Table 7.2 reveals that literacy rate in general in Madhya Pradesh has increased both for males and females over the period 1991 to 2011. But there exists a gender gap of 20.5 between the male and female literacy during the year 2011.

Table 7.3 reveals that literacy rate in general in Maharashtra has increased both for males and females over the period 1991 to 2011. But there exists a gender gap of 14.34 between the male and female literacy during the year 2011.

Compared to the State of Madhya Pradesh, the State of Maharashtra is much better in terms of total literacy, male and female literacy and even gap between male and female literacy.

With regard to literacy among the tribes, as per 2001 Census,

Table 7.2: Literacy Rates in Madhya Pradesh—1981-2011

Sl. No.	*Census Year*	*Total Literacy/ Persons Literacy*	*Male Literacy*	*Female Literacy*	*Gap between Male and Female Literacy*
1.	1991	44.7	58.5	29.4	29.2
2.	2001	63.7	76.1	50.3	25.8
3.	2011	70.6	80.5	60.0	20.5

Note:

1. Literacy rate for 1981, 1991, 2001 and 2011 Census relate to the population aged seven years and above.
2. The 1981 Literacy rates exclude Assam where Census could not be conducted. The 1991 Census Literacy rates exclude Jammu and Kashmir where Census could not be conducted due to disturbed conditions.

Source: Census of India.

Table 7.3 : Literacy Rates in Maharashtra—1951-2011

Sl. No.	Census Year	Total Literacy/ Persons Literacy	Male Literacy	Female Literacy	Gap between Male and Female Literacy
1.	1991	64.87	76.56	52.32	24.24
2.	2001	76.88	85.97	67.03	18.94
3.	2011	82.91	89.82	75.48	14.34

Source: Census of India.

Bihar (28.17%) has the lowest literacy among the States under review. Madhya Pradesh has 41.16 per cent of tribal literacy (much below the national average 47.08%) whereas Maharashtra has 55.21 per cent of tribal literacy (much above the national average).

The progress over the years on the literacy front of the Scheduled Tribe is depicted in Table 7.4. During 2001, there were 14 million tribal children enrolled in elementary schools as against 20.24 million in the 6-14 years age group. The cohort dropout rates among tribal children was as high as 52.3 per cent for primary and 69.5 per cent for upper primary.

Table 7.4 Literacy Level of Scheduled Tribes and Total Literate Population—1961-2001

(*in percentage*)

	1961	1971	1981	1991	2001
Total literate population	24.0	29.4	36.2	52.2	64.84
Scheduled Tribes (STs) population	8.5	11.3	16.3	29.6	47.10
Total female population	12.9	18.6	29.8	39.3	53.67
Total Scheduled Tribes (STs) female population	3.2	4.8	8.0	18.2	34.76

Source: Census of India, 2001.

The two main issues in education of tribal children that emerged were inadequate physical access and socio-cultural differences which came in the way of their participation in schooling. The Seventh All-India Educational Survey 2002 shows that a total of 80 per cent of tribal habitations have schools within or less than 1 km radius at primary level. Similarly, at upper primary level a total of 67 per cent habitations have been provided upper primary school within a radius of 3 km. Thus, for 20 per cent of the habitations at the primary stage and 33 per cent at the upper primary stage, access was still an issue (Table 7.5).

One of the challenges in providing education to tribal children relates to setting up school facilities in small, scattered and remote tribal habitations. The majority of the Scheduled Tribes live in sparsely populated habitations in the interior and in inaccessible hilly and forest areas of the country. Nearly 22 per cent of the tribal habitations have populations of less than 100 while more than 40 per cent have population of 100 to 300. The rest have population of 300 to 500 (Sujatha, 2000).

Table 7.5: Habitations with Primary Schools and Upper Primary Schools

	Habitations with Primary Schools		*Habitations with Primary Schools*	
Total Habitations	Up to 1.0 km	More than 1.0 km	Up to 3.0 km	More than 3.0 km
242993	192624	50369	163308	79685

Source : Seventh All India Education Survey 2002

One of the reasons for poor access to schooling in tribal areas before the 1980s was the high norm on population, number of children and distance for opening new schools. Most of the States have relaxed these norms to enable setting up schools even in small tribal hamlets. This, along with other measures has improved access in tribal areas. For instance, Andhra Pradesh has relaxed norms to set up schools in habitations even with 20 school-age children. Some States have lowered the population size norm, especially for tribal areas. EGS Centres can now be established even with 15 children. In remote tribal habitations in hilly areas of North Eastern States and Jammu and Kashmir, EGS schools can be opened with only 10 children. The Sixth All India Educational Survey (1993) showed that 78 per cent of the tribal population and 56 per cent of tribal habitations have been provided primary schools within the habitation. In addition, 11 per cent of the tribal population and 20 per cent of tribal habitations have schools within less than 1 km radius. About 65 per cent of rural habitations covering 86 per cent of the total rural population have primary schools within the habitation or within a distance of half a kilometre, as against 56 per cent of tribal habitations with 79 per cent of tribal population. Mizoram and Gujarat have the highest

Table 7.6 : Gap between Scheduled Tribe and General Literacy Rates (Census Reports)

Sl. No.	*States*	*1961*	*1971*	*1981*	*1991*	*2001*
1.	Andhra Pradesh	16.78	19.23	22.12	26.93	23.43
2.	Bihar	9.24	8.30	9.21	11.70	18.83
3.	Gujarat	18.76	21.67	22.56	24.84	21.40
4.	Karnataka	16.88	16.67	18.32	20.03	18.37
5.	Madhya Pradesh	12.03	14.52	17.19	22.66	22.58
6.	Maharashtra	22.70	27.44	24.89	28.08	21.67
7.	Orissa	14.30	16.72	20.27	26.78	25.71
8.	Rajasthan	11.24	12.60	14.11	19.11	15.75
9.	West Bengal	22.73	24.28	27.73	30.42	25.24
	India	15.49	18.15	19.90	22.59	17.28

percentage of population and habitations covered by primary schools within the habitations. Up to 95 per cent of the tribal population and 85 to 90 per cent of the tribal habitations in the States are provided with schooling facilities within the habitation.

The gap between the scheduled tribe and general literacy rates have been exhibited in the Table 7.6. It is found that while in all India level the gap is 17.28 per cent, the gap in Orissa is the highest (25.71%) among the selected States in our study. In Madhya Pradesh the gap is 22.58 whereas it is 21.67 in Maharashtra.

Table 7.7 provides a glimpse of the Enrolment Pattern of the ST from 1980s to 2001. The enrolment of scheduled tribes at the primary and upper primary from 1980-81 to 2000-01 increased by 2.4 and 4.2 times respectively. The enrolment of girls has increased by 3 times at primary and 6 times at upper primary stage during the same period. The share of tribal girls in the total school-going tribal children at the elementary stage increased from 32.1 per cent in 1981 to 41.2 per cent in 2000-01. It is, however, a well known fact that enrolment ratio cannot be taken as best indicator due to over-reporting and underage and overage children studying in each class[1]. Hence, it is also important to juxtapose the dropout rate among the ST population (Table 7.8 , 7.9 and 7.10) to provide a clearer picture of the actual situation.

Physical access to schooling, especially at the upper primary stage, is still an issue in some parts of the country in remote tribal areas. But targeted coverage of all eligible habitations for the upper primary school facilities will be a priority.

Table 7.7 : Enrolment of ST Students during 1980-81 to 2000-01

(in million)

Year	*Primary (I-V)*			*Upper Primary (VI-VIII)*			*Elementary (I-VIII)*		
	Boys	*Girls*	*Total*	*Boys*	*Girls*	*Total*	*Boys*	*Girls*	*Total*
1980-81	3.1	1.5	4.6	0.5	0.2	0.7	3.6	1.7	5.3
1985-86	4.2	2.4	6.6	0.9	0.4	1.3	5.1	2.8	7.9
1990-91	4.9	2.9	7.8	1.1	0.6	1.7	6.0	3.5	9.5
1995-96	5.6	3.8	9.4	1.5	0.8	2.3	7.1	4.6	11.7
1996-97	5.2	3.6	8.8	1.6	0.9	2.5	6.8	4.5	11.3
1997-98	5.1	3.9	9.0	1.5	0.9	2.4	6.6	4.8	11.4
1998-99	5.3	4.0	9.3	1.6	1.0	2.6	6.9	5.0	11.9
1999-00	6.1	4.5	10.6	1.8	1.1	2.9	7.9	5.6	13.5
2000-01	6.3	4.7	11.0	1.9	1.2	3.1	8.2	5.9	14.1

Source: Selected Educational Statistics, 2000-01.

Table 7.8 : Dropout Rates of Scheduled Tribes at Primary and Elementary stages—2001 to 2004-05

Year	*Primary (I-V)*			*Elementary (I-VIII)*		
	Boys	*Girls*	*Total*	*Boys*	*Girls*	*Total*
2001-02	51.0	54.1	52.3	67.3	72.7	69.5
2002-03	50.8	52.1	51.4	66.9	71.2	68.7
2003-04	49.1	48.7	48.9	69.0	71.4	70.1
2004-05	42.6	42.0	42.3	65.0	67.1	65.9

Source: Selected Educational Statistics, 2004-05.

Table 7.9 : Dropout Rates of Scheduled Tribe Students at Primary, Elementary and Secondary Stages—2003-04

Year	*Primary (I-V)*			*Middle (I-VIII)*			*Secondary (I-X)*		
	Boys	*Girls*	*Total*	*Boys*	*Girls*	*Total*	*Boys*	*Girls*	*Total*
1990-91	60.3	66.1	62.5	75.7	82.2	78.6	83.3	87.7	85.0
1994-95	56.9	61.3	58.6	74.5	80.0	76.7	N.A	N.A	N.A
1995-96	55.0	58.9	56.6	62.3	71.2	66.0	N.A	N.A	N.A
1996-97	54.4	60.0	56.5	73.0	78.3	75.2	82.5	86.8	84.2
1997-98	52.9	58.1	55.1	71.3	75.5	73.0	72.5	80.4	75.8
1998-99	54.8	56.8	55.7	70.1	75.7	72.4	79.8	85.1	82.2
2001-02*	51.0	54.1	52.3	67.3	72.7	69.5	79.9	82.9	81.2
2002-03*	50.8	52.1	51.4	66.9	71.2	68.7	78.4	83.0	80.3
2003-04*	49.1	48.7	48.9	69.0	71.4	70.1	77.9	81.2	79.3

Source : India, Department of Secondary and Higher Education. Abstract of Selected Educational Statistics—2003-04.

Table 7.10 : Percentage Distribution of Dropouts of Scheduled Tribe Students in Rural Areas by Reasons—July 1986 to June 1987

States/Reasons	*Not interes-ted in education/ further studies*	*For particip-ation In household economic activity*	*For other econo-mic reasons*	*Busy in attending domestic chores*	*Failure*	*Others*
Andhra Pradesh	31.55	28.55	26.07	–	5.72	8.11
Bihar	16.45	54.33	10.82	6.13	4.98	7.3
Gujarat	36.31	25.51	5.02	10.21	21.84	1.11
Karnataka	11.33	37.67	34.00	2.08	4.50	10.43
Madhya Pradesh	32.25	26.82	17.53	3.68	11.44	8.28
Maharashtra	39.87	20.33	19.97	5.01	10.10	4.71
Orissa	23.23	17.34	25.88	3.77	13.31	16.47
Rajasthan	30.01	40.90	11.28	3.68	8.61	5.52
West Bengal	15.00	19.34	27.55	11.69	21.09	5.33

Sources : NSSO 42nd Round Report No. 365, Participation in Education, Part II, Vol. II, 1989.

In some remote sparsely populated areas, it may be difficult to set up primary schools due to small number of children. This may necessitate residential schools/hostels. Seasonal migration is common in several tribal areas. Facilities like seasonal hostels may need to be provided in all such Blocks with high level of migration to help retain children in villages when parents migrate.

Literacy Trends among Tribal Women

Literacy is a significant indicator of development among tribal groups. Among women in general, high literacy rates lead to lower infant mortality rates (Kingdon, 1999; Dreze, J. and G. Kingdon, 2000; World Bank, 1997), reduce the number of pregnancies and enhance the status of women both in domestic life and society. Additionally, the mother's literacy status and educational attainment have significantly positive effects on the child's human capital attainment (Sengupta and Guha, 2002; Colclough, 1982).

Table 7.11 demonstrates the level of female literacy in general during the census periods and the percentage of literacy among the tribal females in India. Undoubtedly, there exists a wide gap between the general female literacy and tribal female literacy. The gap is 21.85 per cent in Madhya Pradesh whereas it is 23.95 per cent in Maharashtra.

Table 7.12 shows the percentage of tribal male and female literacy in some of the tribal dominated districts of Maharashtra as per 2001 census. It is revealed that the district Dhule has the highest concentration of tribal population (26.14%), and the

Table 7.11: Progress of Female Literacy between Scheduled Tribe and General Literacy Rates

Sl. No.	*States*	*General*			*Scheduled Tribe*		
		1981	*1991*	*2001*	*1981*	*1991*	*2001*
1.	Andhra Pradesh	24.16	32.72	50.43	4.09	8.68	26.11
2.	Bihar	16.52	22.89	33.12	9.19	14.75	15.18
3.	Gujarat	38.46	48.64	57.80	14.00	24.20	36.02
4.	Karnataka	33.17	44.34	56.87	12.10	23.57	36.57
5.	Madhya Pradesh	19.00	28.85	50.29	4.36	10.73	28.44
6.	Maharashtra	41.01	52.32	67.03	14.39	24.03	43.08
7.	Orissa	25.14	34.68	50.51	5.53	10.21	39.35
8.	Rajasthan	14.00	20.44	43.85	1.46	4.42	26.16
9.	West Bengal	36.07	46.56	59.61	5.88	14.96	29.15
	India	29.76	39.19	53.05	9.63	18.19	34.75

Table 7.12 : Disparity in Tribal Female Education in some Selected Districts in Maharashtra (As per 2001 Census)

Districts	*Percentage of total Tribal/ Population*	*Percentage of Tribal Male Population*	*Percentage of Tribal Female Population*	*Percentage of total Tribal Literacy rate*	*Percentage of Male Tribal Literacy rate*	*Percentage of Female Tribal Literacy rate*	*Gap in the level of Tribal Male and Female Literacy*
1. Thane	14.75	13.72	15.94	37.78	47.69	27.84	19.85
2. Nashik	23.92	23.32	24.55	40.88	50.33	31.20	19.13
3. Dhule	26.14	28.29	24.25	37.00	45.49	28.27	27.23
4. Chandrapur	18.12	17.93	18.32	55.20	65.11	44.97	20.14
5. Yavatmal	19.26	19.08	19.44	51.94	62.03	41.43	20.60
Maharashtra	8.85	8.63	9.10	45.28	54.93	35.37	19.56

Table 7.13 : Disparity in Tribal Female Education in Some Selected Districts in Madhya Pradesh (As per 2001 Census)

Districts	*Percentage of total Tribal Population*	*Percentage of Tribal Male Population*	*Percentage of Tribal Female Population*	*Percentage of total Tribal Literacy Rate*	*Percentage of Male Tribal Literacy Rate*	*Percentage of Female Tribal Literacy Rate*	*Gap in the Level of Tribal Male and Female Literacy*
1. Jhabua	86.85	86.55	87.14	23.24	31.64	14.78	16.86
2. Mandla	57.23	56.33	58.14	42.10	54.79	29.75	25.04
3. Dhar	54.50	53.77	55.26	28.58	38.07	18.91	19.16
4. Shahdol	44.48	43.67	45.32	36.54	47.64	25.36	22.28
5. West Nimar	35.48	35.02	35.98	32.32	40.34	24.09	16.25
Madhya Pradesh	20.27	19.70	20.89	32.34	42.09	22.33	20.76

Table 7.14 : Literacy Rates of Tribal Dominated Districts in Maharashtra—1991-2011

Sl. No.	*Tribal Dominated District*	*Census Year*	*Total Literacy/Persons Literacy*	*Male Literacy*	*Female Literacy*	*Gap between Male and Female Literacy*
1.	Nandurbar* (65.93)	1991	—	—	—	—
		2001	55.78	66.16	45.18	20.98
		2011	63.04	71.98	53.90	18.08
2.	Gadchiroli (38.31)	1991	42.90	56.60	28.90	27.70
		2001	60.10	71.86	48.07	23.79
		2011	70.55	80.21	60.66	19.55
3.	Dhule (25.97)	1991	51.60	63.60	39.10	24.50
		2001	71.65	81.40	61.39	20.01
		2011	74.61	82.59	66.21	16.38
4.	Nashik (23.92)	1991	62.30	74.00	49.90	24.10
		2001	74.36	83.65	64.35	19.30
		2011	80.96	88.03	73.43	14.60
5.	Yavatmal (19.26)	1991	58.00	70.40	44.80	25.60
		2001	73.62	84.09	62.52	21.57
		2011	80.70	88.58	72.41	16.17

Note: Figures in brackets indicates Percentage of Tribal Population of district as per 2001 Census.
* Indicates newly created district since 1991 Census data is not available.

Source: Ministry of Tribal Affairs and Census of India.

disparity between tribal male and tribal female literacy is also the highest (27.23%) among the districts under review.

Table 7.13 shows the percentage of tribal male and female literacy in some of the tribal dominated districts of Madhya Pradesh as per 2001 census. It is revealed that the district Jhabua has the highest concentration of tribal population (86.85%). But the disparity between tribal male and tribal female literacy is also the highest in Mandla (25.04%) followed by Shahdol (22.28%) among the districts under review.

Table 7.14 depicts the literacy of males and females and their gender gap in total in the State of Maharashtra. It is revealed that the gap between the male and female literacy in general is the highest in Gadchiroli (19.55) followed by Nandarbar (18.8) as per 2011 Census.

Similarly, Table 7.15 depicts the literacy of males and females and their gender gap in total in Madhya Pradesh. It is revealed that the gap between the male and female literacy in general is the

Table 7.15 : Literacy Rates of Tribal Dominated Districts in Madhya Pradesh—1991-2011

Sl. No.	Tribal Dominated District	Census Year	Total Literacy/ Persons Literacy	Male Literacy	Female Literacy	Gap between Male and Female Literacy
1.	Jhabua (86.85)	1991	19.0	26.3	11.5	14.80
		2001	41.4	53.9	28.6	25.30
		2011	44.5	54.7	34.3	20.40
2.	Barwani* (67.02)	1991	—	—	—	—
		2001	41.7	51.1	32.0	19.10
		2011	50.2	57.3	43.1	14.20
3.	Dindori* (64.48)	1991	—	—	—	—
		2001	54.2	70.0	38.2	31.80
		2011	65.5	77.6	53.5	24.10
4.	Mandla (57.23)	1991	37.3	52.2	22.2	30.00
		2001	59.6	73.7	45.5	28.20
		2011	68.3	79.5	57.2	22.30
5.	Dhar (54.50)	1991	34.5	47.6	20.7	26.90
		2001	52.5	65.7	38.6	27.10
		2011	60.6	71.1	49.7	21.40

Note: Figure in bracket indicate Tribal Population percentage of district as per 2001 Census.

* indicates newly created district since 1991 Census data is not available

Source: Ministry of Tribal Affairs and Census of India.

highest in Dindori (24.10) followed by Mandla (22.30) as per 2011 Census.

However, in recent decade, in Madhya Pradesh, there have been remarkable developments in the sphere of primary education due to governmental initiatives. The significant gains in literacy made by Madhya Pradesh can be enlightened by the twin-pronged strategy of the Madhya Pradesh Government: (a) provision of schools and guaranteeing access; and (b) a model for spreading literacy that makes use of the synergies between the community, the local and the State governments. Between 1997 and 1998, under the newly initiated Education Guarantee Scheme (EGS), Madhya Pradesh established 26,000 new schools, most of them in areas inhabited by Scheduled Castes and Scheduled Tribes. This made possible for Madhya Pradesh to declare universal access to education. In order to address the challenge of mass literacy, Madhya Pradesh moved away from the Total Literacy Campaign (TLC) model at the national level and pioneered a new scheme, the 'Padhna Badhna Andolan' (PBA). The PBA uses the organizational support provided by the institution of the Panchayati Raj (village councils) to broker the spread of education at the level of the community.

In his trend report on research in the education of the disadvantaged, Sachchidananda (1990) has viewed that education has been acclaimed as the primemover of development. The governments central as well as State are expected to take special care of educating tribal children. This involves both protective and promotive measures. Notably, education to tribal children is constitutional obligation of both State as well as central governments is to freely and compulsorily provided to children up to 14 years of age as enshrined in the Constitution of India. The challenges in achieving universal education[2] for tribal children can be categorized as external, internal, socio-economic and psychological. The external constraints are related to issues at levels of policy, planning and implementation while internal constraints are with respect to school system, content, curriculum, pedagogy, medium of instruction, etc. The third set of problems relates to social, economic and cultural background of tribes and psychological aspects of first generation learners. The major reason for low educational attainment till this period[3] had been challenges encountered with respect to setting up schooling facilities in small, scattered and remote tribal habitations. This is because the majority of the Scheduled tribes live in sparsely populated habitations in interior and inaccessible hilly and forest areas of the country. Nearly 22 per cent of the tribal habitations have population less than 100 while more than 40 per cent have population of 100 to 300. The rest have population of 300 to 500 (Sujatha, 2000). However, at present the major problems pertain to internal and cultural constraints.

Added to the above problems, age-old poverty of the tribal people is yet another stumbling block in the way of tribal education. The tribal parents always seek the assistance of their children in various activities rather than sending them to schools. Even when the children fail to clear the school examination, tribal parents never take pains to send their children again to school. Educated persons, leaders and the like must voluntarily assume, besides their own duties and responsibilities, the work of counselling and the guidance of their parents to make them aware of the importance of tribal education, particularly tribal girls. In this context, we cannot ignore the role of non-government organizations in the tribal areas.

Special economic incentives should be provided both to the tribal learners and their parents in order to curb the problems like rampant child labour and illiteracy in the tribal areas (Pasayat, 1997, 233-4). A balance has to be maintained between the needs of education programmes should have schemes for 'earning while learning', so that a student is to supplement whatever small it may be, the earning of his parents (Ratha and Behera, 1990, 237).

The 86th Amendment to the Constitution of India (2000) made education a fundamental right, calling for the State to provide free and compulsory education to all children between 6 and 14 years. At the same time Article 51 of the Constitution was amended to parents and guardians to provide education to their 6-14 years old children. Recognizing that the scheduled tribes count among the most deprived and marginalized sections of Indian society, a host of welfare and developmental measures have been initiated for their social and economic development. Tribal Sub-Plan approach came into existence as the main strategy for the welfare and development in the Five Year Plans. Along with core economic sectors, elementary education has been accorded priority in the tribal sub-Plan approach. Elementary education is considered important, not only because of constitutional obligation, but as a crucial input for total development of tribal communities, particularly to build confidence among the tribes to deal with outsiders on equal terms. A second important development in the policy towards education of tribes came with recommendations of the National Policy on Education (NPE) in 1986, which specified, among other things, the following:

1. Priority will be accorded to opening primary schools in tribal areas.
2. There is a need to develop curricular and devise instructional material in tribal language at the initial stages with arrangements for gradually adopting to regional languages.
3. Promising ST youths will be encouraged to take up teaching in tribal areas.
4. Ashram schools/residential schools will be established on a large scale in tribal areas.

Incentives schemes will be formulated for the STs, keeping in view their special needs and lifestyle.

The two foremost challenges in education of tribal children are physical access to schooling at upper primary level and diverse socio-cultural context. In 2001, there were 14 million tribal children enrolled in elementary schools as against 20.24 million in the 6-14 years age group. Thus 6.24 million were still out of school in 2001. The cohort dropout rates among tribal children was as high as 52.3 per cent for primary and 69.5 per cent for upper primary. For 20 per cent of the habitations at the primary stage and 33 per cent at the upper primary stage, access was still an issue in 2002.

Conclusions

We can briefly summarize that reaching those still out of reach does not mean merely expanding existing education system. It is imperative for designing and developing new models and delivery systems tailored to specific groups, in a concerted effort to ensure relevant high quality basic education for every child and adult. Social group disparities particularly gaps between Scheduled Castes and Scheduled Tribes and general caste group are excruciatingly distressing (Tripathy, 2010). The dysfunctional school system in the tribal regions coupled with the mind set of the decision-makers tends to exacerbate the inequities. Some of the factors responsible for such an inequitious situation for tribal children as reported by Tilak (2003) are: pervasive teacher absenteeism, psychological and social distance between teacher and the taught, lack of concern on the part of teachers for children, unsuitable school-timing, lack of involvement of parents in school affairs and so on.

An overall analysis brought to light some useful conclusions. The Constitution (86th Amendment) Act 2002, has been enacted by the Parliament of our country to provide free and compulsory education to all children in the age-group of 6-14 years. The necessary condition for the efficiency of the basic education system relates to geographical accessibility as well as availability of a school to the children of the relevant age-group. With the fulfilment of this necessary condition as the basis, one moves into the realm of identifying the sufficient conditions. Since schooling facilities have children as the target group and further, since the family plays a crucial role in the upbringing of the student in the school age-group, the accessibility of the school is of prime importance and physical access becomes crucial in determining whether or not a child joins school and is retained therein. Experience as well as empirical evidence show that the utilization of school facilities is subject to distance decay, whereby the nearer a person lives to this facility, the more likely it is that he or she will use it assuming of course that there are no socio-economic barriers to access.

Apart from physical distance, socio-cultural distance between the scheduled and non-scheduled children prevents children of the former group from getting themselves enrolled and continued participation. This implies need for locating a school at a place that ensures its accessibility to the children from the SC and ST communities.

Simple availability of a school even within the habitation itself dose not ensure enrolment of all school-age-children. From supply-side perspective, interventions such as building enough schools and classroom and hiring and deploying enough competent is making a full-fledged well staffed and well-functioning school available in the village or its neighbourhood.

The problem of accessibility could be effectively addressed

through a number of demand side interventions: improving the quality of schooling, enforcing compulsory attendance and offsetting the cost of children's labour. Parental demand for schooling of their children is to a large extent dependent on their perceived benefits of education. This perception of parents depends in turn on their literacy levels. Therefore, feeble and fragile social demand for schooling in educationally backward districts with low female literacy levels is a major challenge. In view of this; short term demand generation activities can be effective in raising enrolments. The problem of accessibility acquires significance in the case of habitations which are predominantly inhabited by disadvantaged groups like Scheduled Castes and Scheduled Tribes. These habitations are generally isolated from the main settlement site. Thus, the children of these communities are handicapped in availing themselves of the schooling facility.

According to Vinoba Gautam the interventions being promoted in States under Janshala include:

> Schools, education guarantee centres and alternative schools in tribal habitations for non-enrolled and dropout children; textbooks in the mother tongue for children at the beginning of the primary education cycle, when they do not understand the regional language. Suitably adapted curriculum and the availability of locally relevant teaching and learning materials for tribal students; special training for non-tribal teachers to work in tribal areas, including knowledge of tribal dialect; special support to teachers as per need; deploying community teachers; bridge Language Inventory for use of teachers; school calendars in tribal areas appropriate to local requirements and festivals, etc., will go a long way in developing the literacy of the tribes. *Anganwadis* and *Balwadis* or creches in each school in tribal areas need to be established so that the girls are relieved from sibling care responsibilities; special plan for nomadic and migrant workers. Engagement of community organizers from ST communities with a focus on schooling needs of children from specific households; ensuring sense of ownership of school committees by ST communities through increasing representatives of STs in VECs/PTAs, etc., are urgently required. Involving

community leaders in school management; monitoring attendance and retention of children; providing context specific intervention, e.g., Ashram school, hostel, incentives, etc., are also essential.

Most of the States recognize the need to address issues related to teachers' attitudes, medium of instruction, textbooks and materials, curriculum and pedagogy and teaching-learning process in tribal areas. An increasing number of researchers strongly advocate the use of the mother tongue or home language as medium of instruction in early stages of education. This assumes greater significance in the context of education of tribal children because their mother tongue is often quite distinct from the prominent languages in the State or regional languages. Tribal children face problems wherever teachers do not speak their dialect at all. From the perspective of language, it is desirable to have a local teacher from the same tribal community.

A programme of schooling, which does not pay attention to the ecological, cultural and psychological characteristics of tribal children, is highly unlikely to make any significant impact. The educational system of the dominant non-tribal population is of very limited value in the tribal cultural milieu because it does not match with the lifestyle of individuals and the needs of the tribal community. Linking school education with life in general and the needs of the tribal communities in particular is a most important step that requires serious attention. The evidences suggest that tribal children do possess the basic cognitive abilities and psychological dispositions necessary for successful participation in school. Yet tribal children have very low levels of participation and success in school education programmes. This indicates to our failure to develop a sensitive model of education that is rooted in the psychological strengths of tribal children. Studies indicate that, in comparison to other groups, hunters and gatherers possess a high level of visual and tactual differentiation; they demonstrate capacity for fine judgment of shape and size of stimuli as well as spatial relations and they produce fine categorization of an array of objects.These abilities are required for success in science, art, music, dance, athletic activities, and vocations like carpentry, tailoring, wood and stone crafts. These skills need to be utilized not only for education of tribal children in schools, but also in the broader economic spheres of tribal life. Such attempts will be helpful in generating and promoting the sense of competence, self efficacy, self-respect and positive self-image among tribal children in general.

Such attempts are also highly likely to provide tribal children with a culturally meaningful, ecologically valid and economically viable alternative to life by reinforcing the dignity of their culture and identity. Ever increasing contact of tribes with the outside world over the years has introduced several changes in their culture and life. These changes are reflected in their psychological characteristics also. Studies indicate that their ways of perceiving the world, categorizing objects, interpreting pictures, and strategies of learning and memory become more similar to those with whom they interact and negotiate their life in these changed circumstances. This suggests that tribal children can acquire all those skills that the members of other groups of the society possess. What is important on our part is to develop a positive frame of mind about tribal children. This is possible only through sensitivity to tribal culture and life, recognition of the cognitive strengths of tribal children, and appreciation of their personality qualities. Efforts in these directions will be very helpful in organizing the programme of tribal education as well as promoting economic and other aspects of tribal development.

Similarly, a clear policy for language use in schools has to be developed. Research suggests that significantly fewer students drop out of schools in which the language of tribal groups is used for instruction at the primary level. Development of primers in the tribal dialect involving content from the local context will go a long way in ensuring children's active participation in the learning process in school. While there is a general need for improvement in physical facilities in all schools in remote tribal regions, change in perceptions and outlooks of teachers about tribal children are equally important. Teachers must be sensitized to the cultural and behavioural strengths of tribal children and motivated to do their best for them in schools. Incentives should be initiated to attract effective teachers to work in tribal schools and to retain them there. Only such motivated teachers are likely to generate interest among tribal children towards schools education by attempting to link the contents of the curriculum with the existing realities of tribal communities through the use of innovative technologies.

The most urgent priority is to ensure access to, and improve the quality of education for tribal girls, and to remove every obstacle that hampers their active participation. Education must help learners live their lives with greater competence and greater confidence, developing behaviour based on positive values, understanding and respecting for other people of all kinds, for their rights, for the natural world, for the past and the future.

NOTES

1. It is said that official enrolment statistics bear little relation to actual attendance of students in the classrooms; that enrolment figures are often inflated because there is so much more money for a State making vast enrolment claims.
2. A programme of universal education has three components, namely, universal facilities, universal enrolment and universal retention. Universal facilities may not ensure universal enrolment and universal enrolment may not guarantee universal retention. On the other hand, differential participation may render the growth of education instrumental in social differentiation. In that case education becomes an instrument of change but in a different direction.
3. One of the reasons for poor access to schooling in tribal areas before 1980s was the high norm on population, number of children and distance for opening new schools. Most of the States have relaxed these norms to enable setting up schools even in small tribal hamlets. This, along with other measures has improved access in tribal areas. For instance, Andhra Pradesh has relaxed norms to set up schools in habitations even with 20 school-age children. Some States like Karnataka, etc., have lowered the population size norm, especially for tribal areas. EGS Centres can now be established even with 15 children. In remote tribal habitations in hilly areas of North Eastern States and Jammu & Kashmir, EGS schools can be opened even with 10 children.

REFERENCES

Census of India (2001) Children in West Bengal, *Economic and Political Weekly*, Vol. 37, No. 17, pp. 1621-37.

D.K. Behera (ed.) (1997): *Contemporary Society: Tribal Studies* (Vol. II), New Delhi: Concept Publishing Company, pp. 228-234.

Dreze, J. and G. Kingdon, (2000): "Fertility, Education and Development: Further Evidence from India", Development Economics Discussion Paper Series, STICERD, London School of Economics.

Kingdon, G.G. (1999): "Gender Gap in India's Schools: Is the Labour Market a Factor?" *Insights*, Vol. 29.

Pasayat, C. (1997): "Literacy situation among Tribal Females in Orissa", in Gorge Pfeffer and Ratha, S.N. and D.K. Behera (1990): 'Problems of Education among Tribals: An Appraisal", *The Eastern Anthropologist*, 43 (3); 213-40.

Sachchidananda (1990): "Research in the Education of the Disadvantaged," in the *Fourth Survey of Research in Education*, M.B. Buch, NCERT, (II): 1414.

Sengupta, P., J. Guha (2002): *Enrolment, Dropout and Grade Completion of Girl.*

Sujatha, K. (2000): *Education among Tribals*, New Delhi: Ministry of HRD and NIEPA.

Tilak, J.B.J. (2003): *Education in Orissa—A Review of Progress, Problems and Perspectives for Future on School Education*, New Delhi: NIEPA.

Tripathy, S. N. (2010): *Literacy for Tribal Women*, Delhi: Abhijeet Publications.

World Bank (1997): *Primary Education in India*, Washington D.C.

8

Primary Education in a Tribal Village of Madhya Pradesh: Myth and Reality

S.N. Chaudhary

This chapter is divided into three parts. Opening part covers historical overview of tribal education with reference to Madhya Pradesh alongwith the methodology followed in the study. Second part deals with status of literacy and education among tribe in the studied district and Block. It also covers state of literacy and education in the studied village, functioning of primary school, enrolment and absenteeism, quality of learning, functioning of MDM, parents attitudinal change in favour of education and difficulties in course of providing education to children. In the third part an attempt has been made to suggest action agenda to improve the state of primary education among tribes in qualitative and quantitative terms.

I

Perspective

The history of social education among tribes, no matter at what level of modernization and development they are, is very old. However, its nature was informal in the past. It was demand ridden. Therefore, it was highly localized with having legitimacy from local ecology and environment. The content of such education was based on tribals felt experience. This education was neither supposed to introduce new and alien world view nor it was supposed to promote only conservatism. The main purpose was to equip learners with those set of knowledge which was logical, behavioural and, therefore, practical in day to day life. Locals were not only involved in the establishment and functioning of such institutions which were doing both educational and social functions but also they were involved in the formulation of the so-called content of the education which was seldom written. Hence, the education was totally informal but completely functional and, therefore, relevant. One can take the institution of *ghotul* historically found among Gonds of Bastar, as an example of informal educational institution. *Ghotul* type institutions were also found in many more tribes across the country. Needless to mention that *ghotul* stood for complete practical education and promoter of cooperation, harmony, collectivism and conservation of natural resources.

But as the process of acculturation between tribes and outside forces increased in a massive manner, especially with the introduction of the British Raj, gradually the existing educational system lost its importance. A new and alien education system was introduced by both state and civil society organizations in the tribal world. This education is methodical and totally alien to their culture and tradition. The foremost aim of this education is to facilitate their mainstreaming in the light of the development parameter and culture imposed by the outside forces. It was assumed that the methodical education will improve their quality of life and shall contribute to their integration with the rest of the society, as a result of which they will be able to reap benefits of protective benefits of the state which will ultimately lead to their overall development. Now the history of this protective discrimination process is about 65 years old and, therefore, it is high time to take stock of development especially in the field of literacy and primary education among them.

Needless to mention that the new education system is neither the construct of the local culture nor controlled at the local level. There is no scope and space for the local requirements and features in the content of the ongoing education system. It is rightly said that today in many schools tribal students at the primary and middle level know the name of Mahatma Gandhi and such other big leaders and events because they are included in their syllabus, but hardly any of them know about traditional healers, reformers and locally available social and ecological heritage because these issues and items are not taught in the class room. Earlier the informal education system used to take care of the local features but today it has become the thing of the past. How, to what extent and up to what level of education local features shall be included in their syllabus? This question needs to be debated. Also, there is need to debate about medium of instruction through which tribal children may feel comfortable as well as it may be helpful to them in the globalized situation. There is a point of view that at least at the primary level, tribal children should to taught through their mother tongue. But what about those, who drop out after completing primary education and their number is very big. How they will learn languages which are in demand outside the tribal territory?

Earlier door of informal education was practically opened for all the households in a tribal village. All the boys and girls of a specific age group used to avail informal education. But today we have different types of schools even in the villages. Earlier tribes were economically to a great extent, homogeneous. Hence, most of them were dependent on *ghotul* type of institution. And also for centuries there was no alternative. But today among many of the tribes of central India the process of class formation, although slowly, is taking place. The affluent and occupationally mobile tribes do not like to send their children in government run schools at the local level primarily because it is generally perceived that the type and quality of education provided in these schools are extremely poor. And if their children are not enrolled in these schools they do not take interest in the functioning of these schools. The issue of quality of education received by tribal children in these schools is alarming. It is apprehended that how after completing such education tribal youth will even compete with tribal children who are from relatively well to do families and who have received quality education in good schools? This is a pertinent question which needs to be addressed.

Literacy and Education among Tribe: State Scenario

The overall literacy rate of the STs at the national level has increased from 18.4 per cent at 1991 census to 41.2 per cent at 2001 census. Despite this increase, the literacy rate among the tribes of Madhya Pradesh is lower if compared with that of all STs at the national level (47.1 per cent). Male and female literacy rates among the tribes (53.5 per cent and 28.4 per cent) are also lower in comparison to those at the national level (59.2 per cent and 34.8 per cent).

Among the major tribes of Madhya Pradesh, only Gonds have registered the higher overall literacy as well as female literacy if compared to those of the national average. Sahariya (PTG) have returned the lowest overall literacy and female literacy both.

Among ST literates, 57.3 per cent are either without any educational level or have attained education below primary level. The proportion of literates who have attained education up to primary and middle levels constitute 24.8 per cent and 9.7 per cent respectively. Literates, who are educated up to Matric/ Secondary/Higher Secondary, constitute 6.6 per cent only. Graduates and above are 1.4 per cent while non-technical and technical diploma holders constitute a negligible proportion. *(Madhya Pradesh, Data Highlights: The Scheduled Tribes, Census of India 2001, Office of the Registrar General, New Delhi).*

The data on the education levels attained by all STs show that the dropout rate is high after primary level. It declines sharply from the middle level onwards. Similar trend has been shown by the major STs in attainment of education.

In short, it is apparent that in terms of literacy and education tribes of Madhya Pradesh, not only lags behind tribes of India but also within the State itself tribal women lags behind tribal women, primitive tribes lags behind the dominant tribes and there is high dropout level among them at all the levels of education. And this state of affair also exists at the district level. Therefore, as we move from State to the tribal dominated district and from district to tribal dominated Block and villages the level of literacy and education decreases. Why it is so? Why it is so that in spite of number of institutional initiatives the level of literacy and education is low among tribes. Why it is so that quality of teaching and learning is inferior? Why it is so that the rate of absenteeism is very high? Why it is so that the rate of dropout is high? These are some of the pertinent questions which needs to be probed. For this purpose in mind the present study was carried out.

Methodology

The study was conducted in a village of one of the forty-six districts of Madhya Pradesh namely Betul. The district is predominantly rural because about 81 per cent population lives in villages. The average household size is 6.0. The district has 66.4 per cent literacy rate but female literacy rate (55.6%) is much lower in comparison to male literacy rate (76.8%). Of the total workers 41.8 per cent, 37.7 per cent, 1.8 per cent and 18.7 per cent are cultivators, farm labourers, engaged as labourer in household industries and other works respectively.

There are 10 Development Blocks in the district. 4 Blocks are tribal dominated. The study was conducted in Sahpur Block which is inhabited by 64.40 per cent tribal population. Largely it is inhabited by Gond tribe but certain villages are also inhabited by Korku tribe. Within the Block there are 131 inhabited villages. The study was conducted in one of these villages namely Pathai. 91.8 per cent households are of Gond tribe in the village. All the tribal households of the village, school teachers of primary and middle school of the village, selected number of students of these two schools and other relevant stakeholders participated in the study. Semi-structured interview schedule, interview guide and documentary sources were the main instruments of data collection. Major findings are as under.

II

Situation in Betul : Historical Overview

So far as the history of both primary and middle education in Betul district is concerned it is very old. A beginning was made by British rule for the expansion of education in the district in 1854, when *tehsil* and village schools were opened and supported by private subscription or a voluntary *cess* on the landowners. As a result of these efforts during 1870-71 there were 29 government and 17 private schools with having 1,878 students in the district. With slight fluctuation patterns of growth in the number of both schools and enrolled students retained the positive trend in the decades to come. During 1890-91, three schools were opened especially for Gond children. Also, during 1885-86, one girl school was opened at Betul. The net result of these efforts were an increase in the number of literate population. For instance, in 1901 Betul stood 14th among the districts of the Province in respect of the literacy of its population, 39 per 1,000 of males being able to read and write as against the Provincial average of 54. Only 118 women were returned as literate (Gazetteer of India, Madhya Pradesh, Old Betul District, reprint 1999; pp. 226-228). In 2001, there were 45 districts in Madhya Pradesh while the State had 64 per cent literacy rate, Betul district had 66.87 per cent literacy rate. During 2001, Betul stood 15th among the districts of the province in terms of literacy rate.

Situation in Pathai

Like other tribal villages of Betul district Pathai is also deprived of fruits of education in the historical perspective. And this state of affair exists in spite of the fact that the village is near to the National Highway No. 69 as well as Block Development Office at Sahpur. It has also a primary school since 1957. It is amazing to note that in spite of the existence of Primary school in the village since long, number of illiterate and out of school children in the past was high. Today 53.65 per cent villagers are literate and educated, 27.47 per cent have received education up to primary level and as we move from primary to higher level of education the figure drastically decreases. Only 4 villagers have received education up to graduation level but they too are not graduates. And the number of small children, out of school children and those who are illiterate is around 46.37 per cent.

This statement is supported from the fact that as we move in the descending order from old to the young generation, the number of illiterates decreases. For instance, there are 61 senior citizens in the village of which 52 (83.6%) are illiterate. Relatively high level of enrolment of school going boys and girls today, rapid decrease in the number of out of school children and increasing rate of literacy among young population definitely reflect sustained effort by the State today and in the recent past. Number of State run schemes especially Mid Day Meal, increasing number of infra-structural facility at the school level, special incentives for girl students, coupled with increasing awareness among guardians in favour of education is responsible for this encouraging state of affair.

Primary School

As stated above, within the village there is one primary and one

Table 8.1 : Literacy and Level of Education in terms of Age

Age	*NA/Not gaing to School*	*Enrolled but not attending school*	*Illiterate*	*Literate*	*Anganwadi*	*Primary*	*Middle*	*High School*	*Higher Secondary*	*Under Graduate*	*Total*
up to one year	33	—	—	—	1	—	—	—	—	—	34
1-3 years	37	—	4	—	15	1	—	—	—	—	57
3-6 years	—	18	8	—	36	34	—	—	—	—	96
6-14 years	—	4	30	—	17	158	36	9	—	—	254
15-25 years	—	—	93	13	—	61	41	29	12	3	252
25-35 years	—	—	86	13	—	39	23	6	2	—	169
35-45 years	—	—	88	13	—	13	6	4	—	—	124
45-55 years	—	—	52	3	—	5	5	2	—	1	68
55-60 years	—	—	30	6	—	2	1	—	—	—	39
above 60 years	—	—	52	2	—	4	—	1	2	—	61
Total	70	22	443	50	69	317	112	51	16	4	1154
Percentage	6.07	1.91	38.39	4.33	5.98	27.47	9.71	4.42	1.39	0.35	100

middle school. Primary school is located in a newly constructed building since 2007 with some of the essential infrastructural facilities like drinking water facility, toilet facility, separate kitchen, separate class rooms, sitting arrangements, sufficient number of teachers, regular functioning of MDM, separate cook, blackboard in the class room, proper opening and closing time of school and so on. There are 9 teachers in the school and all of them are permanent. Earlier it was in the middle of the village but now the new building is located in the extreme southern side of the village.

If we see enrolment of tribal children in this school from 2001-02 onwards there is always an increasing trend. For instance, during 2001-02, 191 students were enrolled but during 2008-09 its number have increased up to 241. However, the rate of enrolment of tribal girls is higher than the rate of enrolment of tribal boys.

This does not mean that number of girl students has increased because number of boys have decreased for some of the boys have been enrolled in other schools outside the village, rather, girls enrolment have increased due to number of facilities provided by government along with increasing awareness among villagers in favour of girl's education. Actually most of the villagers are in favour of education of their children, no matter they are boys or girls.

But, as we move from class third onwards, girls enrolment rate gradually decreases. For instance, it was 133 and 123 at Class IV and V which is lower in comparison to enrolment of boys at these two levels (Table 8.2). This is primarily because of patriarchal bias against girls. As girls reaches class IV and V their involvement in domestic work increases. Also if parents have to withdraw any of their two kids from the school they prefer to withdraw their daughter.

Absenteeism

There is gap between enrolled students and students present in the classroom in all the classes at the primary level. This is apparent from the fact that of 254 enrolled students in the school only 194 (76.37 per cent) were present during the course of our visit to the school (Table 8.3). But the gap is wider at class one and as one move towards class V gender gap decreases. In terms of gender, enrolment is higher at the entry level among girls. The rate of absenteeism is also higher among them. But as one move towards

Table 8.2 : Class, Year and Gender-wise Enrolment in Primary School

Year	*I*			*II*			*III*			*IV*			*V*			*GT*
	Tribal			*Tribal*			*Tribal*			*Tribal*			*Tribal*			*M/F/T*
	M	*F*	*T*	*M*	*F*	*T*	*M*	*F*	*T*	*M*	*F*	*T*	*M*	*F*	*T*	
2001-02	20	20	40	17	33	50	20	19	29	22	17	39	16	17	33	191
2002-03	30	18	48	19	16	35	11	17	28	24	13	37	22	14	36	184
2003-04	18	15	33	30	19	49	15	12	27	17	17	34	30	15	45	188
2004-05	28	31	59	28	14	42	27	20	47	18	10	28	22	21	43	219
2005-06	25	50	75	25	28	53	34	19	43	23	17	40	30	19	49	260
2006-07	34	33	67	20	42	62	29	27	56	33	04	37	17	17	34	256
2007-08	39	32	71	23	28	51	24	45	69	22	14	36	25	06	31	258
2008-09	25	28	53	26	22	48	20	26	46	23	41	64	16	14	30	241
Total	*219*	*227*	*446*	*188*	*202*	*390*	*180*	*165*	*645*	*182*	*133*	*315*	*178*	*123*	*301*	*1797*

Source : Admission register available at Pathai Primary School.

Table 8.3 : Gender-wise Number of enrolled Students and their Presence in Classroom for One Week

Day	*Sex*	*I*		*II*		*III*		*IV*		*V*		*Grand Total*		*Percentage of present students*
		E	*P*	*E*	*P*	*E*	*P*	*E*	*P*	*E*	*P*	*E*	*P*	
17/11/08	M	26	13	27	09	22	12	24	11	17	15	116	60	51.72
Monday	F	33	13	24	12	26	13	41	21	14	14	138	73	52.89
	T	59	26	51	21	48	25	65	32	31	29	254	133	52.36
18/11/08	M	26	14	27	19	22	13	24	13	17	16	116	75	64.65
Tuesday	F	33	25	24	18	26	15	41	24	14	12	138	94	68.11
	T	59	39	51	37	48	28	65	37	31	28	254	169	66.53
19/11/08	M	26	15	27	19	22	09	24	14	17	16	116	73	62.93
Wednesday	F	33	21	24	17	26	16	41	24	14	13	138	91	65.94
	T	59	36	51	36	48	25	65	38	31	29	254	164	64.56
20/11/08	M	26	15	27	19	22	16	24	16	17	15	116	81	69.82
Thursday	F	33	23	24	15	26	16	41	32	14	12	138	98	71.01
	T	59	38	51	34	48	32	65	48	31	27	254	179	70.47
21/11/08	M	26	16	27	21	22	15	24	18	17	17	116	87	75.00
Friday	F	33	22	24	15	26	17	41	32	14	14	138	100	72.46
	T	59	38	51	36	48	32	65	50	31	31	254	187	73.62
22/11/08	M	26	17	27	20	22	15	24	18	17	17	116	87	75.00
Saturday	F	33	25	24	18	26	17	41	33	14	14	138	107	77.53
	T	59	42	51	38	48	32	65	51	31	31	254	194	76.37

Note: E= Enrolled, P= Present, M=Male, F=Female and T=Total

Source: Admission and attendance register available at Pathai school

class V enrolment becomes boys centric. But gender gap in terms of presence in classroom at class V decreases in comparison to the situation at the entry point. This shows increasing inclination of parents in favour of primary education to their daughters.

Villagers' and Teachers' Perception about Absenteeism

Different stakeholders have different views on absenteeism. According to parents and guardians, whose wards are currently enrolled in the primary school, some of the specific reasons responsible for absenteeism among their wards are the following:

Fear to go alone in case colleagues also do not go to school, fear from school teacher, younger child do not go in case older also do not go and *vice versa*, fear of being humiliated by colleagues on the way to school, lack of encouragement from parents in case they are not informed by school that their children have been directly admitted form *Anganwadi* register, lack of motivation from parents in case they go to wage work early in the morning leaving children uncared, to graze goat and other cattle which provide constant income to families, engagement of school-going children in wage work at the rate of Rs. 30 per day, engagement in farm activities, parents seasonal outmigration for wage work along with school-going children, rainy season, due to stay at relatives house for many more days, illness, physical deformity since birth, death or accident in family and their regular involvement in collection and marketing of firewood with mother. These reasons shows that both economic and non-economic factors are responsible for absenteeism. More or less similar reasons are also responsible for absenteeism at the State level.[1]

According to Headmistress of the school, students of class I and II are too young to come to school daily on foot from a distant place. Needless to mention that one of the *mohallas, lamba dhana* is located at a distance of about 1 km from the school. The approach road is lonely and there is one *nallah* on the way. Hence, she suggested that one EGS school should be established in that area to ensure high enrolment as well as satisfactory presence of small children in the classroom. Another teacher of the school made comments on each items of the school and its function. Some meaningful suggestions was also provided.

"Large number of students attend school during July and

August. Their presence is also high when quarterly, half-yearly and annual examinations are held. Their presence decreases during festival days. It also decreases during harvesting days of *rabi* and *kharif* crop. *Deepawali* is celebrated on different dates in the season. It all reduces students presence in the classroom. Even PTA meeting is failed to solve this problem. Mid-Day Meal has brought improvement in health status of children. But it also failed to increase attendance rate. If biscuit and other ready made food items are provided, it may bring some improvement. There are 5 teachers in the school. One of them have to go to Block office at his own during the afternoon for official purpose. Teachers are asked to do non-teaching work. Four of us hired a physically handicapped person at our own by paying Rs. 400 P.M. to teach class third students. Students are satisfied. Teachers are transferred on the basis of their political affiliation. It should be discontinued. Also, like girl students boys should also be provided dress and scholarship by the government. Looking to the size of students, peon facility should also be provided in the school" (*Awaz*, Vol. 2, p. 4, 2008).

Quality of Learning

So far as quality of learning is concerned, it is far from satisfaction. This is apparent from the fact that most of the students of class V who were interviewed, responded to very simple questions relating to general knowledge, English, Mathematics, History, etc., incorrectly. For instance, only 44 per cent students know the name of capital of Madhya Pradesh (Table 8.4). Their knowledge about basic science is highly poor. They do not have skill to translate a simple Hindi sentence into English. However, with those simple issues which are familiar to them, such as number of teachers in their school, they have by and large correct response. Roughly all the respondents correctly know the total number of teachers in their school. In other study of non-tribal villages by the author more or less similar observation was made (Chaudhary and Chaudhary, 2007).

Parents Perception about Quality of Primary Education

About 80 per cent villagers (Chaudhary, 2010) expressed views

Table 8.4 : Level of Knowledge

Sl. No.	*Question*	*Answer*		
		Right	*Wrong*	*No response*
1.	Capital of India	45	22	33
2.	Capital of Madhya Pradesh	44	31	25
3.	Name of Prime Minister of India	34	32	34
4.	Stanza of 12	33	14	53
5.	Name of Chief Minister of Madhya Pradesh	58	18	24
6.	State where Mahatma Gandhi was born	10	14	76
7.	Name of Iron man	1	16	83
8.	Independence Day	51	4	45
9.	Republic Day	55	3	42
10.	Hindi translation "I eat Mango"?	17	83	–
11.	Add of 5+7+7+5+3–10=?	65	21	14
12.	Why rubber ball flow on water?	4	96	–
13.	Why silver coin go inside water?	3	97	–
14.	Number of teachers in school?	99	1	–
15.	Name of Sarpanch	42	14	44
16.	District where this village fall	69	20	11
17.	Year when Chhattisgarh State was formed	–	2	98
18.	Number of districts in Madhya Pradesh	33	41	26
19.	State where Makhanlal Chaturvedi was born	4	6	90

about quality of today's education in comparison to education imparted about 20-25 years ago. Most of them have looked upon today's education in a negative manner. Some of the criticisms are as under.

Earlier quality of teaching was better, today teachers are not faithful, class second standard students of yesteryears and class X standard students of today are equal, earlier V pass students got job, today V pass students cannot write application. Today number of schools, number of teachers, infrastructural facility, incentives, etc., have increased but quality of teaching have deteriorated. Earlier teachers had more understanding and insight of subjects and syllabus was hard but today it has gone down. Education is costly affair today. In the case of indiscipline behaviour students were beaten by teachers in the past but today this practice has totally disappeared from Pathai school. Today teachers are more qualified but they do not have interest in teaching. They are simply doing their jobs in the mechanical manner.

Mid Day Meal (MDM)

There are a number of State run schemes to promote primary education in the villages. Mid Day Meal (MDM) is one among these. Today MDM is managed by *Durga Self Help Group* in Pathai. Earlier it was managed by Parents-Teachers Association (PTA). Under this scheme meal is provided to all the enrolled students who are present in the school. But Headmaster of this school said that many times even those who are not enrolled but if they come to school with their enrolled brother or sister, they are also served meal.

Under MDM scheme wheat is provided free of cost to all the primary schools by the government through PDS shop. In P*athai* there is one PDS shop which is responsible for providing wheat. About 4 quintals wheat is provided to this school in each month. It is the responsibility of school itself to collect and carry wheat from PDS. In this case all the three women cooks engaged for this purpose in this school, collect, carry and clean wheat and get it grinded by carrying it on their heads. Many times they have to get wheat grinded on credit, especially when grant is not released in time. And grant is seldom released and received in time.

Usually school remains open for 25 days in a month. Today there is a provision of Rs. 2 to each student for meal per day. This amount is besides the free supply of wheat. Hence, for one enrolled student Rs. 50 is provided in cash in each month along with free supply of wheat. Grant is directly transferred to the account of Headmaster of the school. But it is transferred at an interval of three months. As a result, many times food items are obtained on credit. From the account of Headmaster it is transferred to the respective Self Help Group responsible for MDM management. This amount is spent to get fuel wood, wages to cook, vegetable, oil, spices, salt, milk, sugar, pulse and so on. Headwise details of four months expenditure are as mentioned in Table 8.5

Kitchen Management/Food Quality and Cleanliness

School has a separate kitchen shed. Cooking work begins at around 11 a.m. immediately after counting number of students present in the classroom by cook themselves. Food is never prepared for all those who are enrolled. It is only prepared for those who are

Table 8.5 : Expenditure during Four Months in 2008 (in Rs.)

Sl. No.	Items	March	April	May	June	Total
1.	Floor Grinding	256	52	62	282	652
2.	Vegetable[2]	540	55	220	550	1365
3.	Fire wood[3]	600	100	50	550	1300
4.	Wages to Cooks[4]	1800	250	1550	1500	5100
5.	Ration (except wheat) all items[5]	3665	528	1999	2605	8797
	Total	6861	985	3881	5487	17214

Source: Data obtained from the school record.

present in the class room. During June 2008, a 3 days training programme, meant for cook, was attended by cooks working in this school. During training cooks were advised not to serve potato vegetable on the regular basis. But due to economic reason coupled with unavailability of green vegetable the above instruction is overruled. Green vegetable is very costly and easily not available in the village on each working days.

Kitchen has proper space and sunlight facility. There is no problem of kitchen related water. There are two hand pumps just in front of the school. Children clean utensils after taking food themselves resulting thereby water logging and subsequently creation of unhygienic environment around the place.

Food is served at around 1.30 p.m. in the school. There is sufficient cooking utensils but there is shortage of plates. Usually around 190 students take meal but only 80 plates on record and 60 when we counted, are available. Out of these, 4 plates are used to facilitate cooking work. As a result, either some students take meal jointly, i.e., two students in one plate or they have to wait. Usually food is served by cook. Students either eat under the open sky or inside the school building. In the case of shortage of pulse and vegetable, those who take food late they have to suffer. They are forced to eat *chapatti* without pulse or vegetable. Menu of meal is decided at least one week in advance and usually it is displayed on the notice board (Table 8.6).

There is an increase in the number of enrolment from 191 in 2001-02 to 241 in 2008-09 but on this basis alone no direct relationship may be established between Mid Day Meal intervention and increased enrolment rate. This is because there is gap between enrolment and attendance. For example, total 254 students were enrolled in this school in 2008 but in one week their attendance differ from 63 per cent to 78 per cent. There is not even 80 per cent presence in the classroom and that too when the school is located in the village itself, road connectivity is good and essential infrastructural facility like toilet, drinking water and play ground, etc., is available in the school. All the students present in the classroom take meal. This calls for an analysis of factors and conditions, which are student and family centric, which contributes to absenteeism in such a large scale.

Table 8.6 : Day-wise Menu of Meal for One Week, Students Presence in Classroom and Meal taken

Day/Date	*Enrolled*	*Present*	*Meal taken*	*Meal cooked*
08/12/2008	254	202 (78%)	201	Moong-Dal/Roti/Alu-Matar vegetable
09/12/2008			Holiday	
10/12/2008	—	166 (63%)	166	Moong Dal/Roti/Alu Rajma vegetable
11/12/2008	—	199 (78%)	199	Moongdal with Palak/Roti/Alu-Bringal vegetable
12/12/2008	—	197 (77%)	196	Tuardal/Roti/Gram-Potato vegetable
13/12/2008	—	188 (74%)	188	Kheer-Puri with Potato-Bringal vegetable

Source : As revealed from relevant papers provided by Headmaster of the school.

No specific effort is made by the school management to ensure food quality served to students under MDM. They only supervise at the time when the food is being cooked. However, it was assured that food is cooked as per the fixed menu. But some efforts are made by cook to make food tasty. For example, occasionally cook prepare either mixed vegetable or cook pulse mixed with suitable variety of vegetable. In order to make food more tasty, they opined that at least once in a week rice should also be served. Current amount of Rs. 2 earmarked for one student per day for meal should be increased up to Rs. 4. This increased amount will increase quality of pulse and vegetable served today. Needless to mention that there is no free supply of any edible item to the school even by the households whose children are enrolled in this school. Also, till date no effort was made by the Panchayat in this matter.

From cleanliness point of view the place where MDM is both cooked and served the situation is pitiable. Although floor of kitchen is cemented but it is seldom washed with detergent. It is simply cleaned. Open space around the kitchen is used by male student to pass water. It is almost like an open toilet. It generates bad smell around the place. Also, to meet shortage of plate students clean use plate in hurry without using detergent. This is unhygienic. In short, the entire area of the school, where food is cooked and served, is dirty and full of flies and other insects.

Students Perception about MDM

Students have mixed opinion about quality and type of food served under MDM scheme. Roshni, a student of class fifth is happy with the menu served under MDM. But she advised that rice should also be served. This suggestion was made by most of the students. She also accused poor quality of pulse served to them. *Chapati* served to them is also many times not properly cooked. Surkant Dhurve of the same class opined that quality of *kheer-puri* which is served once in a week, should be improved and it should be served twice in a week. So far as quality of *Puri* is concerned, students are satisfied. But quality of *kheer* is not upto the mark. Sufficient amount of milk is not used for this purpose. For instance, on December 13, 2008 total 188 students took meal. *Kheer* was prepared for all of them and only 2 litres of milk was used for its preparation. On this basis one can easily realize quality of *kheer* dish. Lakhan Lal Parte said that instead of serving wheat made *chapati*, bread made out of maize and *jowar* should be served. To him green vegetable should be served on maximum days, quality and quantity of pulse should be improved and vegetable should be properly cooked with proper amount of spices.

Attitudinal Change among Parents

Changing attitude of parents in favour of education to their wards is also one of the incentives. Most of the respondents, irrespective of their own educational profile which is definitely very low, were in favour of education to their children. However, their argument in favour of education of boys and girls slightly differed. Multiple reasons were provided in favour of education to boys. Maximum (78) said that to get employment of any variety education is essential. Number of parents are of the view that if they wish their children to join government jobs reserved for them, they must provide education to their children. They lamented that due to lack of education their family members are not in job. 41 reported that education will ensure their bright future in both economic and non-economic terms. Other responses which were made by relatively small number of respondents are: for making them good citizen, for dealing with financial matter, for proper understanding, for business purpose and so on children are receiving education. This means instrumental goal of education, especially job, is the main motive behind providing education to boys.

About girls education also more or less similar opinion was expressed. 61 said that since their girls are intelligent, therefore, they wish them to provide education. 40 respondents wish to send daughters in job and, therefore, they are imparting education to them. For many education will ensure better marriage, will teach and take care of their own children, will make children informed and knowledgeable, they will be capable enough to read and write and there will be overall improvement in their personality once they receive education.

Historical reasons are held responsible for positive attitudinal change among parents in favour of education to their wards. They are aware of the erosion of their support base over the time. They are now more dependent on outside world for their ever increasing economic and non-economic demands. They are peeping towards both government and non-government jobs for both economic and social reasons. And these jobs can only be availed provided formal education, especially college education of all types, expands among them. This is not available today. As a result of this many positions reserved for them in government services are lying vacant for decades. It is because of these reasons that they wish to provide education to their children. Recently induced institutional incentives coupled with their constant exposure to outside world, especially with the forces of modernization, motivate them to think in this way. It is because of realization of increasing importance of education in today's world they wish to provide education to their children. However, Matriculation level education was their ideal limit for both boys and girls. Education of above Matriculation level was not choice of any of the respondents for boys but for girls at least 5 respondents said that they wish to educate their daughter up to graduation level.

Table 8.7 : Expected Level of Education for Boys/Girls (Multiple Response)

Sl. No.		*Boys*	*Girls*	*Total*
1.	Couldn't respond	12	23	35
2.	As long as they study	87	42	129
3.	Upto 8th Standard	4	14	18
4.	Upto 10th Standard	11	45	56
5.	Upto 12th Standard	46	36	82
6.	Upto Graduation	–	2	2
7.	Upto Marriage age	–	5	5
8.	Upto level of doctor (means nurse here)	–	3	3
	Total	160	170	330

Since education is not an end in itself, therefore, for specific and practical purposes villagers are imparting education to their wards. Government job is the most preferred choice for both boys and girls. Some of the occupations where they wish to see their wards are doctor (nurse), teacher, any type of government job, police inspector, army man, *anganwadi* worker and so on. 14 respondents wish their daughter to become nurse. It is interesting to note that villagers at large are themselves engaged in wage or farm work but only 11 of them wish to send their sons in wage work. In short, objective behind imparting education to them is to get government job of different varieties. Since most of the time they are in contact with nurse, teacher, *anganwadi* worker and police, they know their dominance and influence in day to day life, therefore, they wish to send their children in these occupations.

Difficulties

About 60 per cent respondents had one or another type of difficulties while providing education to their children. All the students were receiving either primary or middle level education. Their problems were either family or school based. Family based problems were narrated by more respondents than the school level problems. Lack of proper home work and self study at home and incapability on the part of parents to teach their wards, lack of time for children due to wage work, unavailability of coaching facility in the village, lack of proper clothes, lack of proper reading space at home, transportation problem for those who attend school at Sahpur, are some of the problems faced by most of the villagers whose wards are attending schools.

Absence of visit to the school by parents, lack of interaction with teachers and their own wards on school matter and quality of education taught to their children, lack of time and interest in education on the part of respondents on academic issues keep villagers ignorant about functioning of school. Only few respondents perceived that teaching is not proper in terms of quality.

In short, in spite of the availability of one primary and one middle school in the village, since long, educational status of inhabitants of Pathai could not improve. This statement can be validated if we see high level of illiteracy among adults and senior citizens. But in the recent past number of institutional interventions have been made to ensure expansion of primary and middle education. It has resulted into high enrolment and retention at the primary level, low level of dropout and decreased number of out of school children. But the rate of absenteeism from class room is still alarming. It is alarming even when parents at large know importance of education in the current scenario. Number of economic and non-economic factors, primarily available at both primary and middle school level negatively influence quality of education received by students. The quality is far from satisfaction. Their level of knowledge is very low. They cannot avail education based benefits with this type of education, no matter how honestly protective discrimination measures are implemented (Chaudhary, 2011). This calls for the formation of comprehensive planning and action agenda.

III

Action Agenda

Under the given situation when the process of class formation among tribes in general and tribal households of the studied village in particular is very slow, their exposure to outside world, market forces and consumer culture is high, process of social capital formation is very low and slow but the presence of institutional arrangement is satisfactory, the level of the dependence on the state is high and local resources are incapable to meet their ever increasing aspiration, it is very difficult to prescribe action agenda for their educational development especially in isolation from other streams of development. However, some of the efforts, suggested below may be experimented as a pilot project for the educational development of tribes.

1. All the school-going children necessarily be enrolled in the school. This responsibility shall be entrusted upon Gram Panchayat as well as Anganwadi Kendra. Today as soon as children attain 5 years of age their names are forwarded to the local school for admission by the Kendra even without intimating about it to the concerned parents. Many parents do not know whether their wards are enrolled somewhere. This thinking contributes to apathy on their part. This practice must be discontinued once for all. Parents must be informed about enrolment of their children. They should also be provided necessary instructions which can contribute to reading and learning habit among children in a proper perspective.
2. During the current decade there is substantial improvement in infrastructural facility in many of the government schools in villages. However, schools located in tribal villages like Pathai are not properly equipped. For instance, number of plates, bathroom, etc., are inadequate in comparison to the number of students. It should be increased.
3. There is a serious criticism about the course content taught to students. Contents are highly alien for them. It has nothing to do with the local reality. There is no any course content relating to preservation and protection of the local forest. Also, there is no course content against the consumption of *mahua* liquor by most of the villagers and its economic and non-economic implications. As a result, interest of children in reading and learning is negatively conditioned. Hence, there is a need to introduce mixed course content. Local issues must receive proper place in the existing syllabus along with the ongoing course content.

4. Teachers are backbone of the primary education. This is because at this stage self reading and self learning habit remain alien to most of children. Hence, teachers must be sensitive, emotional, friendly and intelligent. Their number should be sufficient. Every now and then they should be imparted training and orientation. Also, as far as possible they should not be deployed for non-teaching activities by the local level administration. Currently in spite of tall promises by the state, these teachers are deputed for non-academic activities every now and then. This practice should be discontinued at the earliest.
5. Most of villagers wish to impart education to their children. They also know importance of education today. But they do not know how to approach this issue. Due to a number of reasons they do not properly motivate and encourage children in favour of education. Because of indifference on their part absenteeism as well as non-seriouness among children in favour of reading and learning increases. This tendency is contributed by children's involvement in family activities as well as apathy on the part of neighbourhood, friends and class mates. To deal with this problem on constant basis, awareness programme should be initiated, especially by the school teachers, among parents and other villagers. If the parents are well informed about importance of education in the life of their wards, they will definitely come forward.
6. In order to make class teaching interesting, not only teachers should cite local examples, know each and every student personally, intimate parents about capability of students but also an effort should be made to initiate coaching/tutorial classes in the evening. Some of the students especially poor performing students and physically challenged students should be encouraged to attend the evening classes. The locally available unemployed but educated youths, with proper training, may be deployed for this purpose.
7. Attempt shall be made by the school to ensure proper functioning of Welfare/Development activities going on in the village so that there is some improvement in social and economic condition of parents. If the parents are

socially and economically capacitated, definitely they will take special interest in reading and learning behaviour of their wards.

8. Discipline is the key of success. The school must remember this formula. For this purpose at any cost all the stakeholders, viz., students, teachers, members of parents-teachers association etc; must maintain discipline. Whatever responsibility have been assigned to all of them, they all should perform it sincerely and honestly.
9. Currently there is no in-door and out-door game facility for students in both the schools. Also, there is no *yoga* facility. To increase discipline, self-confidence, health status, etc., such facilities must be made available at the earliest.

NOTES

1. According to M.P. Human Development Report (2007:397) field/wage work, sibling care, cattle grazing, poverty, lack of educational facility, negative social belief, disease, non-conducive school environment and outmigration are responsible for absenteeism in the case of 25,18.5, 15.9, 11.2, 6, 5.9, 3, 2.8 and 12.6 per cent enrolled students.
2. Potato and Onion is purchased from the *kirana* shop from where ration is taken. All items are taken on credit. However, green vegetable is purchased from village itself or from weekly bazar at Sahpur on cash payment.
3. Firewood is also taken on credit. One tribal woman has been contracted to supply fuel wood. Each day one bundle of fuel wood of 30-35 kg is consumed. Its price is Rs. 25 only.
4. Cook is paid at Rs. 25 per working days. They are not paid on regular basis. They claim that they have to work in school from 11 a.m. to 4 p.m., therefore, their wage rate should be enhanced upto Rs. 50 per day. They should not be treated as part time worker.
5. Ration shop of Sahpur supply all related items on contract and credit. Ration is carried either on head by the SHG members or by tractor. Since it is not safe to store ration in the kitchen, therefore, it is stored in one of the rooms of the school building.

REFERENCES

Chaudhary, S.N. and P. Chaudhary (2007): *Primary Education through Sarva Shiksha Abhiyan: A Study of its Status and Functions with reference to*

Sehore District, Project Report, Sponsored by Rajya Shiksha Kendra, GoMP, Bhopal.

Chaudhary, S.N. (2011): "Exclusion within Inclusion: Functioning and Implications of Sarva Shiksha Abhiyan in Madhya Pradesh" in (eds.) *Excluded People in India: Problems and Prospects*, by R. Parchure, S.N. Tripathi and J.R. Ambewadikar, New Delhi: Manglam Publishers and Distributors.

Chaudhary, S.N. (2012): *In Search of Sustainable Development: Scenario in a Tribal Village of Madhya Pradesh*, New Delhi: Serials Publications.

9

Educational Scenario among the Tribal Children of Hazaribagh

Chaturbhuj Sahu

Introduction

Education remained a vitally important aspect of every society since time immemorial in the form of non-formal way. Subsequently it became the formal way in the schools. After becoming institutionalized way of education it has been changing its shape and scope according to the demand of the society and for the cause of scientific growth in the country. Gradually, it has expended in its shape and number with specializations covering the larger areas of the country including the tribal belts to bring them in the mainstream of the national life (Soni and Soni, 2001). Now education has become part of the economic foundation of modern society, a major avenue of social mobility, a control agency of social distribution and consequently an object of political debate and social policy as urgent and as important as poverty, sickness or unemployment. The development of nation is not measured through the buildings it has built, the roads it has laid down, the bridges it has constructed and the like but by the human resources the nation has developed and produced through well defined system of education, because it has become the most crucial factor not only to equip the new generation with skills so essential for earning livelihood but also to create among them an awareness to social and environment realities.

Thus, the importance of education in terms of literacy has been universally recognized irrespective of diverse societal patterns.

This is more essential for tribal because even after more than 64 years of independence only a handful of tribal people are educated. The tribals require not only general literacy but also other skills which equip them to face the exogenous forces of modernization.

The educational backwardness of the tribal people has its roots in the socio-economic and cultural setting in which they live. Consequently they remained isolated for a long time and were confined their traditional economic activities such as food gathering, hunting artisan work, shifting cultivation, settled agriculture and agricultural labour. The primitive as well as poor condition of the tribal people, their vulnerability to exploitation and the existing different kinds of barriers developed through prolonged isolation, had clear manifestation in the life they led.

In this way we find that education varies according to time, space, society, pattern of culture and the individual. In all societies whether tribal or non-tribal, the basis of all education has been to impart knowledge to pass on knowledge from one generation to another and to show ways and means for improving upon the existing knowledge.

Today we are having numerous means of spreading up knowledge, but during the prehistoric era humanity could have no considerable and esteemable means of acquiring imparting and spreading up of knowledge. Those days people were almost toys of nature having very little knowledge of the nature. They knew one thing, i.e., the sense of equality in the form of freedom of knowledge because knowledge was not bureaucratized by any particular section of people (Sahu, 2001).

At the global level, considerable work has been done on the sociology of education. Karl Menheim's study was the pioneering one followed by Brameld's *Cultural Foundation of Education* and the *Remarking of a Culture: Life and Education in Purerto Rico*, Jule's Henry's *An Outline for the Study of Education*, Margaret Mead's *Coming of Age in Samoa*, Spindler's (ed.) *Education and Culture*, etc. In India some important works have been done in this direction like those of K.P. Chattopadhyay, M.N Basu, T.N. Madan, Sachchidananda, L.P. Vidyarthi, D.S. Nag, Hilda Raj, Chaturbhuj Sahu. They have felt the need of remodelling the educational pattern for the tribal people (Samanta, 1997).

The education imparted to the tribal children is alien in nature and hardly attract the tribal children. The subject matter of the text book mainly related elf, angles, gods, pilgrimage, fairly tales, magic, *Ashwamegh Yagya* and so on. In this way we find that even now the rural's world has been protecting and preserving the very feudal values at the root (Jha & Sahu, 1998).

Now, it has become the concern of the educationists, planners and development agencies to impart education harmoniously to all sections of the people with special provision for scheduled castes and scheduled tribes. This is equally true for the tribal children of Hazaribagh district in Jharkhand.

Hazaribagh District

Hazaribagh is one of the famous districts of tribal Jharkhand. It is the home of socially and culturally important tribes. They are having some special salient features which make them unique. The cultural identification or way of living is still strong among them. Some of the tribes still cling to their abodes in forests and crude technology and simple way of life while at the same time there are others with higher levels of economy. Some others depending on simple industries having some sort of socio-economic symbiosis with their neighboring communities.

The district of Hazaribagh lies between 23°25′ and 24°48′ north latitudes and between 84°26′ and 86°38′ east longitude. Hazaribagh town, situated at an elevation of about 2000 feet, is the administrative headquarters and principal town of the district. Hazaribagh literally means the place with "thousand garden and thousand *bagh*" (Sahu, 1995).

The tribal communities living in the district show heterogeneity in their social and cultural life, although some salient features are shared commonly by all. They were very happy in their respective territories up to the interference of colonial rule. The British Government did not take any attention towards development of tribal communities because it mainly aimed at regulatory functions, such as maintenance of law and order and collection of revenues. They treated the tribals differently from the rest.

When India declared independence, the question of socio-economic and educational development in respect of scheduled tribes came into being under Article 46 of the Constitution to prevent their exploitation by other groups of the society. To tackle these problems, various committees the constituent assembly were set up by the constituent assembly. With the recommendations of the committee the government initiated widespread Tribal Development Programmes effectively since the Fifth Five Year Plan (1974-79) under the new name Tribal sub-plan (TSP) to improve their socio-economic condition, quality of life and asset accumulation.

The primary occupation of the tribals of the district under study is primitive, single cropped agriculture for Santhal, Munda, Bedia, Oraon and Kherwar. Karmali and Mahli are the artisan tirbes while Birhor's primary occupation is food gathering and hunting. All tribes of this district are economically and educationally very backward.

Pattern of Education

Non-formal system of education was the main pattern for the Tribal people but after 1950 the Government of India introduced formal education system among them.

Non-Formal Education: It is the initial form of education pattern. In this pattern the child acquires knowledge by living with others in the community. There is no limitation of the age for acquiring knowledge as the child starts to get knowledge right from birth and remain continued till death. Youth dormitory is the main centre for acquiring knowledge. In this centre unmarried children learn their traditions, folklore, social and religious codes, music and dancing and the different communal activities without getting strain in mind. Thus non-formal education means the systematized educational activities carried on outside the framework of the formal education system. Through this system the tribal people have become able to preserve their identity, cultural values, language and literature, etc. The children learn to lead for group life rather than individual life (Sahu, 2001).

Formal Education

Formal education has formal means and formal ends. It requires a form of schooling, teaching and instruction. It has a regular course of studies which has to be followed by learning and teaching methods. Thus, it is institutionalized, chronologically graded and structured system of learning. The schools, colleges, Universities and research organizations are the agencies of formal education. This system aims at imparting of knowledge and development of skills suitable to the changed set-up.

This system of education has made very little impact on tribal people because it is comparatively of a very recent origin. Prior to 1950, the Government of India had no direct programme for education of the tribals. It has been found that the earlier efforts in the field of tribal education were made by the foreign missionaries especially during the British period. The growth of formal education among the tribal population may be gauged from the facts yielded by the census data. The census figures of 1931 presented that only 0.7 per cent of the tribal people were literate. This percentage rose to 47.10 per cent in 2001. In 1961 it was 8.54 per cent. The present literacy rate of the tribal people is still much lower than the literacy rate of other communities. Literacy rate of female is lower than that of males and the tribal girls of rural areas are at the bottom of literacy rung. If we exclude the percentage of few tribes of north-eastern region like the Khasi, the Garo, etc., then the figure is not very encouraging.

Education in India in general and tribal areas in particular has spread in a haphazard way without taking care of future needs. Hence, it became failure due to apathy, indifference and lack of interest of the tribal people in formal education.

Government's Efforts

After independence the government opened thousands of schools in tribal areas and gave incentives so that the tribal students may be attracted towards going to schools. But why even after 64 years of independence only a handful of tribal people are educated and why even by now education in not being made common and easily available.

The Government of India has made many constitutional provisions for various development programme from time to time for development of the tribals but the programmes could not achieve the desired goals, particularly in education. The Article 45 of the Constitution of India has provided free and compulsory education for children up to the age of 14 years, another articles is made for promoting educational and economic interests of scheduled castes, scheduled tribes and other weaker sections to protect them from social injustice and all forms of exploitation. Moreover, National Policy on Education, 1986 provided many provisions for educational development of the tribals.

In spite of all these we find that the tribal literacy rate is increasing very slowly and the worst situation is seen for female education. It has been observed that Jharkhand is one of the educationally backward States of the country. All tribal communities except those who have adopted Christianity are found below literacy rate. Tribal development programmes within the sub-plans and outside have specific provision for educating the tribal children, with residential schools, proper stipend, relaxation in age of entry into higher educational institutions and free travel to appear in interview and written examinations. But these provisions have not motivated the tribals to educate themselves or their children in a meaningful manner. The dropout rate at the primary level of education among almost all tribal communities of the district is alarming.

Several studies related to the tribal education in Jharkhand have been made by many scholars like Vidyarthi (1955), Sachchidananda (1964, 1965, 1968); Ambasta (1970), Saran (1978); Toppo (1979); Roy (1989); Verma (1994); Sahu (1995, 2001, 2006); Jha and Sahu (1998) and others. They have identified many societal problems, viz., poverty, socio-cultural dogma, medium of instruction, environmental conditions, subject matter and content of study, educational polity, administration, etc., and suggested for educational development among them.

It is also a notable fact that the tribal education not only for Jharkhand but for entire country has remained problematic for the planner since their intensive efforts from the past five decades. The social scientists have aptly remarked that the cultural diversity of the Indian tribals makes any educational programme directed towards them a very difficult and somewhat risky enterprise. They have made suggestion that the educational schemes should be formulated in such a manner that the adult tribals as well as their children can be benefited from the implementation of the tribal educational programme in the most desired way. Thus, it is the appropriate time to throw some light on the issues of development of education because it enriches world of view, develops the logical reasoning and provide knowledge and skill to a level that would be a gainful creative life.

Factors Responsible for Education

There are so many factors responsible for spreading of education among the tribal communities. These are:

Socio-Religious Factor

Tribal communities of the district present a colourful panorama of religious faith and practices which is the manifestation of adjustments with their cultural and ecological condition. Due to this they feel that education makes their children defiant, insolent and alienates them from rest of their society. They also feel that the *Bongas* will do harmful action for those children who will be losing the tradition and norms of the society after receiving education.

Economic Factor

It has been said that the tribal people are the poorest social group having more than 50 per cent population below the poverty line. Each and every member of the family remain busy in the economic activities. In this acute situation it is not easy for most of them to send their children to schools. Children going to school means that the entire burden of their maintenance goes on the hands of the parents.

Lack of Interest in Formal Education

Formal education means one has to follow the prescribed courses of studies within the scheduled time. Subject matters of courses of studies are outside from the cultural, historical and religious spheres of tribal life. The content of books rarely appeals the tribal children. Srivastava (1968); Sharma (1976); Rath (1981); Sahu (1989, 1995) and others have rightly told that the tribal students should be taught about their neighbouring communities, their village life, belief and practices and then pass on to the national scene.

Lack of Suitable Teacher

The teacher has to perform crucial role for creating interest among the students towards reading and learning. This is more valuable for the teachers being appointed for teaching tribal students. The teachers who have no knowledge about the cultural life of the tribe, will not be able to prove themselves good teachers for them. They always try to remain away from posting place. In this critical situation there cannot be a good harmony between the teachers and students. Teachers always consider superior than the tribal community.

The teacher is one of the basic ingredients for improving the quality of education, so it is prime factor that teachers for the primary stage of teaching should be appointed from the same society. This fact has also been recommended by the Scheduled Areas and Scheduled Tribes Commission's Report.

Language Problem

Language has become a major problem for improving the literacy rate among the tribal people of Hazaribagh district. The district has become educational centre for the past one decade. Majority of the people speak Khortha mother tongue. In this circumstances teaching through Hindi is not considered suitable both for the tribal as well as rural children. The tribal and regional languages of the area under study are the fountainhead of the tribal civilization and the symbol of cultural unity. The validity and usefulness of their languages have been given due consideration for the appointment of primary teachers in Jharkhand.

Education through the respective tribal/regional languages provides opportunity to develop the personality of the child. This concept has already been accepted by the UNESCO in 1952.

Vidyarthi, the then Head of the Department of Anthropology, Ranchi University was contemplating to do some substantive work for the Birhor after seeing their starvation and pathetic condition. So in the second week of June 1976, in order to plan and carry out effective action programmes the author was deputed to teach the young and adult Birhor of Chalkari *Tanda*. The Birhor is a primitive and vanishing tribe of Hazaribagh district. Till now they have about 0.25 per cent literacy. The author started to go to *Tanda* and tried to establish rapport with them. After several visits he could understand that Nago Birhor could help him in achieving his goal. He used to explain the importance of education by giving examples including himself. A few of them convinced and agreed to send their children for study. Thereafter he constructed a Birhor type hut comparatively larger in size as school building right in their *Tanda* with the help of both young and adult Birhor. He then brought all the reading and teaching materials and started school with a strength of seven students.

After his several efforts they realized the benefit of education and started to send their children to the school even bearing loss to their economy.

In the month of March 1977, the Director of the Project received three full length letters written by three Birhor students namely Pandu Birhor (S/o Tuluwa Birhor, died on December 1981), Jagdish Birhor (S/o Tekwa Birhor) and Jatu Birhor (S/o Doman Birhor). It was a landmark in the history of development in the field of education that a community which had 0 per cent literacy only in about 9 months could write a letter. This brought a new zeal among the other children including girls and adults. Total strength of students arose 24. In this way the author concluded that the talented students should be picked up from their cultural settings and be provided proper coaching to cope up with the fields of their specialization in the educational institutes of repute. Free boarding and lodging should be provided to them till they stand on their own footing.

Conclusion

On the basis of the recommendations made by the social scientists for development of educational scenario among the tribal people of the country in general and State-wise in particular, the government have implemented several special programmes for the development of education among all tribal children of the study area. Lack of schools, subject matter of text books, partial involvement, insufficiency of residential schools, lack of motivation and dropout due to various socio-economic reasons are some of the important factors for educational gaps among the tribals.

There is no doubt that the literacy level of the scheduled tribe is increasing but literacy and education are two different things.

UNESCO defines literacy as "ability to identify, understand, interpret, create, communicate, compute and use printed and written materials associated with varying contexts" whereas education is defined as "any act or experience that has a formative effect on the mind, character or physical ability of an individual". Therefore, in order to assess the real educational scenario among the tribals we have to look towards the Gross Enrolment Rate (GER), i.e., percentage of the estimated child population in the 6-14 age group enrolled in classes I to VIII and Gross Dropout Rate (GDR), i.e., percentage of students who drop out from a given grade in a given year. Thus it needs some intervention in the strategies of the government programme so that the basic purpose of education may be achieved. It is also to be noted that no welfare programmes will succeed in a continuous manner without spreading of education among the tribals because education has been accepted as one of the key factors for development.

REFERENCES

Ambasht, N.K. (1970): *A Critical Study of Tribal Education (with special reference to Ranchi District),* New Delhi: S. Chand & Co.

Jha, A.K. and C. Sahu. (1998): "Golden Jubilee Year of Indian Independence and Tribal Education", *Vanyajati,* 46, 4:2-4.

Rath, S.N. (1981): "Tribal Development Programme". In *Tribal Development and Its Administration* (ed.) L.P. Vidyarthi, New Delhi: Concept Publishing Company.

Roy, Kanchan (ed.), (1989): *Education and Health Problem in Tribal Development: A Study of National Integration,* New Delhi: Concept Publishing Co.

Sachchidananda (1964): *Culture Change in Tribal Bihar.* Calcutta: Bookland Pvt. Ltd.

— —, (1965): *Profile of Tribal Culture in Bihar.* Calcutta: Firma K.L. Mukhopadhyay

— —, (1968): "Education and Changes in Social Values", *Man in India.*

Sahu, Chaturbhuj (1989): "Nutrition and Health Problem of the Birhor: A Vanishing Tribe of Birhor", In *Modern Trends in Anthropology* (ed.), A.N. Sharma, New Delhi: Northern Book Centre.

— —, (1995): *Birhor Tribe: Dimensions of Development,* New Delhi: Sarup & Sons.

— —, (ed.) (1998): *Tribal Culture and Identity,* New Delhi: Sarup & Sons.

— —, (ed.) (2001): *Indian Tribal Life,* New Delhi: Sarup & Sons.

Sahu, Chaturbhuj, (ed.) (2006): *Aspects of Tribal Studies,* New Delhi: Sarup & Sons.

Samnta, D.K. (1997): "Tribal Education: The Bhil Case," *Vanyajati,* 45,1:25-29.

Saran, A.B. (1978): *Tribal Studies,* Ranchi: Offset Printers.

Sharma, B.D. (1976): *Planning for Educational Development in Tribal Areas.* New Delhi: Ministry of Home Affairs.

Soni, A. and L.N. Soni (2001): "Educational System and the Tribal: A Rethinking" In *Indian Tribal Life* (ed.) Chaturbhuj Sahu, New Delhi: Sarup & Sons.

Srivastava, L.R.N. (1971): *Identification of Educational Problems of the Saoras of Orissa,* New Delhi: NCERT.

Toppo, Sita (1979): *Dynamics of Educational Development in Tribal India,* New Delhi: Classical Pub.

Verma K.K. (1994): "Education and Rural Development", *Man and Life,* 20, 1&2: 37-58.

Vidyarthi, L.P. (1955): "Education in Tribal Bihar", *Man in India,* 35, 1.

10

Tribal Education in Madhya Pradesh : Identification of Problems and Some Resolutions

Debashis Debnath

Introduction

In India as a country of melting pot of languages, castes, religions and ideas, while cementing indigenous values embracing modernity, is a progressive phenomenon. Within the context of the education of marginalized communities such as tribals, a fine balance between these two ends of the spectrum is necessary to yield results that have an impact on sustainability and underpin a holistic education effort. Education as a means of advancement of capacity, well-being and opportunity is uncontested, and more so among communities on the periphery. Nelson Mandela, the former President of South Africa and a great revolutionary had once said that "Education is the most powerful weapon to change the world". A nation's development depends upon its ability to create skilled human resource through the promotion of quality education among its citizens. Thus, one of the avenues to speedy development is education. This also promotes social mobility to think about their betterment and instrumental in shaping their quality of life. It has always been accepted as an important component in tribal development. Education means the broader process of enculturation and socialization. Hence, Anthropologists and sociologists have always given priority to education in the matter of tribal welfare and development but not merely as imparting of literacy or theoretical knowledge of certain things but also the broader process of induction into the learner's culture (Bhowmick, 1980:145). Robert Redfield, an eminent American Anthropologist in the discussion of social organization of civilization pointed out five important components for discussing civilization, viz., environment, social organizations, human career, personality type and world view. So we find he emphasized two important paradigms, i.e., Human career and personality, which highly depend on education. So, from his thoughts education should be accepted as the first change on available resources for tribal development—financial, material and personnel, since it holds the key to the protection and development of tribal communities during a very critical period of their history. Besides, the rising of literacy level has made the weaker sections of the societies, especially tribals, more discerning and intelligent than before and helped them to protect themselves against all sorts of exploitation. In some cases, it has aroused the aspiration level for quality of life and living standard, political awareness to come in the main stream and better social security.

The education system has been brought in tribal areas, which is the extension of the formal education system developed for general population. Education should be in conformity with the knowledge inherited by a child in house, community or his environment. But, we find that there is increasing uniformity even in the reading material at elementary level with central production of text books and guidance from higher levels in the form of model curricula, guide books, etc. Thus, the text books, therefore, may contain material which may be largely unfamiliar to the children in tribal areas. Hence, learning in this situation becomes a burden with no relevance to the environment in which tribal children are living. B.D. Sharma (1976), Chaturbhuj Sahu (1995), A.K. Jha and Chaturbhuj Sahu (1998) and others have rightly pointed out the urban middle class oriented educational system has got superimposed on the entire nation both in terms of its structure and content and in many States tribal children are taught through the same books which form the curriculum of non-tribal children of the urban and rural areas of the rest of the State. Thus, the content of such books which rarely appeal to the tribal children as they come from different cultural backgrounds. Hence, they told that the tribal students should be taught about the neighbouring communities their village, social organization, belief and practices and then they be taught about the national scene. Again the problems of language or medium of instructions make the situation worse. Teaching in the early classes should be provided in mother tongue. But no satisfactory arrangements have been made in most cases. Even in the primary schools language has not been introduced in the syllabi. Though the Article 29(i) under Central and Educational Rights and article 350A of the Special Directive have enjoined on state and every local authority within the state to provide facilities for instruction in the mother tongue at primary stage of education to children belonging to linguistic minority group (Sahu, 1991). Thus, the children in tribal areas learn without understanding and miss the opportunities of developing the faculty of conceptualization which is essential for learning particularly in Mathematics and Science. It shows differential growth of education amongst different tribes and areas. It has resulted into large dropouts. Excepting same unparalleled situations most of the backward communities, specially scheduled tribes are not able to cope up with such less favourable situation.

Recognizing that the ST's count among the most deprived and marginalized sections of Indian society, a host of welfare and developmental measures have been initiated for their social and economic development. In this regard, particular reference has to be made to the tribal sub-plan approach which came into existence as the main strategy from the Fifth Five Year Plan. Along with core economic sectors, elementary education has been accorded priority in the tribal sub-Plan approach. Elementary education is considered important, not only because of constitutional obligation, but as a crucial input for total development of tribal communities, particularly to build confidence among the tribes to deal with outsiders on equal terms. Since primacy was accorded to elementary education, a broad policy frame for education was adopted in the tribal sub-Plans according equal importance to quantitative and qualitative aspects of education (Sujatha, 2006).

By and large, the improvements in the socio-economic conditions of scheduled tribes measured in increased literacy rates, reduction in poverty, etc., have not been proportionate to the investments made. As compared to other sections of society, the tribal population has the lowest 'Human Development Index' (HDI) amongst the rest of the Indian population in terms of all parameters such as education, health, employment, income, etc. In addition, they suffer from geographical and cultural exclusion, which are not captured in the HDI. Similarly, lack of empowerment to make choices for themselves is also not accounted for. A large segment of the tribal population lives below the poverty line and suffers from a high infant mortality rate, severe malnutrition, various communicable diseases, lower literacy rates and an extremely slow pace of development. Under-development coupled with lack of access to proper administrative and judicial machinery in tribal areas further increases their deprivation.

This chapter attempts to discuss the situation of the Tribal Education in Madhya Pradesh with specific cases in Primitive Tribal Groups and finally identities the problems in the system of imparting education in tribal areas of Madhya Pradesh in specific and general cases.

Tribes in Madhya Pradesh

Madhya Pradesh is better known as 'Tiger' or 'Tribal State'. At present, as per 2001 census the population of Tribals in Madhya Pradesh is 122.33 lakh constituting 20.27 per cent of the total population (603.85 lakh) in comparison to the Census of 1991, when the total tribal population of the State was 96.82 lakh which comprised of 16.03 per cent of the total population. Almost the entire Satpura region in the past constituted the tribal Kingdom of Gondwana whose queen was Rani Durgawati. She ruled virtually the whole of what constituted the Mahakoshal region of the State. There are 46 tribal groups, which have been notified as 'Scheduled Tribes'. Among these the Gonds are the largest group, which contribute nearly half of the total tribal population in the State and are distributed throughout the State. Of them, there are three, who have been identified as "Primitive Tribal Groups" (PTGs) in the State. The differences in the tribal community, spread over in various parts of the State, is clearly seen not only on the basis of their heredity, lifestyle and cultural traditions, but also from their social, economic structure, religious beliefs and their language and speech. Due to the different linguistic, cultural and geographical environment, and its peculiar complications, the diverse tribal world of Madhya Pradesh has been largely cut off from the mainstream of development and the world is ignorant about their indigenous knowledge.

Table 10.1: Levels of Education among Some Major Tribal Groups

Name of STs	Literate without educational level	Below Primary	Educational levels attended				
			Primary	Middle	Matric/Scondary/ Higher Secondary/ Intermediate	Technical and Non-technical Diploma	Graduate and above
All STs	1.8	46 5	24.0	9.7	6.6	0.0	1.4
Bhil	15.5	47.0	2.2	0.2	6.0	0.0	1.6
Gond	0.4	5.0	27.0	10.0	7.0	0.1	2.0
Kol	7.0	47.0	2.9	0.4	6.0	0.0	0.0
Korku	10.0	56.0	2.9	8.0	3.0	0.0	0.0
Sahariya	1.4	0.2	6.1	4.0	1.0	0.0	0.5
Baiga	11.0	50.0	2 0	3.0	3.4	0.0	0.0

Source: Tribal Area Development Project, Ministry of Tribal Welfare, Government of Madhya Pradesh.

Literacy is an important index of educational development. Less than 10 per cent of total tribal population in Madhya Pradesh is educated above primary level. Even among the scheduled tribes, the education level is very low among the Sahariya and Baiga tribe of Madhya Pradesh. 62.2 per cent of Sahariya's are educated below primary and 26 per cent of Baiga are educated up to primary. Similarly just 1.8 per cent of Sahariya tribe is able to continue their education up to Matric or Higher Secondary. And the percentage of tribal undergone through any technical and non-technical diploma comes around 0.1 only.

In Table 10.1 the census figures illustrate the trends in literacy among STs and others:

Ashram schools are residential schools for tribal children from a cluster of habitations. Based on the Gandhian philosophy of self-reliance, it was first experimented by Thakkar Bapa, a Gandhian in Panchamahal district of Gujarat in the pre-independence days. *Ashram* schools were found effective as (i) it was not feasible to open full fledged schools in every small and scattered habitation; (ii) it created congenial atmosphere for teaching and learning as it is assumed that the tribal households do not have such an environment; and (iii) it helped to develop the total personality of the child and impart vocational skills to improve employment opportunities. *Ashramsalas* are one of the key components in the education system of tribal areas. This is an ongoing scheme under which residential schools are operational up to Class V and VIII, managed by non-government organizations and funded by the government. These *Ashrams* are being opened in predominantly populated S.C./S.T. areas and preference is given to the girls *Ashrams*. These are residential schools for primary and secondary education The system of *ashramshalas* was introduced in the early 1950s as low cost, cluster based elementary education for the ST students with the support of reputed and well meaning Gandhian NGOs.

The National Programme of *Sarva Shiksha Abhiyan* (SSA), which aims to achieve Universal Elementary Education (UEE), has a special focus on education of the tribal children. One of the super goals of SSA was to "bridge all gender and social category gaps at primary stage by 2007 and at elementary stage by 2010". The broad strategies under SSA reiterate that there will be a focus on participation of children from SC/ST and minorities, urban deprived children, children with special needs, working children and children in the hardest to reach groups. The *Sarva Shiksha Abhiyan* (SSA) recognizes the varied issues and challenges in tribal education in view of the heterogeneous structure of tribal population in the country. The issues and challenges in tribal education can be categorized as external, internal, socio-economic and psychological. The external constraints are related to issues at levels of policy, planning and implementation while internal constraints are with respect to school system, content, curriculum, pedagogy, medium of instruction, etc. The third set of problems relates to social, economic and cultural background of tribals and psychological aspects of first generation learners. Given that the overall results of *Sarva Shikshan Abhiyan* (SSA) have been good, the question now arises about the role *Ashramshalas* can play in tribal education. Currently, there are about 8,200 primary schools in about 5,000 tribal villages under SSA. These schools are endowed with good infrastructure and extra-curricular activities, better teachers, facilities and quality. In contrast, since *Ashramshalas* were created at a time when there were no primary schools in tribal areas, they lack these features.

The sole focus of SSA programme is on the enrolment of students in the school specially students belonging to scheduled tribes and scheduled castes without ensuring quality education. As a result there is a vigorous hike in the GER [Gross Enrolment Ratio] of children at primary level, i.e., from 129.76 per cent in the year 2005-06 to 143.58 per cent in 2006-07 as per DISE report. This resulted in the downfall of educational outcomes. The Madhya Pradesh educational outcomes shifted from 12th position in 2005-06 to 25th rank in 2006-07 among 35 States in the country. 22.12 per cent schools are single teacher schools providing education to 13.67 per cent students.

Despite all efforts, dropout rates in tribal areas continue to be higher than the State average—it is currently around 3 per cent. Women-headed households, Primitive Tribes Groups and migrant families find it hard to keep their children within the education system. Perhaps *Ashramshalas,* being a residential model, can fill the lacuna for such households by especially focusing on enrolling children of these three groups. The second issue pertains to the present integrated education-cum-hostel model that *Ashramshalas* offer. There are now better choices available at the village level for primary schooling. Thus, is it necessary for *Ashramshalas* to offer both, education and hostel facilities? Could education and hostels be delinked so that parents have the option of sending their children to better schools, if they exist in the village? The *Ashramshalas* could focus on providing only hostel facilities.

As far as the present day relevance of the *ashramshalas* is concerned, undoubtedly, the SSA schools are much better and systematic, their teachers are well trained and the progress of students better monitored. Every village in the tribal area has at least one well functioning primary school and there is apparently no need for the children to attend the *ashramshalas*.

The *Janshala* Programme is a collaborative effort of the Government of India (GoI) and five UN agencies—UNDP, UNICEF, UNESCO, ILO and UNFPA—to provide programme support to the ongoing efforts towards achieving Universal Elementary Education (UEE). *Janshala*, a community based primary education programme, aims to make primary education more accessible and effective, especially for girls and children in deprived communities, marginalized groups, Scheduled Castes/ Scheduled Tribes/minorities, working children and children with specific needs. A unique feature of *Janshala* is that it is a Block-based programme with emphasis on community participation and decentralization. The Blocks have been selected on the basis of different indicators such as low female literacy, incidence of child labour, and concentration of Scheduled Tribes (ST) and Scheduled Castes (SC) populations. The Programme is being implemented in nine States of India—Andhra Pradesh, Jharkhand, Chhattisgarh, Karnataka, Madhya Pradesh, Maharashtra, Orissa, Rajasthan and Uttar Pradesh—with a total of 139 Blocks including ten cities under the Programme. The Programme covers nearly three million children, and 58,000 teachers in 18,000 schools. Out of 139 Blocks more than 75 Blocks have substantial tribal population. The proportion of tribal children is 33 per cent of the total target group children in the project area.

In Madhya Pradesh teachers' handbooks called Bridge Language Inventory (BLIs) have been prepared in 3 tribal languages, viz., Gondi (Shahdol and Betul District), Kuduk, (Raigarh) and Bhili (Dhar). Identified teachers were given training in using BLISs in their classrooms. The teaching-learning package is called *Dham Dhama Dham* was translated into Gondi and supplementary reading material, Kopal, was developed for tribal children. The class I textbook *Bharati* has been translated into tribal languages. Supplementary TLM for tribal children has been developed in Jhabua district using local cultural form, i.e., folk tales, songs, proverbs, riddles, to make the learning process interesting. In all, 450 teachers of 311 schools have been trained to use the supplementary materials. Researches have underlined the need to develop culturally sensitive programmes of school education that can ensure the dignity of tribal groups by providing them with economically viable options for life. Some attempts have been made for linking curriculum with the local needs of the communities. Such curriculum would make tribal children more sensitive to local contexts and sustain them in their respective environments instead of forcing them to move out in search of another life.

Study of Tribal Education

The author conducted a field study to investigate the present situation of literacy and educational status in Primitive Tribal Groups in three districts of Madhya Pradesh. The following Tables 10.2 to 10.7 show the brief village profile for this study at a glance. There are three tables of village profile representing the three PTGs—the Baiga, the Sahariya and the Bhariya. One feature that is common in all the three tables is geographical location of the villages. All the sampled villages are amidst forest. The villagers depend on forest for their survival.

In all the villages of three PTGs the forests are in close proximity and they are in the remote places. All the PTGs' villages are distributed in different topography. In case of Baigas the forest densities are comparatively more than Sahariyas and Bharias. The forests are in the degraded condition in Patalkot, where there are the habitations of the Bharias. In all the villages there are Gram Sabhas or Gram Panchayats through which the decentralized governance of the development administration are working. The infrastructures of school building are available in all the villages.

In Bagas, nearly half of the populations are illiterates—male (49.30%), female (51.70%) and in total (54.41%). Of the literates (45.59%), 36 per cent have crossed the primary levels. Of them, males are 53.57 per cent and females are 46.43 per cent. After that

Table 10.2: Baiga Tribes of Dindori District

Sl. No.	*Statements*	*Name of Villages*					
	Features of villages	Tarwa Tola	Kapoti	Kharideeh	Kandawani	Sarai	Bangla Dadar
1.	Name of Tehsil	Dindori	Dindori	Dindori	Samnapur	Samnapur	Dindori
2.	Distance from District	95 km	102 km	67 km	74 km	45 km	70 km
3.	Distance from Block	25 km	32 km	27 km	25 km	17 km	30 km
4.	Total no. of Households	50	42	92	24	85	51
5.	Forest Range	Karanjiya East	Karanjiya East	Karanjiya East	Kanahira	Kanahira	Karanjiya East
6.	Forest Division	Dindori	Dindori	Dindori	Dindori	Dindori	Dindori
7.	Distance of village from forest	00 kms	00 km	00 km	00 km	00 km	00 km
8.	Place of Gram Sabha/Panchayat	Kharideeh	Chakmi	Kharideeh	Dhurkuta	Samnapur	Chaura Dadar
9.	Electricity	Solar Light	No	Yes	No	No	No
10.	Post office	No	No	No	No	No	No
11.	Bank	No	No	No	No	No	No
12.	School	Yes	Yes	Yes	Yes	Yes	Yes

Table 10.3: Sahariya Tribes of Sheopur District

Sl. No.	*Statements*	*Name of Villages*					
	Features of villages	Upri Khoree	Nichli Khoree	Parond	Chak Bilari	Sonipura	Sironi
1.	Name of Tehsil	Karahal	Karahal	Karahal	Karahal	Karahal	Vijaypur
2.	Distance from District	50 km	58 km	35 km	50 km	45 km	130 km
3.	Distance from Tehsil	10 km	18 km	03 km	07 km	05 km	70 km
4.	Total number of Households	70	33	36	35	110	60
5.	Forest Range	Karahal	Karahal	Karahal	Karahal	Karahal	Khari
6.	Forest Division	Sheopur	Sheopur	Sheopur	Sheopur	Sheopur	Sheopur
7.	Distance of village from forest	00 km	00 km	00 km	00 km	00 km	00 km
8.	Place of Gram Sabha/Panchayat	Meharbani	Meharbani	Karahal	Karahal	Karahal	Moreka
9.	Electricity	Only electric poles no supply	Yes	Yes	Yes	Yes	Solar Light
10.	Post office	Karahal	Karahal	Karahal	Karahal	Karahal	Karahal
11.	Bank	Karahal	Karahal	Karahal	Karahal	Karahal	Karahal
12.	School	Yes	Yes	Yes	Yes	Yes	Yes

Table 10.4: Bhariya Tribes of Chindwara District

Sl. No.	*Statements*	*Name of Villages*					
	Features of villages	Chimptipur	Gal Dubba	Gurhi Chetri	Ghat Linga	Kariyam	Rather
1.	Name of Tehsil	Tamia	Tamia	Tamia	Tamia	Tamia	Tamia
2.	Distance from District	82 km	78 km	82 km	81 km	77 km	82 km
3.	Distance from Tehsil	28 km	22 km	28 km	25 km	25 km	27 km
4.	Total no. of Households	12	40	30	75	50	30
5.	Forest Range	Chindi	Tamia	Tamia	Tamia	Chindi	Chindi
6.	Forest Division	Chhindwara	Chhindwara	Chhindwara	Chhindwara	Chhindwara	Chhindwara
7.	Distance of village from forest	00 km	00 km	00 km	00 km	00 km	00 km
8.	Place of Gram Panchayat	Rather	Gal Dubba	Ghat Linga	Ghat Linga	Rather	Rather
9.	Electricity	Yes	Yes	Yes	Yes	Yes	Yes
10.	Post office	No	No	No	No	No	No
11.	Bank	No	No	No	No	No	No
12.	School	No	Yes	Yes	Yes	Yes	Yes

Table 10.5 : Educational Status of Baiga in Six Sampled Villages

	Male	Female	Total Population
Illiterate	459 (49.30%)	472 (51.70%)	931 (54.41%))
Primary Education	330 (53.57%)	286 (46.43%)	616 (36.00%)
Secondary Education	97 (81.51%)	22 (18.49%)	119 (6.96%)
High School	24 (77.42%)	07 (22.58%)	31 (1.81%)
Higher Secondary	09 (90.00%)	01 (10%)	10 (0.58%)
Graduate	03 (100%)	–	03 (0.18%)
Post Graduates	01 (100%)	–	01 (0.058%)
Grand Total	923 (53.95%)	788 (46.05%)	1711 (100%)

the educational status of females are declining. So larger section, i.e., the 81.51 per cent males of the total literate having the educational status above secondary level, out of 6.96 per cent of total population, who have passed out Secondary levels. Even after that level the males have got opportunities and crossed the Higher Secondary (90%), Graduates and Post-Graduates (both 100%) in larger extent, though in totality the achievement is meagre—in High School level (12th Standard), 1.81 per cent, Higher Secondary 0.58 per cent, Graduate 0.18 per cent and Post Graduates 0.058 per cent of the all total population. Villagers are not any degree holder.

Table 10.6 : Educational Status of Sahariya in Six Sampled Villages

Educational Status	Male	Female	Total Population
Illiterate	619 (49.72%)	626 (50.28%)	1245 (82.67%)
Primary Education	166 (69.75%)	72 (30.25%)	238 (15.80%)
Secondary Education	13 (81.25%)	03 (18.755)	16 (1.06%)
High School	03 (75.00%)	01 (25.00%)	04 (0.27%)
Higher Secondary	02 (100.00%)	–	02 (0.13%)
Graduate	01 (100.00%)	–	01 (0.07%)
Grand Total	804 (53.39%)	702 (46.61%)	1506 (100%)

In Sahariyas, nearly half of the male populations are illiterates, i.e., 49.72 per cent and females are 50.28 per cent and in total it is huge, i.e., 82.67 per cent. Of the rest, those who are literates (17.33% of total population), 15.80 per cent of them have crossed the primary levels. Of them, males are 69.75 per cent and females are 30.25 per cent. So, in the education the male sections are going ahead due to male dominance and more opportunities tendered to them. After that the educational status of females are declining. So larger section, i.e., the 81.25 per cent males of the total literate males (1.06% of total population) have passed out Secondary levels. Even after that level the males have got opportunities and crossed the Higher Secondary (100%), Graduates (100%) in larger extent, though in totality the achievement is meagre—in High School level (12th Standard) 0.27 per cent, Higher Secondary 0.13 per cent, Graduate 0.07 per cent of all the total population. There is not even a single person who are post-graduate/other degree holder.

Table 10.7 : Educational Status of Bhariya in Six Sampled Villages

Educational Status	*Male*	*Female*	*Total Population*
Illiterate	406 (45.72%)	482 (54.28%)	888 (60.45%)
Primary Education	169 (51.21%)	161 (48.79%)	330 (22.47%)
Secondary Education	93 (72.09%)	36 (27.91%)	129 (8.78%)
High School	64 (72.73%)	24 (27.27%)	88 (5.99%)
Higher Secondary	11 (40.74%)	16 (59.26%)	27 (1.84%)
Graduate	04 (66.67%)	02 (33.33%)	06 (0.41%)
Post Graduates	01 (100%)	–	01 (0.07%)
Others	–	–	–
Grand Total	748 (50.92%)	721 (49.08%)	1469 (100%)

In Bhariyas, below the half of the males are illiterates, i.e., 45.72 per cent, but in contrary to others females are going aheads, i.e., 54.28 per cent and in total it is 60.45 per cent of total populations. Of the literates (39.55% of total population), 22.47 per cent of them have crossed the primary levels. Of them, males are 51.21 per cent and females are 48.79 per cent. After that the educational status of females are declining. So larger section, i.e., the 72.09 per cent males of the total literate males (8.78% of total population) have passed out Secondary levels. Even after that level from the Higher Secondary the females have got opportunities and crossed the Higher Secondary, i.e., 59.26 per cent. In comparison to others PTGs, the females' achievements in Graduate level are better, i.e., 33.33 per cent. Of total Graduates, i.e., 0.41 per cent of the Bharias 66.6 per cent are males. At the Post Graduate level the males are 100.00 per cent.

The educational status of the three PTG tribes is very low. The older generation hardly had an opportunity for schooling. The men and women in age group of forty's rarely saw a school in their village. In their times the school was too far off and very difficult to reach, so they could hardly had any formal and informal education. The government introduced Adult Education programme in the PTG villages. In this programme the target was to educate all the adults who were deprived of education. The villagers popularly called Adult education as "Buddha Parahi" meaning education to old people. Through Adult education they could learn to write only their names. Very recently the primary schools are seen in several sampled villages. Few villages had full classes running in the newly constructed school building. In some villages the primary schools were also under construction. The concept of Primary school in the villages were related to mid day meal, free distribution of books, uniform and sweaters, free education to all children, incentive to mothers who sent their girl child to school and teacher appointed from the community. These factors resulted in cent per cent attendance in primary schools. So nowadays The Baiga, Sahariya and the Bhariya children are going to school. The literacy rate found in the Baiga is 22.1 per cent, Sahariya is 23.2 per cent and Bhariya is 22.7 per cent.

Major Problems

Marked improvements in access and to some extent in quality of primary education in tribal areas have occurred. However, the number of out-of-school children continues to be several millions, mainly due to a lack of interest and parental motivation, inability to understand the medium of instruction (i.e., State language), teacher absenteeism and attitude, opportunity cost of time spent in school (particularly for girls), large seasonal migration, etc. Low literacy rates in tribal communities continue to indicate a need for overarching support that tackles issues from health to attitudes of non-tribal populations. The above study shows that the main issues in imparting education in tribal areas are quite complex. There have been a number of measures adopted by the Government of India as a national policy for the development of backward people specially the Scheduled Tribes. For example, as the dropouts are very much high at primary and middle school levels; it was proposed to establish a large number of Ashram School (Residential school). The educational trends among Scheduled Tribes of Madhya Pradesh shows very gloomy picture of education system of the State due to various factors as follows:

The Dropout Rate

Further no efforts are being made to prevent the high dropouts and to retain them to continue their education. But the State's commitment to providing quality education to children can be gauged from high dropout rate at primary and upper primary level. The dropout rate at the primary school level is 15.6 per cent while that at the middle level is 14.7 per cent. These dropout rates further increased to 17 per cent in case of girls. 73.57 per cent schools are not having girls' toilet facility which leads to high percentage of girl's dropout from school.

Physical Access

Physical access to schooling, especially at the upper primary stage, is still an issue access to schools in remote tribal areas.

Though there is a government policy to establish a school in every village. But this has not been possible to implement. Hence, though in our study the schools are found in all villages under study, but in many a village the tribal boys and girls walk a long way to reach the villages in remote tribal areas..

Sarva Siksha Abhiyan

The Sarva Siksha Abhiyan (SSA) is framed to secure the right of the children to education and promote the universalization of education. But in real sense the universalization of education is still a distance dream to achieve. Still deprived and marginalized tribal students are excluded at various levels.

Infrastructural Facilities

The tribal belts not only lie far behind in terms of facilities, infrastructure and the grave problem lies in the curriculum and content taught to the students of Scheduled Tribes and Scheduled Castes.

The tribal societies cannot accept the modern education wholeheartedly because of their apprehension that education could alienate them from their fellow members of the community and their supreme deity could be annoyed if they send their children to the schools run by the outsiders.

It is also important to improve the infrastructure and facilities of education in school with special focus on *dalit* and tribal belts of Madhya Pradesh like Jhabua, Barwani, Mandla, Dindori, Mandla, Dhar, etc. Stress should be given on appointment of teacher from the local community and they should be oriented to use local dialect as medium of instruction to enable the tribal children to participate more enthusiastically. It is imperative that the government should ensure the realization of its plan to open a middle school at a distance of every 3 Km. The Government of India has also sanctioned the upgradation of 595 primary school up to middle in 37 district of Madhya Pradesh. However, it is worth noticing that such upgradation should be designed in a cautious manner with proper planning.

School/Timing/Calendar

The school timings and calendar are quite ill-suited to their life environment, and the language of instruction in most cases being not familiar to the tribal children.

The children of tribal families are the active partners of their livelihoods. Therefore, an average tribal family may not be able to afford the children attending schools during certain busy or peak seasons like sowing and harvesting. Some of the new economic activities like making of handicrafts are also family occupations, where the children may contribute significantly. Collection of non-timber forest products is well distributed but there are some peak periods in collection. For instance, the natural flowers are collected only early in the morning.

Course Curriculum

The most important aspect of tribal education is the planning of its content and its presentation. The curriculum should be suitably restructured so as to have clear picture of the surroundings, be physical and social, and several of occupations along with social structure. The students should get an idea of various institutions, which are relevant to the rural economy. The choices of subjects at the middle and high school levels should be provided keeping in view of local needs. Specialization, however, should not be as narrow as may deter the student from pursuing higher studies in general institutions.

Structural Imbalance

The tribal cultures have strong value systems in the traditional sense, so the new formal arrangements have little significance in this system. In the context of education the two different cultures are coming in contact. In the formal education, the content of education leads to form the consumptive society, which makes alien to the culture of the community. Further, the tribal communities manage its own affairs by traditional association, norms or values. His code of conduct is determined by the tradition rather than the law. The modern education has handed to supersede the system making traditional organization rather weak. Disorganization sets in these areas as an inevitable consequence. Thus, the problem in these areas is so complex that a general educational programme may not be of much help to the community. Therefore, a programme of citizen of education with comprehensive frame covering the needs of all sections of the tribal population is necessary which should basically aim at protecting the community from a sudden cultural shock and enable it to graduate through the transitional phase without any erosion of their economic base. The tribal communities have a rich cultural heritage but their experience is limited to a small area much of which is losing relevance in the modern context (Planning Commission, 1981:60).

Institutional Structures

The number of primary schools has increased substantially even in the remote areas though the level of enrolments has not moved up in proportion. The structure of institutional network at the middle and higher secondary school levels, however, is not very satisfactory. The establishment of *High School* is generally determined by demand. As a result, the distribution of Higher Secondary schools is uneven. Most of the tribal villages are scattered. This entails long travels to attend the school. School building also plays an important role in the growth of education among the tribal population. Due to insufficient fund and the mismanagement of fund the school building is seldom suitable to run an educational institution in tribal belt. The most significant feature of the tribal areas is the sparseness of population and/or small size of habitations. This factor has not been taken fully into the educational programme excepting the establishments of some Ashram and Lower Primary Schools. The establishment of residential schools caters to the needs of the sparsely populated areas and the more backward tribal communities. However, since these institutions provided liberal facilities to the children with free board and lodging as also better education, pressure grew for establishing them even in the comparatively advanced areas and admissions are opened to children from more advanced communities. Thus, better off sections of the populations handed to take advantage and problem of the backward areas of the backward communities got ignored notwithstanding the growing number of their institutions.

Supporting Services

It is generally accepted that establishment of institutions in tribal areas by itself is not sufficient to attract the children and retain them in the educational system. There are a number of contributing factors for this situation, the most important being their economic condition though the State Government has provided a number of facilities and supporting services as a part of the tribal education programme in the tribal areas. In case of PTG in some States a system of compensating the family for the opportunity cost by payment of a fixed amount in cash or kind has also been introduced. But, there is a lot of unawareness and inequality in distribution of the scholarships.

In the literacy mission, the low literacy Blocks and low literacy regions within each Block, should be identified. Similarly, the communities at low literacy level should also be identified at each State for special assistance. The literacy level among women is particularly very low.

As the residential institutions, like Ashram Schools and hostels are found in the more sparsely populated areas they should be treated as an integral part of institutional infrastructure for universal coverage.There are a large number of disparities in allotting post-Matric scholarships.

Quality of Personnel

Lack of suitable teachers is one of the major causes for the slow growth of education in tribal areas. One of the important problems in the spread of education is the non-availability of teachers with many qualifications. Teachers are generally recruited from non-tribal areas that join the posts but soon after they begin to try for transfer outside. Many of them do not know the local dialects and also are unaware of the social conditions. With growing unemployment persons with higher qualifications are becoming available even for primary schools but they become disgruntled. The Scheduled Tribes Commission's report says that a teacher in the tribal belt must have thorough knowledge of tribal life and culture. Absenteeism is high and in many areas schools may be run only on paper. Unless these problems are satisfactorily solved, establishment of new institutions by themselves may mean only additional expenditure without much benefit. Most schools in tribal belt are running by single teacher who is engaged to deal with all the teaching and administrative jobs. Overburdening causes irregularity in his duties. Due to his absence there is no alternative way except to close the school.

Women Education

The reason behind such low literacy level is the role and responsibility of a tribal woman in her family. A boy can be expected to go out and compete for higher places in life for which he may have to go to school and pursue studies for long years. Even here now the tribal is questioning its utility but a girl must ordinarily become a house-wife. She also shoulders a substantial responsibility in agriculture and animal husbandry. In addition to that, the number of residential institutions is comparatively less in number and the proportion of total number of seats for tribal girls in the residential institutions is less than the proportion of tribal girls amongst total tribal students. Even the rates of scholarships for girls are comparatively less in number. Again for the personality development, there is little scope, so for building of career the subjects of fine arts, music, etc., should be included.

Administration

The administration run by the States varies from one State to another. In some tribal areas, the Tribal Welfare Department runs all the educational institutions. In other areas, some of the institutions are run by the Education Department and some by the Tribal Welfare Department and some by the Tribal Welfare Department Ashram Schools and hostels are run by the Tribal Welfare Department.

Social Exclusion

Social exclusion is the denial of the capability of individual or group to participate in, and be respected by society more meaningful. Social exclusion of children in education is an issue of violating their rights to education. Social exclusion in education hampers the holistic development of children. The Constitution of India guarantees the right of equality in education. Social exclusion describes a process by which certain groups are thoroughly disadvantaged because they are discriminated against on the basis of their ethnicity, race, religion, caste or where they live, by the teachers and local community that excludes the tribal from education. Social exclusion describes a process by which certain groups are thoroughly disadvantaged because they are discriminated against on the basis of their ethnicity, race, religion, caste or where they live.

Education Policy

Till 2005 there is no clear educational policy for the tribal areas. In spite of the recommendations and suggestions of various committees and commissions, no policy for the tribal areas has been evolved. In some States, the schools in tribal areas are under the control of Education Department and in some under the several Welfare Departments. Lack of administrative policy regarding the education institution in tribal areas adversely affects the education of the tribals. In the Draft Tribal policy the issues of the tribal education has been thoroughly discussed and the recommendations have been made accordingly.

Conclusion

As education is being the effective instrument for empowering the disadvantaged section, especially the tribals and the tribal education is the most important step for the tribal development, all our efforts should be made to improve the educational status of these groups, especially that of women and girl child. From the beginning various approaches have been adopted as part of community development under general plan or specific tribal sub-plan. The result is not satisfactory in terms of the literacy rate, enrolment ratios or dropout rates. The problem of absenteeism is serious one in tribal areas. The large numbers of the students are on the rolls, but the actual attendance is really low. The problem of the tribal education is wastage and stagnation. Wastage is the withdrawal or dropping out of a student before completing the prescribed period of the concerned school. When a student takes more than one year to pass a class it is considered as a case of stagnation (Shrivastava, 1971). These are the happening among tribal children due to lack of academic atmosphere in society. Most of the tribal families are from blow the poverty line. The teachers are also causing wastage and stagnation among the tribal children because at the time of admission they play important role in approaching and convincing the parents. But once the children got admission the teachers consider that their responsibility is over. They keep aloof of the tribal society. So they do not remain dedicated to their jobs.

Madhya Pradesh has high concentration of different tribal groups. But the education and school system continue to remain quite alien to the tribal culture leading to their low interest in education, early dropout and accounting for their low educational status. Unless we respect and make necessary alterations in the content and curriculum in accordance with their culture, languages and social practices, it would be a difficult task to continuously retain the interest of tribal children in education and preventing their early dropouts.

Some suggestions, in general, can be made in the tribal education of Madhya Pradesh in the concluding remarks:

1. There should be special focus on girl's education, inclusive of context-specific traditional and innovative interventions.
2. In the text books the portrayal of tribal peoples should be imbued with human dignity and empathy.
3. In the residential school about 10-15 per cent non-tribal

students from the neighbourhood should be admitted in the schools mainly for tribal children for encouraging integration and competition.

4. To prevent the teacher's absenteeism in tribal areas, local and tribal teachers from local Panchayats shall be given preference in employment and the teaching and non-teaching staff of primary schools shall be placed under the control of the village management committee appointed by the Gram Sabha and Gram Panchayat.
5. The large number of primary schools should be opened for boys and girls within a radius of 1km of tribal villages.
6. The residential high schools or hostel facilities should be made available in the tribal areas (approximately 600).
7. Appropriate sports infrastructure should be provided in middle and secondary schools for the development of human capital in the field of sports.
8. The scope of Post-Matric scholarships, overseas scholarships for higher education should be broadened.
9. The certificates of vocational training education should be acceptable in both public/private sectors.

The above points should be given priority in the educational development and management of the tribal boys and girls. Some economic factors too are responsible for lack of interest shown by the tribal people in getting education. Since most of them are living in the abject poverty under subsistence economy, it is not possible to bear the expenditure to send their children to the schools. Besides, from the childhood, i.e., from the age of five or six, the boys are made engaged in the economic activities in the field and the girls help their mothers in household work or caring their younger brothers or sisters. In addition, the food insecurity may be another reason for sending their children to the schools as they remain always in hunger or starvation.

Most of the tribal communities are suffering from below the poverty line trauma. The reason behind the maximum dropouts among tribal children is the poverty. The percentage of population among the tribal population is much higher than the rational average of 27 per cent (as per Census 2001). So the education of their children is a luxury which they can hardly afford. The children assist their parents from the very beginning of their childhood in income-generating activities. The family size of the tribal families is big. The gaps between two kids are very less. So, the grown up children of the family look after the younger kids. Absence of child care centres, crèches, Balwadis, etc., in the remote tribal areas, also has to share the blame for depriving the children of the poor parents of the facility of education. The causes of absenteeism and finally the number of students passing out at the final examination are even lower. When the children fail at the final examination, the parents do not persuade them to join schools again. The social pressure compels them to send their children to school, but the economic pressure compels them to withdraw their children sooner or later.

REFERENCES

Bhowmick, P.K. (1980): "Education for the under-privileged—A suggestion" in *Some Aspects of Indian Anthropology.* Kolkata: Subarnarekha, pp. 144-152.

Jha, A.K. and Chaturbhuj Sahu (1998): "Golden Jubilee Year of Indian Independence and Tribal Education" *Vanyajati,* Vol. 46, No. pp. 2-4.

Planning Commission. (1981): *Development of Tribal Areas : A Report of National Committee on the Development of Backward Areas.* New Delhi: Government of India, June.

Sahu, Chaturbhuj. (1995): *Birhor Tribe: Dimensions of Development,* New Delhi: Sarup & Sons.

Sahu, Chaturbhuj (2001): "Tribal Education: Problems and Role of SIEMAT" In *Indian Tribal Life,* New Delhi, Sarup & Sons, pp. 25-39.

Sharma, B.D. (1976): *Planning for Educational Development in Tribal Areas.* New Delhi: Ministry of Home Affairs.

Shrivastava, L.R.N. (1971): *Identification of Educational Problems of the Soars of Orissa,* New Delhi: NCERT.

Sujatha K. (2000): *Education among Scheduled Tribes of India: Education Report,* (ed.) K Sujatha, CED documentation.

11

Problems of Education among the Tangkhul Nagas of Ukhrul in Manipur

J.J. Roy Burman

The Tangkhuls are a major Naga tribe groups inhabiting in most parts of Ukhrul district of Manipur State. The Tangkhuls are famous for their acts of bravery and warring qualities. Ukhrul happens to be one of the hill districts in East Manipur. It covers an area of 4,409 Sq. km. The elevation of the mountain ranges vary between 1,800 metres above the sea level. Khayangung hill has the highest elevation of 2,833 metres. Ukhrul district is mainly is a rural area with only Ukhrul district headquarters, the only urban centre in the area. It has 85 per cent forest region. 96 per cent of the people are Scheduled Tribes—overwhelming majority of whom are of Tangkhul. Almost all of them are Christians. Ukhrul has a sub-tropical climate. It witnesses a long monsoon as the rainy season starts from April and continues till September end. Temperature reaches zero degree at places during the winter. The Tangkhuls are mostly agriculturists involved in swidden cultivation or shifting hill cultivation. Some of them also do wet rice cultivation by cutting terraces in the hill slopes. Many people are also involved in forestry activities—good gathering ways and sell wood for commercial purposes. Quite a few of them are engaged in government jobs and some are involved in business. Women are usually involved in household jobs or work in the *jhum* fields for agriculture. Many of them are also engaged in weaving work—mainly to pass their leisure.

Education among the Tangkhuls

The Tangkhul Nagas are a highly educated people. There is almost no children among them not going to the school. Some of the elderly people among them are, however, illiterate. As per the 2001 census 75.40 per cent males and 61.91 per cent females are literate among them. Thus altogether 68.96 per cent people of the Tangkhuls are literate.

Christianity has been a major factor of spreading western education among the Tangkhuls. Prior to that, the village youth used to be trained into social life through the bachelor's dormitories. In the dormitories no strangers were permitted and the village boys rested and trained themselves in warfare to defend the village from outside aggression. They were also trained to undertake welfare activities. They cleared the jungles surrounding the village and repaired the village road, water points, ponds, houses of the destitute. They also attended the sick and needy and assisted in the functioning of the village council. The dormitories too served as recreation clubs where the boys sang and danced and learnt the stories of the yore, legends and myths from the village elders. Similar to boys, dormitories were also set up for girls and girls were placed under the care of elderly women. The girls were taught in undertaking ordinary household jobs and to learn traditional dances and music.

William Pettitgrew was the first Christian missionary to have entered Manipur and spread western education in due course of time. He reached Manipur first in 1894. He initially started a school in Imphal but due to administrative reasons he had to close it down. Later he shifted to Ukhrul and established a mission school with twenty boys in 1896. By 1911 there were 28 students in the school.

Since the Tangkhuls had no common dialect, Pettitgrew developed the Tangkhul village dialect and popularized it through his writings of Tangkhul primers, translation of gospel, hymns and Bible. Through education Pettitgrew tried to change the way of life of the people by teaching them hygiene and better health care. In this way he also performed his evangelical duties. But the American Baptist Mission faced a setback due to local opposition and its growth became retarded.

In 1946, due to the efforts of A.S. Shomi Dominic, a local boy who adopted Catholic religion after studying in Shillong, a

Catholic priest was invited to Ukhrul. Thus in 1952, Fr. Marochino arrived from Kohima. He could immediately convert a good number of Tangkhuls into the Catholic fold. Later the Catholics opened a Middle school for 150 boys at Hundung—a nearby village. In any case the primary motive of the evangelists for promoting education was to prepare them religious understanding and work rather than for any practical purpose. "The missionaries considered the three R's as the most effective means for winning converts and also for enabling them to learn the basic tenets of Christian faith. According to them, educational institute served double purposes: first, as a means of teaching the Christian truth; and second, as a means for recruitment or training future workers. Naturally, therefore, the missionaries gave priority to the study of local vernaculars as the basis for the formulation of their educational programmes. It hardly mattered even if it would take them long time to master them, because the native vernacular was the most effective and direct medium of communication" (Leishmi, 1993). Naturally the missionaries were interested in imparting primary education and had little interest in promoting higher education among the natives.

As a consequence of the evangelists to promote education only up to the primary level, the urge for higher education received a set back. No good school at that level ever emerge in the district. The middle and high schools are almost entirely run by the government. A few private schools have emerged in between. Consequently, people from the affluent sections feel reluctant to sent their wards to schools in the State. They prefer to send their children to far away cities like Delhi, Mumbai, Bangaluru, Chennai and Chandigarh, etc., for attaining higher education.

The trend of education fostered by the Christian missionaries is not isolated only among the Tangkhuls but among all the tribes of the region as a whole. The Table 11.1 reinforces the conviction.

Table 11.1 reveals that the percentage of ST Christian students at the graduate level or above is extremely low. The situation has not altered much even in almost ten years time. Though there has been a fairly good increase in the high school level. Christian missionaries of late, particularly the Catholic have opened many new high schools in both rural and urban areas. But the impact of the same is yet to be felt in Ukhrul district. The schools particularly run by the government are very shoddy and many of them exist

Table 11.1 : Education Attainment by Social Group if Religion is Christian in NER (in %)

Social Groups	*Illiterate*	*Literate upto primary*	*Middle and Secondary*	*Graduate and Above*	*Total*
ST	34.03	43.43	21.06	1.47	100
ST (Meg. & Miz.)	27.95	48.85	21.45	1.75	100
SC	13.94	30.59	36.61	18.86	100
Others	48.84	32.54	15.80	2.82	100
Total	35.74	42.15	20.46	1.65	100
1999-2000					
ST	24.48	36.04	36.20	3.28	100
ST (Meg.& Miz.)	20.31	43.59	33.04	3.07	100
SC	26.25	27.79	40.67	5.28	100
Others	46.54	35.82	16.59	1.05	100
Total	26.92	36.00	34.04	3.04	100

Note : Figures calculated for persons 15 years and above (Dubey & Pala, 2006).

just for the name sake. More than the missionaries, some of the private parties have been seen running schools even in the interior villages of the district.

Problems

There are many practical problems of imparting proper education among the Tangkhuls which have been identified by Anna Leishimi (1993):

1. *Non-availability of Funds*: There is acute shortage of funds in running schools and colleges in the Tangkhul district. People being poor are not in a position to afford costly education. The government also does not provide adequate funds to the schools. The missionary schools are very few and they too are not in a position to run the schools just by themselves. The parishioners and the laity are mainly dependent on agriculture and they earn very little surplus to be able to support the schools or the trusts that manage them. Consequently the schools lack adequate infrastructure to accommodate the students. Many parents thus do not prefer to send their wards to the schools. This finding is quite in tune with the findings of a survey

conducted on elementary education in India by National Council of Applied Economic Research (1995): "The survey came to the conclusion that lack of finance is the most important reason for non-enrolment and dropout of children throughout the country despite the fact that the government and other public bodies are bearing a large share of educational costs in the form of capital investment in land, buildings, other infrastructure and various subsidies on tuition fees, books and school dresses" (Vanlalchhawna, 2006).

2. *Lack of Uniform and Socially Relevant Curriculum:* In different schools different curriculum are followed and this creates problems in pursuing higher education. Quite often the course also do not match with the requirements of the students. They are not socially relevant or need based. Consequently the students do not feel interested to study them and get detached or alienated from the education. This results in their getting poor marks in the examinations.
3. *Lack of Qualified Teachers:* It is quite difficult to find properly qualified teachers in the interior areas. Thus frequently untrained and unqualified teachers are appointed in the schools. more than this, there is quite often interference of political people who push through their own candidates irrespective of their merit. It is believed that many a time the politicians have vested interests and they make money out of such deals. It is also reported that sometimes the qualified teachers are not willing to attend the interior schools and they provide proxy teachers in their place. Sometimes even the Village Councils themselves do not allow outside teachers to join the schools and they provide their own local candidates instead. The Manipur State 2003 Commission on Higher Education too had made similar observations, "Many teachers get away with absenteeism, irresponsibility and misconduct because they have political godfathers. Politicians interfere routinely in transfer and postings of government college teachers. Morale of the teachers is undermined by such interference. Many of the private Aided and Private college are playgrounds for local politicians. Rivalries among them

cause groupism in the management and even among the teachers and the students. Many unhealthy practices in such college are often linked directly to political influence".

4. *Unchecked Growth of Schools*: In the recent years a large number of schools—particularly private schools have mushroomed in the Ukhrul district. These schools are run by lowly paid teachers and many of whom are unqualified. The management of these schools are interested in generating more personal profits or economic gain than looking into the interests of the students. Yet unfortunately, the parents are more interested to send their children to the private schools than the government schools, as in these schools at least the presence of teachers is much more regular. Besides, there is some more prestige attached to these schools. interestingly a highly ranked central government officer in course of his tour to the district during Sarva Siksha Abhiyan found that the parents prefer to send their boys to the private schools while they send their girls to the government schools.
5. *Faulty Examination and Outdated Teaching Method*: In most of the schools the examination system is unsystematic and faulty. In many schools large-scale mass copying is reported. The faculty examination system is mainly due to the directives of the school boards. Mass copying has become a part of the corrupt culture of the community where a tendency to get more without doing hard labour has become the norm. The government too has pampered the community as a principle of appeasement. The teaching methods in the schools are outdated as there is dearth of modern equipments and teaching gadgets. The teachers too have not been upgraded in skill attainment. The students too are not interested in learning the subjects and they are rather taught to memorise the texts.
6. *Medium of Teaching*: The Tangkhul students are extremely handicapped in their learning as they have to cope up with four languages—their mother tongue, Manipuri, English and Hindi. Their medium of instruction is in all these languages and it creates a heavy load on them. The government policy is mainly to be blamed for this and in

most tribal areas only the mother tongue is used as the medium of instruction. The Tangkhuls, as a result, often feel being oppressed by the Meitei majority who dwell in the valley and control the reigns of power. In order to escape from this ordeal many Tangkhul students have demanded their school board to be merged with that of Nagaland, the adjoining State. But then, many realized that without learning Manipuri they will have no future in the job markets within Manipur and they were compelled to abandon their intentions.

7. *Lack of Seriousness among Students and Family Atmosphere:* The Tangkhul students by and large found to be indifferent towards their education and quite often while away their time. Many of them join their family farms during the sowing and harvesting seasons. There does not exist a congenial atmosphere in the household supporting serious education. The parents too are also lax and do not pressurize the students for doing hard labour. In many households there is no separate space for the children to live and they huddle up with their parents and other family members in the same room. Thus they lack privacy for studying intently. Presently some of the children are taking to substance abuse and diverting away from studies. Some of them are also attracted to the underground movement and stealthily join them.
8. *Apathy of the Government:* Manipur is governed by a very weal bureaucracy. Very few senior officials are interested to visit the interior areas involve in school inspections. Moreover, operation of different school boards too have led to confusions. While on the one hand one has to deal with the State education department, on the other one has to deal with the officials of the District Council. This often leads to confusions and delay in work procedures. Corruption too is rampant and the school management has to bear the brunt after all.
9. *Lack of Science Education:* It has been found that the tribals all over the country lack aptitude for science education and the Tangkhuls are no exception. Science education is in a poor state in the district. Very few students opt for science in the higher education. Even otherwise there is

dearth of good science teachers in the schools. The schools are also ill equipped with science laboratories. Because of this no proper scientific skill is getting generated from the area. This ultimately deters local technological development and general development of the area. The 2003 Manipur State Commission on higher education noted similarly, "When the Commission paid visits to all kinds of colleges, it was apparent that there was great disparity in infrastructure development between colleges in the hills and the valley and also between colleges in the urban and the rural in the valley. This disparity has affected higher education adversely, particularly in the hills. For example, science subjects at the Degree level are not opened in most of the colleges in the hills. Even if they are opened, the basic infrastructure and the minimum teaching staff are found lacking".

10. *High Dropout Rates and Stagnation:* Among the Tangkhuls a high dropout rate is noticed. Many students are found leaving their studies in between. Most of them leave due to failures in the examinations. Failure in the examinations too lead to stagnation and wastage of time and money. Due to failure the poor parents are reluctant to support their wards for long. Devi (2006) too noted the high dropout and stagnation rate among the Scheduled Tribes in Manipur.
11. *Political Disturbance and Education:* Education in the Tangkhul district quite often comes to a complete halt due to political disturbances. Tangkhuls play a stellar role in the political upsurge against the Indian state. For this most of them actively and passively support the NSCN (IM) faction of the underground. Many times they attack the security forces or the government treasury. The NSCN (IM) also levies tax from every individual and trucks carrying goods through the area. As a result, a tense situation always prevails in the area. Quite often the underground calls *bandhs* for long duration and all schools and colleges get closed in those days. The situation gets worse as and when the security forces retaliate and attack the innocent people. Ultimately the Tangkhuls believe that they are not Indians and that they should be given freedom. Many of the young

boys and girls get attracted to such calls and leave their studies to join the underground movement. But ironically, many of the family members of these children are found to leave the State to acquire higher education in many different cities of India. Many of them also seek jobs in these places after having completed their education.

Conclusion

The Tangkhul Nagas are a proud and vigorous race. They dwell in a remote area of Manipur and India. They, for political reasons, feel detached from the country. They have been converted to Christianity and prospered a lot in terms of health and hygiene. *Jhum* or shifting cultivation provides them with enough succour to be self dependent and they are able to withstand the onslaught of the State. But they also want to emerge out and have great cravings for learning. It is in such a situation that education in the area is felt to be lagging behind. Though Christianity had enabled them to gain basic education, much more is felt to be required by them. It is felt that the Indian state has failed to rise to the occasion to meet their requirements and hence an impasse. The state too has its limits and suffers from resource crunch. But political decentralization and tactful handling may resolve the crisis and lead towards a more meaningful education. After all the Tangkhul youth for now do not like to be confined to their villages and after higher education, they seek white collar jobs in cities—who will fulfil this distant dream?

REFERENCES

Devi, J. (2006): *Education in Manipur*, Imphal: Raj Pravina Brothers.

Dubey A. and Pala V. (2006): "Role of Christianity in Fostering Literacy and Education in Northeastern Region: Statistical Evidence" in T.B. Subba and others (ed.) *Christianity and Change in Northeast India*, New Delhi: Concept.

Leishimi, A.S. Anna (1993): *Educational Development in Ukhrul District*, M.A. Dissertation, Manipur University: Department of Education.

The Department of University and Higher Education (2003): *Report of the Manipur State Higher Education Committee, Part III.*

Vanlalchhawna (2006): *Higher Education in North-East India*, New Delhi: Mittal Publications.

12

Education System in Manipur : A Comparison between the Tribes and Non-Tribes

Kashnug Zingran Kengoo

Introduction

Manipur is a multi-ethnic, multi-linguistic and multi-religious State. Imphal is the capital of Manipur. According to Census of India (2001), the total population of Manipur is 22,93,896, out of total population, tribal consist of 7,13,813 (31.11%) population and remaining total population 15,80,083 are Meitei's, and some outsiders like, Nepali, Bengali, Bihari, etc. Census of India (2001) recognized 29 tribes in Manipur. Manipur comprises of three major communities, Meiteis, Nagas and Kuki-Chin-Mizo. There are nine districts in Manipur, (see Table 12.1). Imphal east, Imphal west, Bishnupur and Thoubal districts are Meitei's dominated (non-tribal) concentrated in valleys of Manipur, whereas remaining five district are inhabited by tribals. And among tribals, Nagas are the most populated and among Nagas, Tangkhul comprise of highest population inhabiting in Ukhrul district of Manipur. Nagas inhabit in four hilly districts, Ukhrul, Senapati, Tamenglong and Chandel whereas Churachandpur district is dominated by Kuki-Chin-Mizo. Geographical location of Manipur indicates, are settled in hilly areas are surrounded the valleys of Meitei dominated region. Multiple ethnic groups have their own distinct language, tradition and culture. There are four major religious groups Christian, Hindu, Muslim (Manipuri Muslim are called Pangan) as well as the indigenous Meitei religion, Sanamahi.

Table 12.1 : Distribution of Ethnic Groups in Manipur

Sl. No.	District	Ethnic Group
1.	Imphal, Bishnupur and Thoubal	Meiteis, Pangans, and few Settlements of Kom
2.	Ukhrul	Tangkhul Nagas and few Settlements of Kukis
3.	Senapati	Mao Nagas, Poumai Nagas, Maram Nagas, Thangal Nagas, and few Settlement of Kukis
4.	Tamenglong	Zeliangrong Nagas (Zeliang, Rongmei and Zeme), Chiru Nagas, and few settlements of Kukis
5.	Chandel	Maring Nagas, Monsang Nagas, Lamkang Nagas, Chothe Nagas, Monyon Nagas, Tharao Nagas, and Kukis
6.	Churachandpur	Paite, Simte, Raite, Mizos, Hmar, Suhte, Purum, Gangte, Vaiphei, Kuki.

Source: Shimray (2001).

System of Education

In Manipur, the system of education depends upon powers and money that corrupt the system instead of giving fair and quality education to common people. Education has been politicised deliberately. Meitei dominated valley areas are maximally developed in education whereas, the minority tribal dominated areas are leaving behind by minimal educational development. "It is easier to add new educational initiatives than to change the old ones. Why? Because the change of educational practice is a fundamentally political threat in the sense that challenges structures of authority, dominance and control." (Bush & Saltarelli, 2000, p. 32). The problems of tribal education are fallout of a larger problem of cultural upheaval, political unrest, and economic stagnation that has gripped the education system. Meiteis as dominant groups in Imphal, the Capital of Manipur and they exercise power to administer all the development in education. Democratic forms of educational development are in imbalance in the State. The process of equal tribal participative and inclusive in education is unfamiliar in Manipur. Gangmumei (2000) states, "The State has financially and administratively the schools and colleges established by the government or private agencies. In the government schools that are administered by the State bureaucracy there is no question of democracy in management. The aided institutions have to function in accordance to the whims and fancies of the State educational bureaucracy and those who wield political power."(Gangmumei, 2000:195). Due to inequality diversion of educational development, education conflict arises between the two sections of people, since dominant denied the interest of minorities' equality in education. Smith (2003) states, "Irrespective of the degree of decentralization and differentiation between the system, issue of equality carry the potential to inflame or ameliorate conflict between different groups within society. Equality concern may arise in terms of 'inputs' such as equal access of all groups to education, transparency in the allocation of resource and the recruitment, training and deployment of teachers." (Smith, 2003 : 26).

Recruitment of Teachers

Recruitment of teachers are not on the basis of merit and capability of the individuals, it has become the system of money power, recruiting the right person are not in the policies of education department in Manipur. Teachers have been recruited excessively from among the Meiteis which is reserved for the tribals. Naga Youth Front (2010) states, "In the recent recruitment of teachers under the district councils of the hills, 552 posts out of 1,600 reserved vacant posts have been given to Meiteis." (webcasted on 02 June 2010, at www.nagalimvoice.com). The political leaders and bureaucrats are the key person to decide who to offer the post of teachers even though they are not in the field of education department. The more the amount of cash flows into the hands of the leaders by the candidates, the better preference and opportunity to get the position of teachers. It does not pertain only to education sector but to numerous government departments, it is evident to the common people of Manipur. To quote from Singh (2011), "The estimated rates for various posts are discussed in private conversations ranging between Rs. 3-4 lakh for a primary teacher, Rs. 10-15 lakh for a sub-inspector/assistant SI of police, up to 15 lakh for a supervisor (women and child welfare), and Rs. 15-25 lakh (or even higher) for a State civil services post." (Singh, 2011:12). The system of education has been degraded by bribe and corruption in Manipur. Since money and power played important roles to select teachers, the procedure to select the qualified teachers are replaced by unqualified person. Political leaders interfere in the administration of education like transferring of headmaster and teachers are not concern according to the requirement of respective schools, but the inappropriate system of placement and transfer lies in the hands of political godfathers, which in reverse severely affects the schools, particularly in the tribal areas.

Proxy System of Teachers

Most of the Meitei teachers in remote hill areas got themselves transferred in their respective areas, like, Imphal valley and the adjacent Meitei dominated districts, in result, students are left with few teachers. The investigation of Naga Youth Front (2010) report states, "Many teachers under Education department are given to Meiteis for hill areas and almost 100 per cent of them have been transferred with post to the valley with some excuse leaving behind just 3 to 4 teachers in all schools." (webcasted on 02 June 2010, at www.nagalimvoice.com). The non-availability of well-qualified and trained teachers at the rural tribal areas is a serious problem and appointed a substitute teacher paying a minimum amount from the salary; these proxy systems are very much common in tribal areas of Manipur. President, All Tribal Student Union, Manipur (2008) states, "In the valley, teachers are in excess and schools are overcrowded; most of the teachers from valley those who are posted in the remote tribal hilly region transfer themselves by means of bribing the concerned officials and politicians." (Interview, President ATSUM in 2008). The performances of teachers in tribal areas are not satisfactory, leaving the schools with substitute teacher. Teachers leave from their respective schools for their own convenience, withdrawal of monthly salary is considered as their first priority and some are engaged in alternative business in their hometown. Committed government school teachers are found rare. Shimray (2007) states "So, to ensure good education, teacher must be equipped enough to deliver competent services. One important thing about teacher is to uphold the commitment. Commitment means to perform his or her professional duty enthusiastically with the sense of responsibility and dignity. So that, outcome has to be accountable to the society as well as overall social-economic development. No doubt, our society has produced high literate population but few educated persons." (Webcasted on 27 August, 2007, at thohepou.wordpress.com).

Linguistic and Identity Problems

Medium of instruction in primary schools is becoming an issue in tribal areas. In primary stages the first medium of instruction should be their mother tongue; secondly, English, regional and mainstreams as third priority of instruction. Due to non-availability of textbook in their mother tongue in tribal areas, school children are compelled to learn in English as first medium of instruction, whereas Meiteis dominant people have their own mother tongue textbook. Among tribals, every tribe has their own distinct language in roman script. Singh (2000) states, "The soio-cultural milieu of the tribal people of Manipur has its distinctive characteristic. The 29 recognised tribes of the State speak 29 dialects. Hence, there is a need to develop instructional materials in most of the tribal dialects in addition to the 5 major dialects, namely, Hmar, Paite, Tangkhul, Lushai, Thadou (Kuki), which are used as the medium of instruction in primary schools in the hill areas of Manipur." (Singh, 2000:207). In tribal areas, the problems of mother tongue instruction in schools remain unchanged. Tribals remain confined in their respective dialects; they don't know how to read and write Manipuri and Hindi scripts. Therefore, teachers for Manipuri and Hindi subjects are difficult to find among tribals.

One of the core issues of setting the school syllabus, the curriculum that content merely about the mainstream India and the dominant Meitei society. None of the subjects content about the history or culture of tribals, school students are forced to learn the mainstream and Meiteis history which deteriorating the rich culture, tradition and identity of tribal people by the dominant Meiteis educational policy maker. Language and identity are inseparable, it supported each other. Shimray (2007) states, "Indeed, the social co-existent is weakened by the contention of ethnic sentiment, partisan interest, jealousy and individualism. Present language row is a very serious subject and has to be debated across every section of the society and community. Now, the State faces inevitable "counter-productive" from the peripheral hills. Not only the language issue, but it is clear portrays that there is serious socio-economic inequality between hills and valley district as well as tribal and non-tribal. Today, valley districts are rather well ahead in all round economic and infrastructural development. Such economic inequality as well as Metei Mayek issue would further fosters ethnicism and sectarian aspirations. Language is culturally sensitive issue because it touches the core of social element as well as identity. Present language imbroglio is seen as another potential factor that can stir up ethnic hornet." (Webcasted on 3 October 2007, at www.e-pao.net). Traditional tribal arts, literature, music, dance, etc., are excluded from the curriculum; the only dominant Meiteis cultural heritages are available in syllabus from primary to higher level of education in Manipur. Building their own culture ignoring the tribal minority in curriculum triggered conflict between Meiteis and tribals. Such instances are also witness in different parts of the world. Smith (2003) states, "A significant part of the curriculum is dedicated to the arts, music, literature, history and geography and in some countries these are referred to as 'national subjects', that is, they are seen as an important way of consolidating a common sense of national identity. The potential for conflict arises when the cultural heritage and traditions of a majority group dominate the school curriculum and when the art forms, music and literature of minorities are unrepresented. Even where there is little diversity within a population, the curriculum may portray a picture of national heritages that is chauvinist or ethnocentric." (Smith, 2003 : 31).

There are numerous ways leading to conflict in education, specially, when education system that gives importance on dominant group. In the case of curriculum that deals with language, religion, and culture. In Manipur, imposition of dominant Meitei language (Meiteilon) and Meeitei Mayek (Manipuri script) upon the tribals generate conflict, it has also been considered as compulsory subject in Imphal valley, but tribals agitated against the alien subject as a compulsory subject in the indigenous traditional tribal areas. Shishak (1992) states, "But I dare say the Meitei-controlled government of Manipur has no legal and moral right to make Meitei language study compulsory in schools." (Shishak, 1992:4). Against the obligation of Meitei language, the apex tribal student body ATSUM President (2006) states, "respect any movement to restore and revive the indigenous script of any community, we will not accept the imposition of

Meetei Mayek on the tribal people of Manipur." (Webcasted on 5 November, 2006, at delhithurawn.net). The head Naga organization in Manipur, United Naga Council (UNC), All Tribal Students' Union, Manipur, and Kuki Student Organisation, strongly protested to turn down the imposition. Language is an important element of one's own growth in culture associated with identity. Seitz (2004) states, "The formal education system contributes to exacerbating societal conflicts in particular when it (re) produces socio-economics disparities and brings about social marginalization or compartmentation, or promotes the teaching of identity and citizenship concepts which deny the cultural plurality of society and which then lead to intolerance towards "the other". Education is, as numerous examples document, a key medium with which ethnicity is mobilized for the escalation of conflicts." (Seitz, 2004 : 10).

Role of Community in Education

Every tribal district has a government model school which has been established long time ago, inaugurated the schools by the concerned leaders but the operation and activities of schools are not look into by concerned officials. Later the schools remained vacant, since the schools have no infrastructures and bad shape, schools remain unfit for human beings to be used as a school which is not renovated, and undeveloped. Jamani (2006) states, "The inadequate physical facilities and poor communication in the rural and hill areas are the main obstacles in the process of universalisation of primary education. Leaving school by the children before the completion of their full course may be attributed to the unfavourable environment in the school. The quality of the furnitures such as benches, desks, blackboard in many of the schools in Manipur is below standard. In some schools in rural areas, children are to sit on the floor; some of the school buildings have no wall. The approach roads are muddy." (Jamani, 2006 : 65). Inspection of schools from the education department is unknown and negligence of the concerned authority creates poor administration in schools. Village government schools are in pathetic condition. Due to huge difference of government and private school, parents prefer to send their children in private schools. Poor administration leads to dysfunctional of government schools, some of the village schools remain closed throughout the year. One, NGO called International Fund for Agriculture Development (IFAD) of which Project Manager states, "We examined all the schools. Most of the government schools are like animal shelters that are not fit for human beings." On the other side, village churches played an important role to develop education. Approximately 95 per cent of the tribal people professed Christianity, churches and village councils take an initiative together to expand education, majority of the tribal village church set up and run English schools. A Tangkhul village in Ukhrul district called Hoomi village, Pastor states, "Church is the main source of income to run the English school". Apart from establishment of schools, most of the churches in tribal villages sponsored the children of poor parents in school stages and higher studies in different parts of India. The students studied Theological as well as secular studies.

Problems of Higher Secondary Schools

The tribal regions in Manipur lack higher secondary schools, even few secondary schools which are located in tribal areas has been devaluing the quality of education by lack of infrastructure and faculty. Once the headmaster or principal retire, the vacant post remain unfilled. Existence of principal in higher secondary school are rare, the senior faculty of the department is deputed as a principal, likewise one of the chief populated Tangkhul Nagas district, one and only Pettigrew College in Ukhrul district, Mr. Mashun Stone a senior lecturer is deputed as principal in charge of college, the same case happened in Ukhrul Higher Secondary School and Industrial Training Institutes. Some of the newly upgraded high schools to higher secondary schools in tribal areas are found lack in infrastructure, facilities and faculty. The headmasters of the schools are placed as principal in-charges and are not qualified to be principal due to their low profile of educational qualification. Lecturers are appointed on contract basis, since the lecturer did not get their monthly salary on time, they do not fully attend the academic calendar, they are engaged in other activities for their daily needs. Lecturers did not get their monthly salary for five to six months. The Principal in charge of the Somdal Higher Secondary School in Ukhrul district (2010), states, "Since the lecturer did not get their salary on time, they are looking for alternative income for their survival, I cannot force them to stay back for full academic calendar".

Waiting for the State government to uplift the facilities of schools in tribal areas remain hopeless. In order to get better education system in tribal areas, private schools compete to affiliate in Central Board of Secondary Education (CBSE) and Indian Council of School Education (ICSE), but the State government did not encourage and discarded the interest of private schools. The Meitei's dominated Manipur government creates a stumbling block by rejecting private schools affiliation in CBSE and ICSE, which is under the direct control of Central Government. Democratically, it denied the Rights to Education for tribal people in Manipur. Taking an advantage to control and impose State education policies in the will of dominant groups create chaos between tribes and dominant non-tribe Meiteis. The then Member of Parliament (MP) of outer Manipur Mr. Charamanei on 27 May, 2005, wrote to Ministry of Human Resource Development (MHRD), it states, "The most insensible and cruel act of the Manipur Government is the imposition of the ban of private schools from getting affiliation to the CBSE and ICSE which is nothing but violation of rights to education to the tribal people".

Colleges in Tribal Areas

Among the nine districts in Manipur, The Census of India (2001) shows Meitei inhabited areas are high in higher education. Comparing among the tribals in Manipur, Ukhrul score the highest percentage in higher education level followed by Chandel. Tribals are lagging behind in higher education, in comparison with Meiteis due to deprivation of educational facilities and lack of educational institution in tribal regions whereas Meiteis dominated districts have sufficient educational institution and facilities. The only central university is located in Imphal valley and is subjugated by Meiteis thus excluding the attention of tribals. Singh (2006) said, "Manipur is not far behind from other States in tribal education but it shares in technical and professional education is not up to the mark. The hill areas suffer from lack of institutions of higher learning." (Singh, 2006 : 46). All the important colleges are based in Imphal valleys few colleges are located in tribal areas. However, there is lack of college teachers in hilly region, and there are also many posts of teachers lying vacant in tribal areas. The investigated report of the Higher Education Commission (2003) states, "The Commission finds that there is a great disparity in infrastructure development between colleges in the hills and the valley and also colleges in the urban and the rural areas of the valley. This disparity has effected higher education adversely, particularly in the hills where even the basic infrastructure and the minimum teaching staff are found lacking." (Report of the Manipur State Higher Education Commission, 2003, p. viii).

In 2005, there were 57 colleges in Manipur out of which 16 colleges are located in the tribal districts whereas 41 colleges are located in Meiteis dominated districts. Colleges of importance like, Regional Institute of Medical Sciences (RIMS), Law, Polytechnic, Engineering, Management, Business, Dance, Computer, etc., were set up in Imphal and other Meitei populated districts. Few colleges have been set up in tribal region of Manipur. Among them Churachandpur district has 5 colleges including one Law college, making it the tribal district with most colleges whereas other district like Ukhrul have only one college.

Problems of Higher Education

Seitz (2004) states, "One of the key questions for the relationship between education and conflict is the manner in which education systems organize their dealings with diversity." (Seitz, 2004 : 10). Conflict has affected education from various directions in Manipur State, which has multiple ethnic groups within one boundary, i.e., from Meitei, the larger dominant group, and down to the smaller tribal groups among the society. Tribes agitated against the low intake of students in Manipur University. Census of India (2001) depicts, Meitei's population consists of 65.7 per cent and remaining 34.3 per cent comprises of tribals. Tribals protest against the reservation policy which is only 7.5 per cent in Manipur University. Tribal students demand 34.3 per cent, according to the proportion of tribal population in Manipur University as well as job reservation in Manipur but the response remain in vain. Looking for alternative solution for tribal students in Manipur, ATSUM states "Too much energy and resource has been wasted trying to get a dignified share of our rights to education. We do not have any faith in government's will or capacity to develop our human resources. We have reached a limit where we have to look for alternatives." (The Imphal Free Press, webcasted on 9 September 2007, at kanglaonline.com).

Due to Manipur University discriminating and segregating educational rights of tribals, tribals were compelled to demand separate tribal hills university. Facing the problems, tribals struggle for equality cannot be kept in isolation. To solve the problems of tribal students in Manipur, division of separate tribes and non-tribes educational administrative will be effective. Vaunglallian (2010) pointed out two divisional points by setting up of educational department, "the Manipur Hills Education Department (& Service) and the Manipur Valley Educational Department (& Service). To draw maximum benefit for such small and beautiful Departments, we must have two separate Ministers, two separate Secretaries/ Commissioners, two separate Directorates and two separate budgets, etc., so that there can never be any sort of inter-transfer, or 'overlapping (a word very applicable and relevant today). It will also actually help if the officers and buildings of the two Departments/Services are as far as apart possible—one big deep in the Hills and the others in the far corner of the country." (Webcasted on 24 September 2010, at www.thesangaiexpress.com).

Migration

The above mentioned points in this chapter highlight the evident of tribal deprivation in education. There are many stumbling blocks to pursue education in Manipur, the problems of education system compelled to migrate tribal students in different parts of India for better and quality education. Due to lack of educational institution, poor infrastructure, the large number of tribal students leave Manipur at the level of high schools, higher secondary and higher education, seeking admission in different parts of educational institution like Shillong, Delhi, Mumbai, Bangalore, etc. However, the general problems in Manipur, three years bachelor degree course in Manipur University has affected the career of students; as it takes five years to complete. Ethnic conflict, corruption, bandhs, strikes and flexible academic calendar disrupt academic career of the students such as extension of syllabus to be covered, postponing examination, etc. Politicians and bureaucrats do not give priority to education in the States, since, their sons and daughters are outside the States for getting good education.

Conclusion

Government frameworks do not suit to tackle the issues and problems arising in education especially in tribal areas. The attitudes of governments towards education in rural hilly region of Manipur are not satisfactory. The schemes and programmes do not reach in time and the concerned officers who have been given responsibility are largely corrupt. In the present situation, if the educational development depends on government to reform the education system, it will face critical and uncertain future in terms of education. The education system has been considered a State government's responsibility. The role of the Central Government is to formulate broad policy frameworks in order to ensure quality, and setting norms for utilization of resources through various sponsored schemes from time to time. There are huge differences in education between the tribal hill regions and dominant groups in the valley of Manipur. The present problems of education in Manipur represents a crisis of governance, which in turn reflects a crisis across a range of political, social, economic and administrative systems that are in place to adjust the development and management of resources and provision of services to different communities.

REFERENCES

Bush, K.D. and Saltarelli, D. (2000): "The Two Faces of Education in Ethnic Conflict, Towards a Peace building Education for Children" Italy, UNICEF. Retrieved online 19 August 2008, from (http://www.dfid.gov.uk/Pubs/files/edconflictdev.pdf).

Charenamai M.P. (2005): "Letter to Ministry of Human Resource Development" (MHRD). Government of Manipur order vide no. 16/11/02/SE(S). Dated 27 May 2005. Regarding the Imposition of Meitei Language and Meitei Mayek upon the Tribal Students in the Education System.

Jamani (2006): *Education in Manipur*, Imphal: Rai Pravina Brothers.

Morung Express (2008): "Manipur Tribals Demand Separate Hill University", (Retrieved from http://www.tangkhul.com/modules.php?name= News&file=article&sid=2807).

Kamei, G (2009): "Education in North East India: Problems of Democratization", Horam, M. (Ed.). *The Rising Manipur including other North Eastern States,* New Delhi: Manas Publication.

Report of the State Higher Education Commission (2003): "*Report of the State Higher Education Commission, Part I-II,* Manipur: The Department of University and Higher Education, Government of Manipur.

Seitz, K. (2004): *Education and Conflict: The Role of Education in the Creation, Prevention and Resolution of Societal Crises—Consequences for Development Cooperation* German: Deutsche Gesellschaft fur Technische Zusammenarbeit (GTZ) GmbH.

Shimray, U.A. (2007): "Education in Tangkhul Naga Region", (Retrieved online from http://thohepou.wordpress.com/2007/08/22/education-in-tangkhul-nagas-region/).

Shimray, U.A. (2007): "Meetei-Mayek: Uneasy Script", (Retrieved online from http://www.epao.net/epSubPageExtractor.asp?src=news_section.opinions.Opinion_on_Manipu r_Integrity_Issue.Meitei-Mayek_Uneasy_script).

Shishak, T.A. (1992): *North-Eastern Tribals and Language Issues: The Tangkhul Theological Association,* Manipur: Ukhrul.

Singh, L.L. (2000): "Universalisation of Elementary Education in the Hill Areas of Manipur", Horam, M. (Ed.). *The Rising Manipur including other North Eastern States,* New Delhi: Manas Publication.

Singh, N.S. (2011): "State of Education in Manipur", *Economic and Political Weekly,* June 4, Vol. XLVI, No. 23.

Singh, R.M. (2006): *Tribal Development in 21st Century,* New Delhi: A Mittal Publication.

Smith, Alan. (2003): *Education, Conflict and International Development.* Report commissioned by Department for International Development (UK). Retrieved September 12, 2008, from (http://www.dfid.gov.uk/Pubs/files/edconflictdev.pdf).

Vunglallian, T. (2010): "Educating Manipur: The Education District Way", *The Sangai Express,* 24 September.

13

Trends of Higher Education among Tribal Students

K.P. Pothen

Introduction

Education and higher education among the scheduled caste and scheduled tribe students have become very important after the achievement of independence in 1947. The Constitution of India has made special provisions for the benefit of scheduled castes and scheduled tribes. They are included in the weaker sections of the Indian society. There are 13.82 crore people belonging to the scheduled castes in India. This constitutes 16.48 per cent of the country's total population. The population of the scheduled tribes were 6.78 crore according to the 1991 Census of India constituting 8.08 per cent of the country's total population. Their literacy is just 29.60 per cent. The literacy among women is 18.19 per cent comparable to the national average of 39.29 per cent. (cf 'People of India,' *Malayala Manorama Year Book,* 2010 : 580). The tribal population in Madhya Pradesh is substantial especially in districts like Jhabua, Dhar, Mandla, Khargone, and Chhindwara.

Most of the students who came to Indore for higher education (After class XII) belongs to the above district. A representative sample of 300 students were selected from Devi Ahilya University, Indore for the study—219 boys (73%) and 81 girls (27%).

These students study in various colleges and university departments. Most of these students took advantage of the hostel facility provided in the institutions and also special hostels meant for scheduled castes and scheduled tribes.

The method of study including the tools of data collection and the analysis of data, interpretation and conclusions are given below:

Method of Study

The study was conducted in the light of the following hypothesis:

(1) Awareness and interest are increasing among the tribals for higher education.
(2) But, keeping in view the population of the tribals, the number of students coming forward for higher education is less.
(3) Higher education of the tribals depends upon their socio-economic background.
(4) Despite the availability of facilities for higher education, the performance of the tribal students is not appreciable.
(5) Due to higher education among the tribal youth, alienation is observed among them with regard to traditional values and institutions.

With regard to the scope of the study, the following were important :

(i) The socio-cultural background of the tribal students.
(ii) How the tribal students perform in their educational institutions?
(iii) Facilities that were available to the students and how they made use of the same.
(iv) How do the tribal students adjust to the new environment in which they live?
(v) What are the levels of future aspirations and ambitions of the tribal students? And
(vi) How do they maintain their relations with their fellow beings at their native places?

With regard to the *tools of data collection* the following have been followed :

(i) Information from the university, collectorate and various colleges regarding scheduled tribe students.

(ii) Administration of semi-structured interview schedule on students.

(iii) Case study of 20 students

Findings

Table 13.1 : Age Group of Scheduled Tribe Students

S.No.	Age group	No	Percentage
1.	15-17	12	4.00
2.	18-21	158	52.00
3.	22-25	107	36.00
4.	26-28	14	5.00
5.	Above 28	9	3.00
	Total	300	100.00

Thus, it is seen that majority of the students (265 or 88.33%) belong to the age group 18-25) (Table 13.1).

Sex of the Tribal Students

Out of 300 students, 219 (73 per cent) are males and 81 (27 per cent) are females. The number was selected out of the total of the male and female students undergoing higher studies in the Devi Ahilaya University (Table 13.2).

Table 13.2 : Tribe-wise Categorization of Students

Sl. No.	Name of the Tribes	Males		Females	
		No.	%	No.	%
1.	Bhilala	150	50.00	15	5.0
2.	Bhil	27	9.00	14	4.0
3.	Orang	25	8.33	9	3.0
4.	Gond	5	1.60	23	7.6
5.	Barela	10	3.30	7	2.3
6.	Other Tribes (Panika, Pardi, Pradhan)	2	1.00	12	4.0
	Total	219	73.00	81	25.9

Thus, it is found that vast majority of the tribal students belonged to Bhilala, Bhil and Orang Tribes.

Table 13.3 : Various Faculties of the Tribal Students

Sl. No.	Faculty	No	Percentage
1.	Arts	198	66.00
2.	Commerce	27	9.00
3.	Science	16	5.33
4.	Engineering	12	4.00
5.	Medicine	18	6.00
6.	Law	19	6.33
7.	Education	8	2.66
8.	Home Science	2	0.66
	Total	300	100.00

Out of 19 students in law, three are girls. Home science is for girls only. In education, out of 8.3 are boys and 5 are girls.

Arts and commerce are the faculties very popular among the scheduled tribe students of Devi Ahilya University (Table 13.3). It is interesting to note that none of the tribal students had offered English medium, education, although a good number of teachers delivered lecture in English. This, in fact was a problem of the tribal students. None of the students went for private tuitions, may be they could not afford to do so. In spite of the fact that the tribal students had their own languages/dialects, they made earnest efforts to understand the lectures given in English or Hindi (Table 13.3).

Marital Status of Tribal Students

Out of 219 boys, 14 are married; and out of 81 girls, 11 are married. Thus, vast majority of the tribal students are unmarried. There are few cases of child marriage, but, the students were not sure if they will honour it.

Type of Family of the Tribal Students

Out of 300 students, 194 belonged to joint family and 106 belonged to nuclear family. Thus, majority of the students are from joint family. Jointness of the land ownership was important for them. Hence, it is wrong to say that joint family system is not found among tribes.

Languages/Dialects used by the Tribal Students

Various language/dialects like Hindi, Nimari, Bareli, Pali, Urao, Malwi, Bhilali, Bhili, Gondi, Ratvi, Ramgari, Gujarati, Bundelkhandi, and Chhatisgarhi are used by the tribal students as shown in Table 13.4.

Table 13.4 : Languages/Dialects used by Tribal Students

Sl. No.	*Language/Dialect*	*No*	*Percentage*
1.	Nimari	74	24.66
2.	Bhilali	57	19.00
3.	Hindi	52	17.40
4.	Bareli	31	10.33
5.	Bhili	28	9.40
6.	Other Language/Dialects	58	19.33
	Total	300	100.00

In spite of their use of tribal language or dialect the students were able to understand Hindi well, and used Hindi as a Medium of instruction.

Conclusions and Suggestions

As a result of the present study, the main conclusions arrived at are mentioned below :

(1) The number of male tribal students is more than the female tribal students for higher education. The girls lag far behind.

(2) In faculties of engineering and medicine, no female student was found.

(3) In the faculty of law, there were 16 male students and 3 female students.

(4) Most of the students are of the age group 15 to 30. The highest number of the age group is 18 to 21 years.

(5) The tribal students are from various tribal groups. The highest number is from Bhilala tribe (165). Out of these 165 students, 150 are boys and 15 girls.

(6) The highest number of girls is from Gond tribe (23) some of these Gond girls follow Christian Faith.

(7) Bhilala, Bhil and Gonds are the main tribal groups from which the students come for higher education.
(8) Most of the tribal students follow Hindu religion (250 out of 300, that is 83.33 per cent).
(9) 49 students belong to Christian faith out of 300 students (16.3 per cent) among Christian girls, majority belonged to the Gond tribe.
Availability of Christian schools, hostels, and other facilities have encouraged them to be in Christian faith. Christian tribals are good in sports and games too. Sports and games help the tribals to secure good jobs too, after graduation or post-graduation.
(10) Most of the tribal students are unmarried (275) only 25 are married. Child marriage is not popular among them.
(11) Most of the tribal students (194 out of 300) belong to joint family system, which clearly shows that tribal students uphold the traditional family values.
(12) Most of the parents of tribal students are uneducated (160 fathers and 270 mothers) women lag behind in education.
(13) Most of the parents of the tribal students are agriculturists (232 out of 300). They follow traditional farming.
(14) Most of the parents belong to poor families. (224 out of 300). Their economic standard of life is poor.
(15) Most of the tribal students make use of their own language or dialect. Nimari and Bhilala are the most popular ones (74 and 57 respectively out of 300).
(16) The tribal students chose arts faculty (133 boys and 65) for higher education. They find it easy. Next favourable faculty was commerce.
(17) As for studies, 168 students out of 300 faced some difficulty in understanding the subjects in classes (134 boys and 34 girls). Some of the reasons for this are the language of the professor difficult, subject difficult, indiscipline in the class. English as the medium of teaching, and irregularity in classes. Further, the students could not get adjusted to the new atmosphere in Indore also.
(18) Very few tribal students went for tutorials. They cannot afford.
(19) Majority of the scheduled tribe students reside in hostels (285 out of 300). 216 students reside in hostels made for

scheduled tribe students. 63 students reside in college hostels. Most of the students are dissatisfied with hostel life. Some reasons for this are absence of mess, electricity, water, furnitures, etc. In any case, scholarship given by the government and hostel facilities encourage the tribals to have higher education. They resort to part time work, including labour, when scholarship amount is insufficient. Yet, the tribal students do not suffer from any inferiority complex.

(20) Most of the tribal students receive scholarship from Government (295 out of 300). 282 students said that the scholarship amount is insufficient. So, they have to obtain some amount from their homes and take loans too. Some students resort to labour too. Most students said that without scholarship from Government, they cannot study.

(21) As for occupational ambitions, most of the students said that they preferred Government jobs. Most tribal students do not want to continue their traditional habitat too. 10 students work alongwith study. 4 work as telephone operators. 4 boys work as teachers. 3 boys work as labour. Some of them are willing to work in any capacity. They have dignity of labour.

(22) 294 students are in favour of reservation in job and education.

(23) 97 out of 300 students appeared for Public Service Examinations. 33 students have appeared for IAS. They are ambitious. 53 students appeared for banking examinations.

(24) As for marriage, students who had child marriage in the traditional manner refused to adhere to the same in future.

(25) Majority of the students have expressed their desire to live in their own villages after competition studies (184 out of 300). But they are not sure about it.

Suggestions

Certain suggestions may be offered as a result of the above study:

(1) Higher education centres and hostels be provided in rural and tribal areas, so that they need not migrate to city.

(2) Adult education be provided in rural and tribal areas.
(3) Tribal students would secure jobs in their own areas.
(4) Guidance for the choice of courses of study be given to tribal students.
(5) Every educational institution of higher learning be provided special facilities for tribal students.
(6) Special coaching facilities may be given to tribal students.
(7) Feelings of discrimination or preference be get rid of so that the tribal and non-tribal students can live together in a friendly manner.

14

Educational Attitude of Tribal Students in Madhya Pradesh

K.R. Sharma

Introduction

Education is the most important element in the development of any community, particularly when it is faced with a new situation with which educationists are not familiar, particularly in tribal areas where new developmental programmes are being taken up. Ignorance is the biggest reason for weakness. Therefore, the more articulate begins to take advantage of the simple situation in the backward areas. Our developmental efforts, designed for the benefit of the more backward people, may in this situation, on the contrary, result in some kind of disadvantage. In this context, we may take any criteria, education emerges as the most important and crucial investment. The Educational Attitude Scale (EAS): The students' attitude towards education and also the purpose it serves in improving their way of life was studied by using a scale developed by investigator. The investigator was in need of a scale which could be used on the tribal pupils, as their needs, aspirations and problems are not considered very similar to those of the non-tribal students. Therefore, another scale was developed and used. *Attitude Towards Education*: Thurston (1946) defined attitude as the degree of positive or negative feeling associated with some psychological object such as any person, institution, ideal, symbol, phrase or slogan towards which people can differ with respect to positive or negative feeling. One of the easier ways to know how individuals feel about a particular psychological object is to ask them direct questions and to classify them into three groups, that is, those with favourable attitude, those with unfavourable attitude and those may be doubtful or undecided about their attitude towards the object.

Methodology

The Sample

The random sampling technique was used for drawing the sample. Out of the 380 tribal higher secondary schools, the sample was drawn from eight schools of three tribal districts, four schools each of boys and girls were selected for the study. 302 tribal and 78 non-tribal students of classes IX, X and XI were taken randomly. The teachers and the Principals of these schools were contacted and permission was sought for conducting the study. The *Tehsildar* of the concerned Tehsil, the Tribal Development Officer of the District, parents of the pupils, Gram Sewakas and local leaders were also approached for collecting the background data and other information needed for the study. The Tribal Research and Development Institute, the Director of Census Operations, the Tribal Welfare Department, and the State Gazetteer of Madhya Pradesh were also approached with the view of knowing about the welfare activities, scholarships and other plans for the tribal people.

Data Collection: Data was collected with the help of developed EAS tools (Table 14.1). The tools were administered to the students by the investigator.

Hypotheses

The study was conducted in the light of the following propositions :

(1) There will be significant difference between the tribal and non-tribal students with regard to their educational attitude; and
(2) Educational attitudes, as one of the component of education of the tribals, should significantly interact with sex and caste, caste and family size, caste and family

Table 14.1 : Number of Students selected for the Study according to Class and Sex

Class	*Tribal*			*Non-Tribal*			*Total*			*Per cent*
	Boys	*Girls*	*Total*	*Boys*	*Girls*	*Total*	*Boys*	*Girls*	*Total*	
IX	90	39	129	20	08	28	110	47	157	41.32
X	53	18	71	20	07	27	73	25	98	25.79
XI	74	39	103	08	14	22	82	43	125	32.89
Total	217	86	303	48	29	77	265	115	380	100
Per cent	57	23	80	12.60	7.40	20	70	30	100	

education and parental occupation and family income and caste.

Findings and Analysis

The Effect of Sex and Caste upon Educational Attitude

The educational attitude of three sub-groups of the sampled population—tribals (Bhil, Bhilala) and Non-tribals was analysed. The data revealed the following :

Table 14.2 : Summary of Analysis of Variance (ANOVA) showing the Effects of Sex and Caste upon Educational Attitude Test

Source	*df*	*Sum of Square*	*Mean Square*	*F*	*P*	R^2
Model	5	4166.207	833.241	3.42	0.0019*	0.050
Sex (V-1)	1	236.099	236.099	1.11	0.2921	
Caste (V-2)	2	3860.366	1930.183	9.10	0.0001*	
V1 x V2	2	69.74	34.87	0.16	0.8485	
Error	374	79334.979	212.126			
Total	379	83501.187			SD=14.56	

*P<.01

Table 14.2 indicates that F-ratio for the model is 42 which is significant at p = .0019 level. It means that sex and caste of the students have an effect on their educational attitude.

Further, analysis of variance show that F-ratio are 1.11 (for sex), 9.10 (for caste), 0.16 (for the interaction of sex and caste). As such sex does not affect (p = 2921) the educational attitude of the pupils, whereas caste has a significant effect (p = 0.0001). The effects of interaction for sex and caste are insignificant (p = .8485). It means that boys and girls of a particular caste have no effect on their educational attitudes. R^2= values indicates that sex and caste of the students influence their educational attitude to the extent of 5 per cent only.

Effects of Caste and Family Size upon Educational Attitude

Educational attitude of the three groups (Bhil, Bhilala and non-tribal) was analysed on the basis of caste and family size. The results of 2-way analyses are given in Table 14.3.

Table 14.3 : Summary of ANOVA showing the Effects of Caste and Family Size upon Educational Attitude

Source	*df*	*Sum of Square*	*Mean Square*	*F*	*P*	R^2
Model	8	4192.002	524.000	2.45	0.014*	0.050
Caste (V2)	2	3898.526	1949.263	9.12	0.0001*	
Family Size (V4)	2	94.630	47.711	0.22	0.802	
V2 × V4	4	198.845	249.711	0.23	0.920	
Error	371	79309.185	231.771			
Total	379	83501.187			SD=14.56	

*P < .01

Table 14.3 indicates that F-ratio model is 2.45 which is significant at 0.014 level. It means that caste and family size of the students affect their educational attitudes.

Further, analysis of variance shows that F-ratios are 9.12 (for caste), 0.22 (for family size), and 0.23 (for interaction of caste and family size). As such family size and interaction of caste and family size does not influence their educational attitude. The caste, however, shows significant effect (p = .0001). R^2 = value indicates that the variable of caste and family size influence their educational attitude to the extent of 5 per cent.

Effect of Caste and Family Education upon Educational Attitude of the Sampled Population

The educational attitude scores of the three groups were analysed for variance on the basis of caste and family education, the results of the 2 = way analyses are given in the Table 14.4.

Table 14.4 : Summary of ANOVA showing the Effects of Caste and Family Size upon Educational Attitude

Source	*df*	*Sum of Square*	*Mean Square*	*F*	*P*	R^2
Model	7	5468.228	781.175	3.72	0.001*	0.065
Caste (V2)	2	3998.526	1999.263	9.29	0.0001*	
Family Education (V5)	2	425.939	212.970	1.02	0.363	
V2 × V5	3	1143.763	381.254	1.82	0.142	
Error	372	78032.959	209.766			
Total	379	83501.187			SD=14.56	

*P < .01

Table 14.4 indicates that F-ratio for the model is 3.72 which is significant at 0.0001 level. It means that caste and family education of the students exercise an important influence on the pupil's educational attitude.

Further, analysis of variance shows that F-ratios are 9.29 (for caste), 1.02 (for Family education) and 1.82 (for the interaction of caste and family education). As such family education and interaction of caste and family education does not significantly affect their educational attitude (p = .142), whereas caste has a significant effect on their educational attitude. (p = 0.0001). R^2-value indicates that caste and family education of the students influence their educational attitude to the extent of 6.5 per cent.

Effects of Caste and Parental Occupation upon Educational Attitude

The educational attitude of the three groups was analysed on the basis of caste and parental occupation. The result of the 2-way analyses are given in Table 14.5.

Table 14.5 indicates that the F-ratio for the model is 2.40 which is significant at 0.007 level. It means that caste and parental occupation do affect their educational attitude.

Further, analysis of variance shows that F-ratios are 9.21 (for caste), 1.00 (for parental occupation) and 0.84 (for the interaction of caste and parental occupation). As such caste has a significant effect upon the educational attitude (P = 0.0001). Whereas parental occupation (p = .394) and interaction with the caste and parental

Table 14.5 : Summary of ANOVA showing the Effects of Caste and Parental Occupation upon Educational Attitude

Source	df	Sum of Square	Mean Square	F	P	R^2
Model	11	5598.163	508.924	2.40	0.007*	0.067
Caste (V2)	2	3898.526	1949.082	9.21	0.0001*	
Parental Occupation (V6)	3	634.901	211.634	1.00	0.394	
V2 x V6	6	1064.736	717.561	0.84	0.540	
Error	368	77903.024	211.693			
Total	379	83501.187			SD=14.56	

*P < .01

occupation (p = .540) does not affect the educational attitude. R^2-value indicates that caste and parental occupation of the students influence the educational attitude of the pupils to the extent of 6.7 per cent.

Effect of Caste and Family Income upon Educational Attitude

The educational attitude scores of the three groups were analysed for variance on the basis of caste and family income. The results of the 2-way analyses are given in Table 14.6.

Table 14.6 : Summary of ANOVA showing the Effects of Caste and Family Income upon Educational Attitude

Source	*df*	*Sum of Square*	*Mean Square*	*F*	*P*	*R^2*
Model	15	8824.163	588.277	2.87	0.0003*	0.106
Caste (V2)	2	3898.526	1949.263	9.50	0.0001*	
Family Income (V7)	5	1017.587	203.517	0.90	0.4321	
V2 × V7	8	3908.050	488.506	2.38	0.0164	
Error	364	74677.024	205.157			
Total	379	83501.187			SD=14.32	

*P < .01

Table 14.6 indicates that the F-ratio for the model is 2.87 which is significant at 0.0003 level. It means that caste and family income of the pupils do affect their educational attitude.

Further, analysis of variance shows that F-ratios are 9.50 (for caste), 0.99 (for family income), and 2.38 (for the interaction of caste and family income). As such caste significantly affects the educational attitude of the students at 0.0001 level. The family income and interaction with caste does not affect the educational attitude of the pupils. R^2-value indicates that caste and family income of the students influence the educational attitude of the pupils to the extent of 10.6 per cent.

Resume of Findings of ANOVA in respect of Students' Educational Attitude

Table 14.7 indicates that all the social class variables namely, sex, family size, family education and parental income and occupation

Table 14.7 : Resume of Findings in Respect of Educational Attitude

Value	Sex and Caste	Caste and Family Size	Caste and Family Education	Caste and Parental Occupation	Caste and Parental Income
F	3.93	2.45	3.72	2.40	2.87
df	5/374	8/371	7/372	11/368	15/364
p	0.0019*	0.014*	0.001*	0.007*	0.0003*

*P < .01

exercise a powerful influence in developing favourable educational attitude among the pupils. These variables play an important role in the development of attitude towards education both among tribal and non-tribal students. The educational attitude scores show that there is not much difference between the tribal and non-tribal students. Hence, Hypothesis 1 is not retained. Hypothesis 2 is accepted. These prove that educational attitude of the tribal students is an important factor in determining the education of the tribal students and it also interacts with various independent variables, that is, sex, caste, family size, family education, parental occupation and family income.

15

Reasons for Increase in Dropout Rate among the Scheduled Tribe Students at Primary Schools

R.S. Shrivastava

Introduction

One-eighth population of the country and one-fifth population of the State belongs to the Scheduled Tribes. In Madhya Pradesh, the Scheduled Tribes, Scheduled Castes and Other Backward Classes form 20.27 per cent, 15.17 per cent and about 50 per cent of the total population of the State, respectively. The nomadic, semi-nomadic, Denotified Groups and people in unclean occupations have been recognized separately. The total population of the Scheduled Tribes in the State is 1.23 crore, 1.15 crore living in Rural Areas and 0.08 crore in Urban Areas. The total number of Households of the STs is 22.78 lakh, 2.16 lakh in rural areas and 0.16 lakh in Urban Areas.

The predominant tribal pockets are either in the middle of the State or in the western side. The Scheduled Tribes are otherwise dispersed in the whole of the State. The tribals in the middle of the State occupy areas having rich natural resources both on the ground and underground. But those who live in the western side of the State have poor natural resources depleting further with the passage of time. Facing very tough living conditions, they have managed since times immemorial their distinctive tribal identity. These people have more or less a self-sufficient economy, cut off from the mainstream, very hard work including periodical migrations with the family in search of employment, always overburdened with the indebtedness and caught tightly in the clutches of the moneylenders.

The Problem

While quoting the survey done by IPMS in 2006-07, the Rajya Shiksha Kendra in its Annual Work Plan and Budget 2007-08 (pp. 23) have mentioned that 42 per cent ST boys, and 45 per cent ST Girls, total 43.5 per cent in the age-group of 5 to 14 years are out of school. Out of school children include the dropouts also. Separate figures in respect of STs for dropouts have not been given. These figures are higher than the SCs among whom the comparative figures are 17.7 per cent boys, 16.3 per cent girls and 17.0 per cent total. Nine reasons have been enumerated for Out of School Children in all the categories. Out of School Children are highest amongst the Scheduled Tribes as compared to all the social categories as shown below (Table 15.1):

Table 15.1 : Percentage of Out of School Children

Age Group	%SC			%ST			%CWSN		
	Boys	*Girls*	*Total*	*Boys*	*Girls*	*Total*	*Boys*	*Girls*	*Total*
Total 5-14 yrs	17.7	16.3	17.0	42.0	45.0	43.5	8.1	5.7	6.9

Source: IPMS Information Planning and Management Service.

The reasons given for out of school children and their percentages are given in Table 15.2 :

The reasons have been given in general and not specific for the Scheduled Tribes which needs to be studied.

However, this situation is when a number of schemes are being run for the education of the Scheduled Tribes. The schemes worth mentioning are :

Availability of access to primary schools was improved through Madhya Pradesh Education Guarantee Scheme (EGS), launched in January 1997. This scheme acknowledged the necessity for making a primary school available to all the habitations (*majras, tolas,* or *phalias*) of a village. In addition, the Government has followed a liberal policy for private schools allowing opening of a

Table 15.2 : Reasons for being Out of School

Reason Number	*Reasons*	*%Out of School Children*
1.	Working in field, agricultural labour or other labour work	19.1
2.	Sibling care	15.9
3.	Cattle grazing	15.1
4.	Weak financial condition	13.3
5.	Lack of educational facilities (MS)	8.9
6.	Social beliefs due to which parents are reluctant to educate children	5.8
7.	Handicapped or prolonged illness	6.4
8.	School environment not conducive	2.3
9.	Migration	13.2
	Total	100.0

primary school just by an affidavit. A network for improving the quality of academic inputs through ensuring a suitable Pupil and Teacher Ratio (PTR), a suitable review of the curriculum of primary level in 1994, a comprehensive programme of teachers' education and learner evaluation.

It is on these foundations that the Government of Madhya Pradesh highlighted their resolve in the field of education as a part of the "policy thrust for economic development of Madhya Pradesh" a policy document of the Government issued in 2001. The document said "the Government was committed to universalisation of primary education and proposed to continue the employment guarantee scheme. The process of establishing middle schools at 3 km from every habitation was to cover the entire State. Similarly, a high school/higher secondary school was to be established within a distance of 5 km of habitations." The Government also planned to establish schools of excellence in all the districts. In the field of higher education, Bhopal was being envisioned as a "University", i.e., a city of universities of various kinds. In addition to the institutions run by the Education Department the Tribal Welfare Department also is running the following institutions to boost the educational activities among the STs :

1. Junior Primary/Primary Schools	12,643
2. Middle Schools	4,369
3. High School	585

4. Higher Secondary Schools	483
5. Model Higher Secondary Schools	04
6. Girls Educational Campus	02
7. Games Campus	16
8. Eklavya Model Residential Schools	12

In 19 Tribal Districts, Excellent Schools have been established. At 30 Block Headquarters also Excellent Schools have been opened.

State Scholarship is provided at the following rates to the children of our target groups, i.e., 5-14 years :

	Scheduled Tribes	
Class	*Boys*	*Girls*
1-5	150 (PTG)	150

Cash Incentives for Girls' Education

Those girls who pass V, VIII and X Board Examination are given cash incentives of Rs. 500, Rs. 1,000, and Rs. 2000 respectively. Those girls who take admission in Class IX are provided with cycle.

Special Scholarship to the Primitive Tribal Groups

Special scholarship is admissible to the Boys of the Special Primitive Tribal Groups. Bharia, Baiga and Saharia at the rate of Rs. 15 per month for 10 months, i.e., Rs. 150.

Free Uniform to Girls

Under Sarva Shiksha Abhiyan in those Blocks in which the percentage of literacy of females is less than 10 per cent free uniforms are provided to girls studying in Class I-VIII. In 268 such Blocks the uniforms to girls have been provided by the Rajya Shiksha Kendra and in remaining 45 Blocks by the Tribal Welfare Department to 1.31 lakh girls.

Residential Institutions

Residential institutions have been opened under Tribal and Scheduled Caste Development as given in Table 15.3 :

Table 15.3 : Hostel Facility for Tribal Boys and Girls

Sl. No.	Type of Institutions	Boys		Girls		Total	
		No.	Sanctioned Seats	No.	Sanctioned Seats	No.	Sanctioned Seats
(1)	(2)	(3)	(4)	(5)	(6)	(7)	(8)
1.	Pre Matric Hostels	969	30709	223	9365	1192	40074
2.	Post Matric Hostels	55	3305	38	1910	93	5215
3.	Ashram Schools	461	24315	403	23855	864	48170

Boys taking admission in Hostels and *Ashrams* are paid stipend at the rate of Rs. 350 per boy while girls taking admissions in Hostels and *ashrams* are stipend at the rate of Rs. 360 per girl.

Mid-Day Meals (MDM) programme is also being run. In *Anganwadis,* also besides supplementary nutrition, health care and pre-school education are also given to children in age-group 0-6. The presence of pregnant and nursing mothers by way of care and protection provided to them in the *Anganwadis* also attract the children. The norms for opening *Anganwadis* have been lowered down to 150 population as compared to the children which is on the population of 700. Out of 69,238 *Anganwadis* 3,363 *Anganwadis* which is 4.85 per cent are running for the tribal children.

Early Education and Care Centres are also being run under the SSA and NPEGL.

However, it is little disturbing that, in spite of all these efforts Ministry of Human Resource Development, Government of India fact-sheet laying down the Educational Development Index (EDI) based on the effectiveness of action translating the goal of education for all (EFA) still lists Madhya Pradesh as one of the States where the EDI is less than ten. It means that, still there are critical gaps in the school education sector which need to be addressed adequately. The fact sheet reveals that the top seven States accounting for the most "out of school children" are Bihar, U.P., West Bengal, Madhya Pradesh, Rajasthan, Arunachal Pradesh and Jharkhand. It further reveals that "these school children are from socially marginalized groups, specially girls, working children, children of very poor families, children with special needs and children with multiple disadvantages." (based on EDI fact-sheet issued by Union Ministry of Human Resource Development—as reported in the *Pioneer*, 13th February, 2006.

Literacy

Percentage of literacy in all the communities of Madhya Pradesh has gone up from 22.14 per cent in 1971 to 44.20 per cent in 1991, i.e., it has nearly doubled while among Scheduled Tribes it has risen from 7.62 per cent to 20.54 per cent showing nearly three times increase during the same period. But if the literacy percentage of 1981 to 1991 is compared it is observed that among all communities the increase is only by 16.33 per cent as compared to 10.86 per cent among tribals. It shows that both in absolute and relative terms the growth of literacy among Scheduled Tribes is slower than all communities during 1981-1991 decade. But during 1991-2001 the situation has changed a lot as shown in Table 15.4.

Table 15.4 : Decadal Increase in Literacy (Percentage) during 1961-2001

Year	General			Scheduled Tribe		
	Total	Male	Female	Total	Male	Female
1961	17.13	27.03	06.73	05.10	09.52	00.97
1971	22.24	32.70	10.92	07.62	13.05	02.18
(% of growth)	29.83	20.98	62.28	49.41	37.08	124.74
1981	27.87	34.49	15.58	10.68	17.74	03.60
(% of growth)	25.31	05.47	42.67	40.16	35.94	65.14
1991*	44.20	58.42	28.85	21.54	32.16	10.73
(% of growth)	58.59	69.38	85.17	101.69	81.29	198.06
2001**	64.11	76.80	50.28	32.30	42.10	22.03
(% of growth)	45.05	31.46	74.28	—	—	—

*Undivided Madhya Pradesh.
** Divided Madhya Pradesh.

A comparative picture of growth in literacy in general population as compared to the Scheduled Tribe population has been shown in the Table 15.4 from the year 1961-2001. The comparison of growth in literacy in general population to Scheduled Tribe population during the last forty years shows that the growth of literacy among Scheduled Tribes has been more as compared to the growth of literacy amongst general population.

In respect of female literacy among the Scheduled Tribes, in the decade of 1961-1971, the growth has been 124.74 per cent as compared to 62.28 per cent among the general female literacy. Similarly, in the decade of 1971-1981, the growth of female literacy among the Scheduled Tribes is 65.14 per cent, while in general female literacy it is 42.67 per cent. The growth of female literacy in Scheduled Tribes is quite high during the decade of 1981-1991, as it is 198.06 per cent as compared to general female literacy of 85.17 per cent.

In the context of districts, only one district Jhabua has literacy rate below 20.00 per cent. There are 10 districts namely, Bhind (41.80%), Ujjain (43.90%), Shajapur (47.70%), Bhopal (47.80%), Raisen (42.40%), Jabalpur (42.70%), Dindori (40.90%), Mandla (42.10%), Seoni (43.50%) and Balaghat (44.40%) with literacy rate between 40.0 per cent and 50.0 per cent. There is only one district namely Narsinghpur having literacy rate above 50.0 per cent (52.80%).

The distribution of districts by literacy percentage is given in Table 15.5.

Table 15.5 : Distribution of Districts by Percentage among the Scheduled Tribes

Sl. No.	*Literacy Percentage Range*	*No. of Districts*
1.	Below 20.0	01
2.	20.0 to 25.0	05
3.	25.0 to 30.0	12
4.	30.0 to 35.0	09
5.	35.0 to 40.0	07
6.	Above 40.0	11
	Total	45

Tribal Areas of the State have been divided into four Zones viz. Western, Central, North Eastern, and North.

The analysis of Scheduled Tribe population vis-à-vis literacy reveals that:

The zone-wise population vis-à-vis literacy ratio shows that it is higher in the Central Zone and lowest in Northern Zone. Zone-wise Scheduled Tribe population and literacy ratio is given in the Table 15.6.

Table 15.6 : Zone-wise Scheduled Tribes Population vis-à-vis Literacy Ratio

Sl. No.	*Zone*	*Sch. Tribe pop. Vis-à-vis literacy ratio*
1.	Western	79:21
2.	Central	72:28
3.	North-Eastern	76:24
4.	Northern	81:19

Within the zones, the district wise vis-à-vis literacy rate reveals that:

(a) In the North-Eastern Zone, literacy percentage is more than the State average literacy ratio (32.30%) in the districts where population is more than 40.0 per cent

(b) In the Northern Zone the situation is that districts having Scheduled Tribe population below 20.0 per cent, have a literacy percentage more than the State average except Gwalior in which the Scheduled Tribe population is 3.50 per cent while literacy is 28.20 per cent.

(c) In the Central Zone, the literacy percentage in almost all the 17 districts is more than the State average irrespective of population except in Harda (29.10%), Sagar (30.10%) and Vidisha (22.70%).

(d) In the Western Zone, the literacy percentage is more than State average in districts having low population except Neemuch. It is below the State average in districts with very high Scheduled Tribe population.

Under the Constitution of India, the State governments have been given the responsibility to provide free and compulsory education at the elementary level to all children of school going age. Education as an expression of human development is seen to have both intrinsic and instrumental value. The Tenth Five Year Plan 2002-07 of India records—"performance in the field of education is one of the most disappointing aspects of India's development strategy. Out of approximately 200 million children in the age group of 6-14 years only 120 million are in schools and net attendance in the primary level is only 66 per cent of enrolment."[1] The Tenth Plan further emphasizes the need for "education for all" as one of the primary objectives of the Tenth Plan with a prescription to pass over "control over schools and teachers to local bodies, which have a direct interest in teacher performance" and "implementation of 73rd and 74th Amendments of the Constitution, which facilitate the transfer of management of primary and upper primary schools to Panchayats/local bodies."[2]

Remedial Measures

The reasons for dropouts have been given above. The remedial measures could be :

1. Attendance in the Anganwadis could be increased. The spread of Anganwadis have increased and it has universal coverage. The siblings should be sent to the Anganwadis to free the children specially girls to attend the schools. The Anganwadis look after not only the educational needs of the children but also the health needs and provide recreative and healthy atmosphere to the children. The pregnant and lactating mothers also get nutritious food.
2. Effective implementation of MGANREGA (Mahatma Gandhi National Rural Employment Guarantee Act) will provide sufficient income to the people and children may not have to work for earning and go to the grazing, etc. They thus will be able to attend the school. As work will be available in the village and its surroundings itself, it will curb the migration which takes place in search of employment and deters children from going to school.
3. The Panchayati Raj especially known as PESA (Panchayati Raj Extension to Scheduled Areas) has been set up in every village. The responsibility of Panchayati Raj is for providing education to children and specially girls. In so far as providing infrastructure in schools specially toilets etc. for girls the Panchayats could effectively look after it as they have sufficient funds for it. The Panchayats could also tackle the problem of absentee teachers by providing residential facilities on the village itself and imposing strict discipline on teachers in looking after the schools in every respect.

4. The Parents Teachers Association has been formed in each village with the primary objective of providing necessary help and assistance from the villagers in ensuring cent per cent attendance of children, effective implementation of mid-day meals programme and ensuring strict discipline in educational matters in respect of teachers. It has been observed that frequent meetings of parents and teachers do not take place and, therefore, the problems connected with schools do not come up. Periodical meetings of parents and teachers will definitely bring the problems of schools to two important stakeholders of education, i.e., parents and teachers.
5. In so far as handicap and prolonged illness is concerned efficient health facilities through *Anganwadis* could be provided to the handicapped and sick children. A good amount of educational facilities exist for handicapped children which could be provided to them.

As has been discussed above education, especially tribal education, both boys and girls have shown better results as compared to general population. It the bottlenecks coming in the way of education are removed as suggested, the education of the tribal people will definitely improve to a greater extent. A good cooperation and cohesion is required among the departments namely School Education, Mahila and Baal Vikas (Anganwadis and Mid-Day Meals) and Panchayati Raj specially PESA (Panchayati Raj Extension to Scheduled Areas).

NOTES

1. Tenth Five Year Plan 2002-07, Vol. I, Dimensions and strategies para 1.72.
2. *Ibid.*, para 1.73.

16

Tribes and their Education with reference to Madhya Pradesh and Chhattisgarh : An Appraisal

V.K. Shrivastava

Introduction

Man is known from history. The history of man begins in social groups. Even in Vedic age the tribe has been known by various names—*'Adivasi', 'Vanvasi and Janjati'*, etc. During the span of time, gradually these communities started displaying their distinct characteristics and got separated from the main society by the rulers of time. Undoubtedly considerable differentiation can be perceived among the tribal people with reference to differential rates of spread of education, urbanization, intensity of outside contact, access to productive resources, life style and so on. But as the outcome of common experiences of disposition from age old rights of access to control and management of resources, marginalization of significant spheres of decisions in the process, intended or unintended assault on deeper structure of their culture and history. 'Tribal people are emerging as a unified social category'. According to Burman (1996) right from pre-colonial to post-independence period these tribal communities have passed through three stages of development, i.e., isolation, assimilation and integration. Still they have yet not, themselves found in the Indian mainstream of life. They have dispersed all over the country, not only speak different languages, they also differ from one another in race, language, socio-economic and cultural patterns.

Thus, these tribal communities belong to different ethno lingual groups and profess diverse faiths and occupy about 15 per cent of the area of the country in various ecological and geo-climate conditions ranging from plain to forests, hilly and inaccessible areas. They are at different stages of social, economical and educational development.

As regards the identity of tribes, no scientific definition has been evolved to define tribe. Article 366(25) of the Constitution of India refers Tribes as those communities, who are scheduled in accordance with Article 342 of the Constitution. This Article says that only those communities who have been declared as such by the President through an initial public notification or through a subsequent amending Act of Parliament will be considered to be Scheduled Tribes. The tribal population of the country, as per the 2001 census, is 8.43 crore, constituting 8.2 per cent of the total population. The population of tribes had grown at the growth rate of 24.45 per cent during the period 1991-2001. More than half of the Scheduled Tribe population is concentrated in the States of Madhya Pradesh, Chhattisgarh, Maharashtra, Orissa, Jharkhand and Gujarat. As per annual administrative report 2007-08 of Ministry of Tribal Affairs, Goverment of India, there are 700 Scheduled Tribes notified under Article 342 of the Constitution of India.

The present States of Madhya Pradesh and Chhattisgarh have about 20.3 per cent and 31.76 per cent Scheduled Tribe population of their total State population (2001) occupying about 30.19 per cent and 65.12 per cent geographical area of the respective States. About 34.14 per cent and 19.31 per cent Scheduled Tribes population fall under the category of 'Dispersed Tribe' (Living outside of Schedule/ TSP Area) in Madhya Pradesh and Chhattisgarh States respectively. Total Scheduled Tribe population of Madhya Pradesh and Chhattisgarh is 42.5 per cent of total population of Central India.

The tribes of Madhya Pradesh and Chhattisgarh States are not ethnically a unit on the basis of physiographic conditions and distribution, tribes living in different parts of both the States form a large central tribal belt depicting mosaic picture, consisting variety of culture. Thus, the tribal areas of Madhya Pradesh and Chhattisgarh can be divided into five cultural Zones/Regions, viz., western, central, north-eastern and southern. The dialect of these tribal communities have also regional variations, only in Bastar,

Datewada and Bilaspur districts of Chhatisgarh State five dialects viz., Halbi, Madi, Bhateri, Dorli and Parji are spoken. In other regions of both the States Bhili, Korku, Kurakh, Gondi, Koli and Mundari are spoken.

According to the present level of the socio-economic development, the tribes of both the States fall in three broad categories—Developed tribes, Developing tribes; and most backward-primitive tribal groups (PTGs)—poor than average tribal group like, Sahariya, Kol, Paharikorwa, Abujhmaria, Baiga, Kamar, Birhor, Bhinjhwar, Dhangar, Bjujia, Pando and Dorla and Bharias.

Tribal Education

The tribal scenario of India and the tribes living in Central India, particularly of Madhya Pradesh and Chhattisgarh reveals that education has hardly been a subject of importance for the tribals. During the British rule in India, no serious thinking was given for the education and for that matter even social and economic development for the tribal. As per 1931 Census, the percentage of literacy amongst the tribals was as low as 0.7 compared to the general literacy rate of 8.3, corresponding figures of literacy among the tribal women being 0.2 per cent only as compared to the general female literacy rate 2.3 per cent. The percentage of literacy amongst the tribals of the Central Province (C.P.) and Barar (Present Madhya Pradesh including Chhattisgarh) was only 0.5 and for female literacy it was negligible. Because the educational grants for the tribal areas were meagre with the result the number of high schools, middle schools and primary schools were of course, negligible, if not all together zero. The British Government had appointed an officer on special duty Mr. M.V. Grigson[1] in 1940 in the then Central Provinces and Berar to investigate the conditions of tribals. He made some useful suggestions, viz., opening of schools, hostels, mid day meals and grant of scholarships and stipends, but nothing could be done.

After independence during all Five Year Plans, education in general and tribal education in particular has been the priority of the Central as well as the State governments. The Constitution of India through Article 45 has laid down 'Free and compulsory education for all children upto age of 14 years' as of the Directive Principles of State Policy. The time frame for achieving this goal was mentioned in the Constitution as ten years (i.e., by 1960). Further, the Article 46 particularly lays emphasis for the promotion of educational and economic interest of Scheduled Tribes. Unfortunately, still we are relatively far away from reaching this goal.

For the first time the National Education Policy (NEP) was framed in 1968, which marked significant step in the history of education in post-independence India. This policy was framed taking into consideration important aspects which had been examined in depth by Commissions and Committees over a long period, both before and after independence, culminating in the Education Commission (1964-65). "The policy of 1968 aimed at promoting national progress creating a sense of common citizenship and culture and strengthing national integration. It laid down stress on the need for a radical reconstruction of education to improve its quality at all stages, much greater attention to science and technology, cultivation of moral values and a closer relation between education and the life of the people."

The 1968 National Policy on Education had recommended to review every five years of progress made in its implementation. But such reviews were not made till 1985. The new National Policy of Education was again framed in April 1986. For the first time this National Education Policy (NEP) laid emphasis on educational improvement of Scheduled Tribes. This accorded the following :

(i) Opening of Primary Schools in tribal areas;
(ii) Imparting educational training to educated Scheduled Tribe people;
(iii) Tribal youth to take up teaching;
(iv) Promoting residential schools;
(v) Introducing incentive schemes;
(vi) Opening of non-formal educational centres; and
(vii) Curricular for tribal students at all stages of education to create awareness.

The NEP was again reviewed and revised in 1992 laying educational development of Scheduled Tribes and their equalization with the non-SCs. Besides, this has envisaged wide ranging action on a variety of issues and problems, yet it has sought a convergence of such action to secure a total and coordinated impact. It has also reached beyond the education sector to link effectively with other sectors of social development to achieve quick and positive results. But the task of ensuring the effective implementation of the NEP rested on the following factors:

(i) Effective education planning and management system;
(ii) Effective decentralization;
(iii) To evolve priorities and pursue objective oriented programmes;
(iv) Sound personnel management system; and
(v) Performance of routing task, i.e., supply of text books, conduction of examinations and delivery of educational services, etc.

The NPEP suggested that education needed to be managed in an atmosphere of utmost rigour, seriousness of purpose and at the same time of freedom essential for innovation and creativity. NPE also suggested the following strategies :

(i) A better deal to teachers with greater responsibility;
(ii) Provision of improved student services and insistence of observance of acceptable norms of behaviour; and
(iii) Provision of better facilities, institutions and creation of a system of performance appraisal of institutions according to the standards and norms set at the national or State level.

Soon after adoption of Programme of Action (POA) 1986, the Central Advisory Board of Education (CABE) had constituted Committees to recommend measures for toning up educational management, these committees prepared draft report for pursuing action with the States and other authorities concerned. However, due to frequent political changes, action could not be pursued on many of these initiatives.

However, in pursuance of this policy and based on the report of a Committee appointed by the Human Resource Development (HRD) Ministry, GoI in 1990 and the recommendations of the CABE, minimum level of learning (MLL) have been laid down for the primary stage with the intention of reducing the curriculum load and making it more relevant and functional for those children who have not support for learning at home or outside the schools, who are not likely to avail the opportunity of education beyond this stage and who must learn here what is required to sustain them throughout their lives and enable them to function in their world as socially useful and contributing individuals. Another important development was the World Conference on Education For ALL (EFA) held in March 1990 in Jomtien, Thailand. The conference was organized by UNESCO, United Nations system and several donor agencies. The conference adopted a declaration calling upon all member-states and international agencies to take effective steps for achieving Education for All (EFA) by the year 2000. The conference advocated a holistic concept of basic education in lieu of a sectoral approach segregating section like primary schooling, Non-Formal Education, and continuing education in separate compartments. In order to harness increased donor interest in the basic education, as a result of the conference, it was decided to formulate comprehensive basic education project in educationally backward States. The framework for availing external assistance for basic education was involved at the 46th meeting of the CABE held on 8-9 March, 1991 and reiterated in the 47th meeting of the CABE held on 6th May, 1992.

Under the Tribal Sub Plan (TSP) strategy adopted at the eve of Fifth Five Year Plan (1975), the tribal educational plan and the literacy campaign have been geared up, and while implementing the NEP, the objective of universalisation of education has been accepted as the national goal, and since Fifth Five Year Plan the target for each tribal Sub-Plan has been fixed under three broad parameters—universal access, universal retention and universal achievement.

Besides, a national policy for Scheduled Tribes (Draft) has also been formulated by the Ministry of Tribal Affairs, Government of India in the year 2006, laying focus to boost tribal education and literacy, aiming to increase tribal literacy growth 30 per cent per annum.

The Appraisal

While doing the appraisal, it is inevitable first to analyze and highlight those factors, situation and the process acquired, which directly or indirectly posed constraints/hazards in implementation of educational programmes and ultimately to promote the literacy among the Scheduled Tribes. In brief this could be seen as given below:

1. Prevailing of negative attitude towards the Scheduled Tribes that access to education and attain literacy is for upper stratum of the society right from beginning. It is seen that during the first-four decades there have been great changes in the relationship between the dominant groups who are often oppressors and the weaker group specifically the tribals and these changes have their repercussions on the literacy programmes for the oppressed.
2. Type of policy adopted towards the tribal communities in the past three distinct policies, viz., policy of isolation during the period of pre-independence and of assimilation and integration during post-independence and these have marked three state of development in their relation. In broad terms, the development of dominant oppressed group (tribal) relation has followed the following pattern:[4]
   (a) The establishment of dominance;
   (b) The maintenance of dominance; and
   (c) The decline of dominance—this could not be considered as a complete decline of dominance which, however, exists in more subtle forms.
3. Wrong approach of academicians by propounding the theories explaining the cause of poor literacy amongst the tribal people and they are :
   (a) *Native Endorsement Theory*: It explains that ethnic minority and the oppressed learners are genetically inferior;
   (b) *The Deficit or Cultural Deprivation Theory:* It explains that the oppressed (S.T.) has been attributed to their environment, i.e., the home, the social and ethnic structure to which they belong; and
   (c) *The Institutional Deficit Theory*: It blames on the institution rather than culture or the environment of the oppressed.
4. 'No literacy is better than wrong literacy'. Since the tribal area is vast and regional variation is wide to cover under the literacy programmes a well planned and effective implementation of educational programme is different. As a result, the literacy programme is failed to produce

desired results and much of money and energy go waste. Besides, the following factors have also posed constraints:

(a) *Narrow View of Literacy*: It is often confined to only acquiring the basic skills of language. At times its scope is still further narrowed to only learning how to write one's own name. This failed to empower the illiterate as it does not help them develop the awareness of their positive strength and the strength of their environment;

(b) *Dominant Culture Bias*: The literacy Programme are biased in favour of dominant culture, because the machinery involved in planning and execution of these programmes has been from the non-tribal dominant group of persons; and

(c) *Reinforcement of Negative Stereotypes*: It has been found that the literature published by the State Resource Centres (SRC), National Literacy Programme reinforce the negative stereotypes of women as subservient to men and establish their traditional role as housewives and nurturers. Similarly, the literacy primers for the tribal adult learners, instead of developing in them love for their people and culture help reinforce the non-tribal negative stereotypes of them.

5. The materials required for literacy programmes to be used in the tribal areas is very important. The irony of the situation is that all kinds of materials, viz., print, audio and video are not prepared keeping in view the needs of tribals and the regional variations of the tribal areas. Actually as a matter of fact one form of the material should support the other and all three kinds should from a package. There is need to decide in which order and combination these materials are to be used. It may depend on the target group; good to begin with audio and video materials and then to print. Besides, while preparing the teaching materials, the attention is not given and efforts are not made on the following factual sides/areas:

(a) The theme, language style and the format of materials needed to be carefully seen. The theme should be close to the experience and the environment of the target group and should be free from cultural bias, and

(b) The existing tribal oral literature such as, oral narratives, folktales, proverbs, riddles, etc., can be analysed and based on the analysis, reading materials can be prepared for tribal learners using some of the oral features of their literature.

6. Poor teaching method adopted while teaching in the class room. As a matter of fact the teaching method also used to be adopted to the culture of the target group. Culture has great influence on learning. Method of teaching such as, recitation, loud reading, memorization, cooperative and situational learning, poor learning which suit their oral culture are likely to be more effective. There is, therefore, need for research to identify some of the indigenous tribal methods of teaching/learning existing in tribal oral cultures and to develop them for use in formal classrooms to teach tribal learners.
7. The management of the literacy programmes create problems. As a great number of agencies of different kind and nature are involved, there is need to coordinate their activities to avoid duplication and wastage. Particularly, there is need to develop cooperation and understanding between government and the voluntary organization involved in implementation of literacy programmes for the tribals.
8. Poor literacy campaign—The National Literacy Mission (NLM) is intended to be a societal mission for bringing about qualitative changes and improvement by mobilizing the various cross-sections of society. The NLM has not achieved its target yet, specially in the tribal areas. The principal aim of National Programme of Adult Education (NPAE) is to provide education including literacy to the population in 15-35 age group. Within a policy context it is appropriate to compose schooling to children with adult literacy campaign which essentially means night schools devoted to attainment of literacy in vernacular. The object of any literacy campaign should accordingly be taken to send illiterate children to primary school alongwith imparting functional literacy to the higher age groups through short-term course. The latter in fact should have an impact on the former because of the new environment of community participation.

9. There is gender bias. The need and effort required for female literacy are all the more compelling. It is said that of all the disparities, none is of greater impediment to progress than that based on gender. In formulating women's literacy campaigns, a basic question pertains to whether the traditional values should be eroded or retained?
10. Lack of understanding of the basic requisites of tribal literacy. As regards the tribals, many of them have long abandoned their own mother-tongues and have taken to local dialect. In such cases, the literacy drives for tribals do not encounter any language problem. However, tribals who have retained their own language that are incomprehensible to others, literacy programme entail for them the additional burden of learning the local language which are usually the medium of instruction for such programme. It would be seen prudent to prepare literacy manuals in the local tribal's language in that, language difficulties constitute a cognizable hindrance to the trainees progress, cultural programmes—both musical and histrionic performed by tribal groups in their own language do help bolster awareness and appreciation of literacy campaigns amongst them. Moreover, in formulating the content of tribal literacy programmes, it is of utmost importance to stress the human values inherent in tribal culture (Sarkar, 1994).
11. *Lack of Motivation*: Motivating the learners for demand for literacy is probably the most overriding issue regarding literacy drives for the tribal communities. As generally said there are two vital obstacles in this sphere—one originating from below and other from above. The latest campaign approach to literacy even based on an earnest, intensive and multifaceted environment building programmes, would not succeed in the absence of a deficit demand for literacy. The problem essentially is not one of lack of opportunities and information but of the willingness of the tribal people[7]. So the toughest job in the earlier literacy effort among the tribals, is to provide adequate motivation to illiterate mass. The urge to learn or reach has to emerge from within as there are no material rewards or incentive except those of appreciation and

respect from the community and a feeling of self fulfilment (Batna and Lokesh, 1998).

12. The other constraints/problems against literacy drives for the tribal are important and numerous. The delivery mechanism becomes ineffective owing to inability to find for literacy projects enough voluntary instructors with reasonable education, training and competence, a sense of dedication and commitments. As regards the 'role and participation of voluntary organization' in promoting the literacy programmes in the tribal areas, it is limited and the number of whole time workers insufficient. The another issue is the community participation' through Panchayats which is central component of decentralized approach to eradication of illiteracy. The problem once again lies in the power structure in the tribal areas. In many places the Panchayats are now entrusted with the implementation of illiteracy eradication programme, but there is a clear antithesis of this with those popular institutions also being dominated by the entrenched rural elite and by class and political bias. So, it indeed is a grim irony that with few notable exceptions the Panchayats have become centres of power struggle rather than genuinely caring and sensitive to the need of the tribal communities. Further, it is also experienced and observed that during Post-Literacy Campaign (PLC) the level of literacy achieved by illiterate adults is at best fragile. It is generally feared that many non-literate would relapse into illiteracy if they were not put immediately through a meaningful post-literacy programme.

The constraints discussed above have played dismal role directly or indirectly in presenting the literacy scenario of the tribals in the tribal areas of the States of the country. The fate of the weakest of the weak (tribal) continues to be deplorable and pathetic even after six decades of independence.

Educational Status of Tribes

Literacy

The literacy rate for the total population in India has increased from 52.21 per cent to 64.84 per cent during the period from 1991 to 2001 whereas the literacy rate among the Scheduled Tribes has increased from 29.60 per cent to 47.10 per cent. Among ST males, literacy increased from 40.65 per cent to 59.17 per cent and among ST females, literacy increased from 18.19 per cent to 34.76 per cent during the same period. The ST female literacy is lower by approximately 21 percentage point as compared to the overall female literacy of the general population. However, the increase in total as well as female literacy among STs is significant.

Literacy rate has increased from 8.53 per cent in 1961 to 47.10 per cent in 2001 for STs while the corresponding increase for total population was from 28.30 per cent in 1961 to 64.84 per cent in 2001. The details are given in Table 16.1.

Table 16.1 : Literacy among STs and all Social Groups (%)

Year	*STs*			*All Social Groups*		
	Male	*Female*	*Total*	*Male*	*Female*	*Total*
1961	13.83	3.16	8.53	40.40	15.35	28.30
1971	17.63	4.85	11.30	45.93	21.97	34.45
1981	24.52	8.04	16.35	56.38	29.76	43.57
1991	40.65	18.19	29.60	64.13	39.29	25.21
2001	59.17	34.76	47.10	75.26	53.67	64.84

Source: Registrar General of India.

It is also clear from the above Table 16.1 that—

(1) Despite growth of literacy rate of Scheduled Tribes, the gap in literacy rate of Scheduled Tribes and the total population has not narrowed down significantly; and
(2) In case of female the gap in the literacy rate of the total population and Scheduled Tribes female has widen.

Further, the position in regard to female literacy of Scheduled Tribes is particularly of great concern. As a large number of districts in the country still have less than 10 per cent literacy rate.

Eleventh Plan Targets and Special Focus Areas are as under :

- Achieve 80 per cent literacy rate;
- Reduce gender gap in literacy to 10 per cent;

- Reduce regional, social and gender disparities and extend coverage of NLM programmes to 35+ age group;
- Special Focus Areas;
- A special focus on SCs, STs, minorities, and rural women; and
- Focus also on low literacy states, tribal areas, other disadvantaged groups and adolescents.

Gross Enrolment Ratio (GER)

Gross Enrolment Ratio (GER) for elementary stage (Classes I-VIII) is defined as percentage of the enrolment in elementary state to the estimated child population in the age group of 6 to below 14 years. GER has increased from 88 per cent in 2000-01 to 102.4 per cent in 2004-05 for all STs and from 81.6 per cent in 2000-01 to 93.5 per cent in 2004-05 for total population. The gross enrolment ratio in respect of all categories and Scheduled Tribes at elementary stage (I-VIII) is given in the Table 16.2 below.

Table 16.2 : Gross Enrolment Ratios (GER) for Elementary Stage (I-VIII)
(Figures in percentage)

Year	*Scheduled Tribes*			*Total Population*		
	Boys	*Girls*	*Total*	*Boys*	*Girls*	*Total*
1995-96	105.7	75.1	90.9	86.9	69.4	78.5
1999-2000*	99.3	70.9	85.2	90.1	72.0	81.3
2000-01*	102.5	73.5	88.0	90.3	72.4	81.6
2001-02*	99.8	77.3	88.9	90.7	73.6	82.4
2002-03*	86.7	73.9	80.5	85.4	79.3	82.5
2003-04*	90.6	81.1	86.1	87.9	81.4	84.8
2004-05*	108.5	95.8	102.4	96.9	89.9	93.5

*Provisional.
Source: Ministry of Human Resources Development, Government of India, New Delhi.

(The enrolments in these stages include underage and overage and hence the total percentage may be more than 100 per cent in some cases.)

However, these high enrolment ratio cannot be taken on their face value. Public Report on Basic Education in India (PROBE) after a study in some of the tribal dominated States, viz., Madhya

Pradesh, (including Chhattisgarh) Rajasthan and Bihar (including Jharkhand, 1998) found that GER present a grossly exaggerated picture in respect of enrolments.

As per the Eleventh Five Year Plan (2007-12) document of the Planning Commission, Government of India, the G.E.R. for the year 2004-05 is 11 per cent, which is quite low and for Scheduled Tribes it is 6.52 per cent. There is increased disparities in GER that too area/gender and social category-wise. It is shown in the Table 16.3 below.

The secondary education GER for SCs and STs 45.4 per cent and 37.2 per cent are respectively, as compared to the overall GER of 51.6 per cent indicating a substantial social gap in enrolments for these groups. The GER for girls belonging to SCs and STs is 37.6 per cent and 30.5 per cent, respectively, indicating a substantial gender gap in enrolment for these groups.

Table 16.3 : Disparities in GER, 2004-05

Disparities	*GER*
Areas:	
Rural	3.70
Urban	19.90
Gender:	
Male	12.40
Female	9.10
Social:	
SCs	6.57
STs	6.52
OBCs	8.77
Others	17.22
All	11.00

Source: UGC—Based on the Study of 370 districts of India.

Dropout Rate

The fact that children dropout school early or fail to acquire basic literacy and numeracy skills partially reflects poor quality of education (UNESCO, 2007). The average school attendance was around 70 per cent of the enrolment in 2004-05. In States like UP and Bihar, the average attendance was as low as 57 per cent and 42 per cent respectively. One-third of the teachers in Madhya Pradesh, 25 per cent in Bihar and 20 per cent in UP do not attend schools.

Besides, the repetition rates in such States are also very high, resulting in wastage of human and material resources. Teacher attendance ability and motivation appear to be the weakest links of elementary education programmes. Lack of universal pre-schooling (Early Childhood Care and Education, ECCE), and consequent poor vocabulary and poor conceptual development of mind makes even enrolled children less participative in the class, even for learning by rote (Erickson, 2007).

The dropout rates at primary levels for SCs (34.2%) and STs (42.3%) are substantially higher than the national average-29 per cent (Table 16.4). The gap in respect of SCs is very wide in Goa, UP, Tamil Nadu, West Bengal, Haryana and Himachal Pradesh. The gap in respect of STs is very large in Maharashtra, Andhra Pradesh, Orissa, and Gujarat. The social gap in dropout rate is acute in respect of girls. Two-thirds of the tribal students just do not go beyond class VIII (Planning Commission, 1998-99).

Table 16.4: Dropout Rates by Social Composition, 2004-05

Categories	*Primary (I-V)*			*Elementary (I-VIII)*		
	Boys	*Girls*	*Total*	*Boys*	*Girls*	*Total*
SCs	32.7	36.1	34.2	55.2	60.2	57.3
STs	42.6	42.0	42.3	65.3	67.1	65.9
All	31.8	25.4	29.0	50.5	51.3	50.8

Source : Selected Educational Statistics, 2004-05—Eleventh Plan document.

Retention Rate

It is increasingly realized that retaining the disadvantaged children enrolment in schools is far more challenging task than enrolling them into educational system. Around 22 per cent children dropped out in classes I and II. Several factors, apart from their adverse socio-economic conditions are responsible for this. The opportunity cost of girl-child education is quite high in the rural set-up and she is often a 'nowhere child' neither in the school nor in the labour force but doing domestic work, mostly sibling care. It is well documented that the presence of female teacher often serves as a role model for girls and positively influences their enrolment and attendance. But, then, in the educationally backward States, there are few women teachers to particularly attract girls to school and retain them.[13]

As regards the availability of the schooling facilities within the habitations predominantly populated by Scheduled Tribes continue to be a relatively disadvantaged position. The relative deprivation is evidently more in case of location of upper primary schools. In terms of percentage whereas 49 per cent of all habitations have a primary school, only about 46 per cent Scheduled Tribes habitations have such a school. As regards the upper primary schools 7.9 per cent Scheduled Tribes habitation have them. Further, as regards the position of teachers in the schools Scheduled Tribes teachers are only 5.7 per cent (NCSCST, 1998-99).

Special Interventions for the Disadvantaged Groups

Young learners from socially marginalized sections experience education in a distinctly different form than those who occupy mainstream positions of power and privilege.[15] They face overt and covert forms of rejection in schooling. The Twelfth Plan will lay special focus on disadvantaged groups and educationally backward areas. This focus will include not only higher resource allocation but also capacity building for preparation and implementation of strategies based on identified needs, more intensive of monitoring and supervision, and tracking of progress. Specific measures will include :

- Top priority in pre-primary schooling to habitations of marginalized sections.
- Setting up additional 500 KGBVs in Blocks with higher concentration of SCs, STs, OBC, and minority population.
- Special attention to districts with high SCs, STs and minority population. Innovative funds for SFDs to be doubled.
- Focus on improving the learning levels of SC, ST, minority children through remedial coaching in schools and also in habitations through educated youth of Nehru Yuva Kendra Sangathan (NYKS), NSS, Self-Help Groups (SHGs), and local Non-Governmental Organizations (NGOs).

- Special schools for slum children in 35 cities with million plus population.
- Special intervention for migrating children, deprived children in urban slum areas, single parent's children, physically challenged children and working children.
- Creation of capacity within the school for dealing with students lagging in studies.
- Setting up 1000 hostels in EBBs with the resident PG teacher as the warden to provide supplementary academic support.
- Sensitizing teachers for special care of weaker sections and CWSN.
- Intensive social mobilization in SCs, STs, OBCs and predominantly tribal and minority habitations through community support.
- Housing for teachers in tribal and remote habitations.

C. Situation in Madhya Pradesh and Chhattisgarh

Educational Situation/Status

The formal education has opened comparatively a new dimension to tribal society projecting different kind of situations and sometimes conflicting problems in the socio-religious life of the tribal communities due to drastic regional variations during early fifties and sixties. Conflicting because all the tribal communities have the richest socio-economic and magico-religious tradition interwoven with cultural heritage thoroughly built of the informal education imparted by the seniors to the juniors. Classical mode of informal education is imparted in the traditional institutions. Training in hunting, fishing, dancing, singing and farming have been imparted to young tribal folk in their social institutions such as, *ghotul*, dormitories and night clubs. Among the most important functions of Oraon Youth Dormitories is the 'Pacha-Service' by which services of 'Dhunkariya' could be requisitioned by any villager who wants labour for thatching his house or for working on agricultural field for a token payment. Similar is the role of *ghotul* among the Muria tribal community in Bastar and Dantewada districts. Role of such centres for informal education and training has been well defined (Planning Commission, 2007-12).

After independence the efforts of the State and Central governments to introduce formal education in a planned manner in the tribal areas of old Madhya Pradesh in early decades could not succeed as desired, as the grip of the cultural compulsion proved to be great hindrance in introducing the process of modern formal education. So development of formal education has confronted not only social taboos, but also natural and physical hazards.

It is significant that whereas the National Policy on Education of 1987 (Revised 1993)—stipulated Universal Elementary Education (UEE), the State documents of policy and programme do not talk about UEE till about 1994. Prior to 1994, the States action for education is evinced in discreet, dispersed, small incremental accretions of schools. These additions too, are on an *ad hoc* basis, without realistic estimates of the size of the problems and the impact of the additional benefits. No goals are set to measure performance against policy. If discourse is an indicator of government commitment which, because the process of development is a continuous one it is, then this absence of a consciously articulated strategy for UEE is a sort of indicator of the level of awareness and commitment to UEE. The year 1994 marks the first ever efforts to address that goal of UEE, beginning with an increasingly growing concern of the state for universal primary education and by 2000 moving up to a concern for universal elementary education. It is significant that this concern sparks off with the emergence in the State of the elected panchayats dotting almost each village with Panchayati Raj Institution (PRI). The idea of universality pushes itself up as an inevitable corollary of the deepening and broadening of the democratic process up to the village level. State educational planning moves from piece meal provisioning to a concern for all and a search for strategies that address all. This was challenging in view of historically entrenched problems (GoMP, 1998).

The emergence of the State Government policy of decentralization and support to community processes coincided historically with the entry in the State of a major externally aided programme in education sector. This was the District Primary Education Programme (DPEP) introduced in 33 districts of low literacy in the State, in 1994 in its first phase and 1997 in its second phase. DPEP's concern of decentralized participatory action aimed at improving primary education was in consonance with the State government's policy. The strategic framework of DPEP was constituted by elements of district based decentralized planning and community participation, emphasis on capacity building of teachers, educators, educational managers, space for contextual innovation, a wide array of strategies ranging from social mobilization material development to infrastructure improvement and adopting a societal mission approach to implementing basic education programme. Decentralization and the resources made available to the State under DPEP created opportunities for innovative action to address long standing problems. Thus decentralization of education has facilitated to some extent the introduction of alternative methods of participatory problem mapping. A system of collective micro planning on a habitation basis to assess the status of children's schooling out of school and educational and infrastructure facilities was initiated to enable disaggregated problem mapping. This was observed in Lok Sampark Abhiyan (LSA). The first LSA was undertaken in 1996 and the second in 2000-01. LSA-I aimed at finding out how many children were going to school, what were the reasons for those not doing so, and what was the outreach of schooling facilities. LSA-I conducted in 1996 covered 55,295 villages and contacted 6.1 million households and 10 million children. LSA-I revealed that only 70 per cent of the habitations had access to primary schools. LSA-I also demolished the myth of universal enrolment. Enrolment was not more than 70 per cent. Most children as dropouts had never been enrolled. The most deprived were girls and children from scheduled tribes. Another round of household survey was carried out as LSA-II in 2000. It identified middle school gaps and measured the progress of educational indicators at the primary level and established a benchmark for the upper primary. It has made possible the formulation of a comprehensive State perspective UEE plan with district specific perspective plans. Lok Sampark Abhiyan (LSA) I and II become important processes for documenting status, drawing attention to gaps and provoking prompt action and demonstrate the efficiency of decentralization, which is the premise for planning. LSA I and II marks possible the measurement of attainments of key educational indicators in a comparative frame of 1996 and 2001—a period of 5 years set of issues for educational planning (GoMP, 2002). The issues that have been addressed on priority by the State working towards universal elementary education are as under:

(i) *Creating Access to Elementary Education*: Lok Sampark Abhiyan (LSA) made visible the large access gaps particularly highlighting the very depriving tribal areas and the tribal communities.

(ii) *Access to Primary Schools*: Responding to the demand for schools the State government evolved an innovative scheme for universalizing access. This was the M.P. Education Guarantee Scheme (EGS). EGS was launched in January 1997. The scheme is sensitive to the habitation pattern in the tribal areas of the State where people reside in hamlets called *majras, tolas or phalias* that are distant from one another. A historical backlog of about 30,000 accessless habitations could be eliminated in 2 years time. The EGS also aimed at time bound provisioning of schools and was, therefore, postulated on Government guaranteeing a school in 90 days EGS works through a tripartite sharing of responsibilities between Panchayats, community and State Government. Now every habitation in the State has a schooling facility within one kilometre. By August 1998, Madhya Pradesh declared universal access to primary education. The benefits of the EGS have gone to the backward areas and the deprived children. About 40 per cent of the EGS schools are in tribal areas, 45 per cent children are from ST families, 91 per cent children are from SC, ST and other backward classes. Universalisation of access through EGS clearly indicates that it is not just a geographical outreach, but also a very significant socially inclusive strategy.

The State government's intervention has been very significant in creating access in the primary sector where the governments share is 84 per cent. The government policy for private schools is liberal. Anyone can open a school, with an affidavit since no prior permission is required. The idea is to encourage a wide network of institutions for primary education.

(iii) *Access to Upper Primary*: A gap of about 7,575 schools was estimated as of 2000. 7,575 schools are being upgraded into upper primary. This will ensure universal access to the upper primary implying that each primary school has an upper primary schooling facility within 3 kilometres. In the case of upper primary, 66 per cent of upper primary access is through government funded schools and 34 per cent through private;

(iv) *The Issue of Quality*: The issue of quality has been comprehensively defined to include diverse factors that impact on school effectiveness. This includes the following :

- Physical infrastructure;
- Academic inputs and processes;
- School management; and
- Physical infrastructure—The quality of learning space;

(v) *Curriculum*: The curriculum of primary level was reviewed in 1994 to introduce elements of competency based, activity based and child friendly pedagogy. Based on the new curriculum, the State has now introduced new teaching and learning materials at the primary state. On the initiative and guidelines issued by Directorate of Adult Education, Ministry of Human Resource, Government of India to provide academic and technical resource support to literacy programme in the State, the State Resource Centres (SRCs) were established in 31 districts of undivided State of Madhya Pradesh. During the year 1999-2000, the activities of SRC have been focused on the training and material development of post-literacy (PL) and continuing education (CE) programme. It is operating in 31 districts in both the States. The adult education programme has been boasted through 'Padhna Bedhna Andolan'. S.R.C. also provided resource support to agancies like Sahayog and 'Mahila Samakhya.

(vi) *Teacher Education*: Since variety of teachers pose challenges for training as the State government has not had policy of pre-service training as a mandatory pre-requisite for teacher recruitment, the strategy for training has been sensitive to these complexities.

(vii) *Learner Evaluation*: The State Government followed the policy of non-detention till the upper primary level with only the District Board Examinations at the end of the V and VIII classes. This policy was changed in the academic year 2000-01 wherein an annual examination had to be cleared for promotion to the higher grade (This also worked in Chhattisgarh).

(viii) *Decentralization of Academic Support*: To strengthen the academic support system, DPEP helped to create a bridge from the school to the academic institutions at the top by establishing 236 Block Resource Centres (now designated Janpad Shiksha Kendra) at the Block level, and 4,325 Cluster Resource Centres (now designated as Jan Shiksha Kendra) located within primary or middle schools and serving groups of 10-15 schools.

(ix) *Restructuring of Academic Support in Institutions*: Restructuring of academic support institutions has been acknowledged as a key area of concern and the State has initiated review of the academic requirements of key institutions. Both the State governments have recently undertaken professional reorganization of academic support institutions (SCERT and DIETs) seeking to restructure these institutions on the following premises to create the necessary pre-condition of quality support.

- Clear delineation of academic criteria comprising of knowledge specialization, academic development for the purpose of staffing;
- Rotational placement between academic support institutions; and school to ensure mutual enrichment of theory and practice;
- Emphasis on subject faculty structure to ensure that core curricular inputs are designed and implemented by competent professionals.

Literacy

Before carving out the State of Chhattisgarh from the State of Madhya Pradesh in November 2000, the State of Madhya Pradesh has been the largest tribal State of the country having poor proportional increase in literacy during the period of four decades, i.e., 1961-2001. It is 05.10 per cent, 7.62 per cent, 10.68 per cent, 21.54 per cent, and 41.2 per cent respectively and for Chhattisgarh it has been 52.71 per cent in 2001 census. The Table 16.5 given

Table 16.5 : Tribal Literacy Rate

(in per cent)

S. No.	Year	India			Madhya Pradesh			Chhattisgarh		
		G.	S.T.	Difference	G.	S.T.	Difference	G.	S.T.	Difference
1.	1961	24.03	6.28	18.15	17.13	5.11	12.02	—	—	—
	Male	34.45	10.00	24.45	27.03	9.24	17.79	—	—	—
	Female	12.96	2.43	10.52	6.73	0.96	5.77	—	—	—
2.	1971	29.45	11.30	18.15	22.14	7.62	14.52	—	—	—
	Male	39.45	17.63	21.82	32.70	13.05	19.65	—	—	—
	Female	18.69	4.85	13.84	10.92	2.18	8.71	—	—	—
3.	1981	36.23	16.35	19.88	27.87	10.68	17.19	—	—	—
	Male	46.89	24.52	22.37	39.49	17.74	21.78	—	—	—
	Female	24.82	8.40	16.78	15.58	3.60	11.98	—	—	—
4.	1991	52.21	29.60	22.61	44.20	21.54	22.66	—	—	—
	Male	64.13	40.65	23.48	58.42	32.16	26.26	—	—	—
	Female	39.23	18.19	21.40	28.85	10.73	18.12	—	—	—
5.	2001	65.38	47.10	18.25	63.70	41.20	22.50	64.70	52.70	11.90
	Male	75.26	59.17	—	76.10	53.50	22.60	77.40	65.00	12.40
	Female	53.70	34.76	19.36	50.30	28.40	21.90	51.90	39.30	12.60

Source: Census Report of India, 1961, 1971, 1981, 2001.

below shows comparative picture of literacy of India vis-à-vis States of Madhya Pradesh and Chhattisgarh.

It is clear from Table 16.5 that the rate of literacy between general and tribal specially the female tribal literacy is widening in last five decades while it is less in Chhattisgarh. The District-wise rate of literacy of Scheduled Tribes in Madhya Pradesh shows different picture as analysed below :

- Madhya Pradesh has a population of over 20 per cent Scheduled Tribes after the division of the State. 13 districts (of 1991) have a population of Scheduled Tribes exceeding 20 per cent of the population.
- Districts with larger than State-share of Scheduled Tribes also do well in literacy in the nineties.
- Here again 8 out of 13 predominantly tribal districts far exceed that State average and national average in the growth rate of literacy between 1991-2001. Only the districts of Barwani, Dindori, Dhar, Khandwa and Jhabua have a growth rate below the State average. All these five districts have a growth rate above the national average. It is clear from Table 16.6.

Table 16.6 : District-wise Literacy Growth in Madhya Pradesh

District	Population of ST in district	Percentage of literacy in 2001 Census	Percentage of growth in literacy
Jhabua	85.67	37.08	18.07
Mandla	60.84	60.77	23.75
Dindori	60.48	54.49	16.75
Umaria	54.84	60.26	27.63
Shahdol	46.32	57.76	22.31
Dhar	53.48	52.70	18.16
Khargone	46.23	63.41	22.18
Barwani	66.50	41.35	13.27
Betul	37.51	66.87	20.98
Seoni	36.95	65.88	21.39
Chhindwara	34.47	66.03	21.13
Sidhi	30.43	52.82	23.67
Khandwa	26.77	61.71	16.22

Source: Census of India, 2001

As per 2001 census, the 31.76 per cent Scheduled Tribes live in Chhattisgarh. District with larger than share of Scheduled Tribes also do well in literacy as per 2001 Census. Rajnandgaon district has the highest rate of literacy for Scheduled Tribes followed by Durg, Dhamtari, Kankare, Mahasumda and Janggeer (Chapa).

The Other Indicators of Education

- In both the States minimum learning level (MLL) is laid down for primary stage to reduce curriculum load.
- Educational attainment in both the States is almost 1.70 which is less than country's average for the Scheduled Tribes.
- As per census 2001 the educational status of Scheduled Tribes population falling in the age group of 19 years in both the States having literacy without educational level is almost in between 4 per cent to 5 per cent.
- Scheduled Tribes persons educationally deprived :

	M.P.	*Chhattisgarh*
Age group 7 above	40 per cent	45 per cent
Age group 15 above	52 per cent	55 per cent

- Share of Scheduled Tribes persons attending educational institutions in the age group 7 to 14 years is 80 per cent for Madhya Pradesh and 85 per cent for Chhattisgarh.
- Percentage of illiterate in different age groups :

	M.P.	*Chhattisgarh*
15-34 years	70 per cent	75 per cent
35-49 years	80 per cent	85 per cent
50 yrs+	90 per cent	95 per cent

Management of Schools

Education in India and in the States of Madhya Pradesh and Chhattisgarh is largely a budget based system where efficiency is rated by ability to consume budget and to demand more. This is the pattern which has been followed by the State Government. The funds budgeted for the educational programmes have been consumed mostly by the class of urban population. The tribal/rural population could hardly get their full share. Thus, the whole education system, including the curriculum, the text books, the reading materials, the educational group and the management system, is addressed to and focused on non-tribal middle class urban population which, ethnocentrically is called the mainstream. Since the tribals are expected to join the mainstream, education is also conceived as a mechanism to enable them to join mainstream and, therefore, incongruity and mismatch between educational system catering to the mainstream and the culture of the tribals is rarely noticed. This, however, is a very significant factor for low participation of tribals in general and tribal women in particular in total educational process. Therefore, the type of educational ambit created within the limited approach and the paucity of funds, the tribal population has been lagged behind in the field of education and have subjected to exploitation.[1]

A brief review of the management of the primary educational system in Madhya Pradesh reveals that after the reorganization of the States in 1956, a common integrated system of education was adopted and the entire system was put under the control of State Education Department. But gradually it was realized that the tribal education needs special focus in order to run the educational programmes in full swing in the vast tribal areas of the State. Therefore in 1964, a policy decision was taken that the educational institutions located in the tribal areas of the State will be managed by the State Tribal Welfare Department[2] who will look after the special needs and problems of the tribal population. Since then, school education in the State is managed primarily by the School Education Department for the general areas and Tribal and Scheduled Caste Welfare Department for the tribal areas. Policy matters are decided by the Department of School Education headed by a Principal Secretary. Implementation of policies and programmes is done by the Directorate of Public Instructions.

Table 16.7 shows the department-wise responsibility of qualifying the educational institutions in the States.

Table 16.7 : Management of Educational Institutions

Sl. No.	*No. of Departments*	*Percentage of schools*
1.	School education department	72
2.	Tribal welfare departments	21
3.	Local bodies	13 (included iin 72%)
4.	Private arrangements	7
5.	Schools receiving aid from the State government	20 (of the 7%)

For this school management has been decentralized to the district and sub-district levels. Recognizing the need to strengthen the school as a unit, the Parents Teachers Association (PTA) and the Village Education Committee (VEC) have been given power to decide on issues that impinge on the daily functioning of the school, such as school timing, local holidays, monitoring the regular functioning of the school. Teachers are now expected to be accountable to the local PTA and the VEC, this is expected to make the school management responsive to the needs of the children. Further, after adoption of TSP strategy on the eve of Fifth Five Year Plan (1975) the following steps have been initiated in the Tribal Sub-Plan/Scheduled Areas to boost the educational activities :

- Distinction between elementary and higher education has been made;
- U.E.E. has been given top priority;
- Providing community knowledge of 3 Rs;
- Residential facilities up to H.S.S. increased—at divisional, district and Block level;
- Operation 'Black Board' adopted in few districts;
- District Institute of Education and Training (DIET) established; and
- Education Guarantee Scheme started.

Problems

A. Management of Educational Activities

- The national education structure is adopted with reference to the facilities available. The result is:
    - Children start schooling at late stage;
    - Children do not get opportunities for pre-primary education;
    - U.E.E. could not succeed in the absence of well thought off educational management system for tribal areas. So regional imbalances and educational disparity at community level have been widened;
    - Lack of coordination between State Education Department and Tribal Welfare Department in the areas of imparting training and inspection;

- Shortage of teacher at primary school and middle school teacher-pupil ratio is not as per norms;
- Teachers are handicapped in transacting their curriculum due to lack of appropriate training, learning materials and teaching aids;
- Shortage of classrooms and school building;
- Text books, not available timely as per requirements of the children and also not up to the mark;
- Language used is often too sophisticated;
- Course content not designed to develop skills in children;
- All the villages/habitations do not have schools within walking distance—inadequate coverage—because of:
    - Small habitation;
    - Sparsely populated area; and
    - Poor participation.

B. Operational Problems

- High rate of dropout and stagnation;
- Classroom process is drab and uninteresting;
- Learning/reading material is not prepared properly accordingly to the needs of children, resulting high dropout;
- Economic factors;
- Health problems/malnutrition;
- Socio-cultural factor-discrimination;
- Dysfunctionality of education system (teacher absenteeism and shortage of other basic inputs);
- Having to work when they ought to be in school; and
- Not having necessary environment at home in order to be inspired to go to school.

Suggestions to take action

In short, the action ahead has to take the following issues into consideration :

- Provision of appropriate infrastructure facilities to schools;
- Focusing on strengthening institutional management processes and strengthening the use of information for planning and management;

- Strengthening decentralized management through capacity development;
- Strengthening community participation especially through institutional means and ways such as, the PTA and the VEC;
- Sustaining the new impetus towards restructuring academic support systems on principles of professional calibre, school experiences as participatory forum of teacher development and motivation, especially at the level of the *Jan Shiksha Kendra*;
- Adopting a more development approach to teacher training, and creating professional incentive for teachers to upgrade their knowledge and skills;
- Ensuring that the curriculum, both respects local knowledge and culture and adds wider dimensions of understanding and accordingly effect improvement in content;
- Establishing a reliable system of learner assessment;
- Develop appropriate incentives for learners mainly of special focus groups; and
- These measures have been initiated. They need to be sustained and strengthened in the light of experiences and in the interest of learners.

The key theme is to continue decentralizing management and academic support to schools so as to redefine the school from its inherited identity as the lowest level appendage to large bureaucratic machinery to school as empowered and autonomous unit. Under National Literacy Mission (NLM). Total literacy campaign (TLC) has generated lots of enthusiasm which needs to be strengthened. Through continuing education the tribal would improve their skills as the main focus of continuing education on the neo-literates, semi-literates and non-literates, school dropouts, and specially tribal women. At last, it is concluded that tribal education is to be thought of rather as an investment in building their human capital, i.e., investment in making.

NOTES

1. In the then Province of Central Provinces and Berar also, an officer on special duty was appointed in 1940, to investigate into the conditions of aboriginal tribes. The officer on special duty, Mr. M.V. Grigson, I.C.S., made useful suggestion, p. 305. Reference "A Historical Review of the Progress of Education amongst the Scheduled Tribes" by Vimal Chandra.. This article was published in the book *Applied Anthropology in India,* Edited by Dr. L.P. Vidyarthi, Kitab Mahal, Allahabad, 1960.
2. Impact of educational programmes on the development of tribal women literacy in Madhya Pradesh. A Study done by Dr. V.K. Shrivastava (1996). p. 10, under a project of Ministry of Human Resource, Government of India.

* On the Recommendation of Narona Committee (1964). Constituted by State Government of Madhya Pradesh for management of the schools located in tribal and non-tribal areas.

REFERENCES

Batra, C. and K. Lokesh (1998): *Outreach Community Learning and Development Programme,* New Delhi: Government of India, Ministry of Human Resource Development.

Burman, B.K. Roy (1996): *Tribal Situation: An Approach to Problem in India,* New Delhi: Rajiv Gandhi Institute of Contemporary Studies.

Government of Madhya Pradesh (1998): *Human Development Report,* Bhopal, p. 6.

Government of Madhya Pradesh (2002): *Human Development Report,* Bhopal, p. 28.

Lynn Erickson (2007): *Concept Bases, Curriculum and Instruction for the thinking Classroom,* California: Sage Publication.

National Commisson for Scheduled Castes and Scheduled Tribes (1989-99): *Fifth Report,* Vol. I, New Delhi: GoI, p. 217.

Planning Commission (2007-12): *Eleventh Five Year Plan,* Vol. III, New Delhi, GoI.

Shankar, G. (1994): "Literacy for Oppressed", in (ed.) *Quest for Change: National Literacy Mission,* New Delhi: Ministry of Human Resource Development, GoI.

UNESCO (2007): *EFA-Global Monitoring Report,* Paris.

17

Educational Status of Tribals of Andaman and Nicobar Islands: A Study

Palash C. Coomar and *S.K. Biswas*

Introduction

The study of Indian tribes has impressed many researchers for a long time. In the first phase, India being a classic homeland of various tribes, castes and other forms of ethnic groups, offers a very good laboratory for empirical observations. India has the second largest tribal population in the world next to African countries. The scheduled tribes accounts for 67.76 million (1991 Census) or 8.08 per cent of India's total population. Of these 1.95 per cent is primitive tribes. The highest concentration of Scheduled Tribes is found in North-East States of Mizoram (94.75%) Nagaland (87.70%), Meghalaya (83.53%) and Orissa (22.21%) and Andaman and Nicobar Islands (8.27%) (Dilip Shah, 2003).

The tribal people are characterized by their inherited dialect and socio-economic practices. Anthropologists like D.N. Majunder, H.L. Chaklader, N.K. Bose, Risley and Radcliff Brown point out and offer a unique case, where more than 600 tribes and sub-tribes, big and small have been found to exist in different parts of the country, (Department of Social Welfare, 1969). The framers of Constitution of India were very much respectful towards the welfare and development of our indigenous tribal people. The Constitution provides various safeguards in favour of Scheduled Tribes (ST). These may be broadly divided into two parts. (I) Protection and

(II) Development. Recognizing the importance of education, the framers of the Constitution of India have made specific provisions in Article 15 (4) and 46 for promoting education among the Scheduled Tribes. Both these Articles have directed and empowered the State Governments to make suitable provision to promote with a special care on educational and economic interest of the weaker sections of the people and in particular of the SCs and STs.

Our first Prime Minister Pt. Jawaharlal Nehru was very much in favour of the integration of tribals with the mainstream of the nation. (Verma, R.C., 1990). The basic approach of the Tribal development of Scheduled Tribes in the line of the constitutional framework was laid down by Nehruji who established Dhaber Commission in 1960.

Education and Tribal Development

Education is the key catalyst to the development of human resources. Education is a crucial part of legitimate entry in the national level participation of development as well as social stream of the nation. In fact, literacy in general and female literacy in particular is the best indicator of the social development also. According to Sachchidananda (1964), education is an integral part of culture, it cannot be divorced from people and the society they live in … .without this, the social heritage of one generation cannot be transmitted to another. In the past education was one of the main considerations for hierarchical classification in Indian Hindu society. Education was out of reach to the poor and backward people and also to tribals. Lack of it is largely responsible for the exploitation and pitiable plight of the tribals. For them, education is the pivot on which their success depends. Education spreads knowledge. Knowledge gives inner strength and creates sense of justice, which is very essential for the tribals for attaining freedom from exploitation and poverty.

According to former Union Minister of Education. Shri K.C. Pant "The role of education is to transform a static society into one vibrant with a commitment to development and change" (Mathur, N.N.G., 1994). In our national perception education is essential for all. India's National Policy on Education (1986) stated that the education is fundamental to our all-round development, material and spiritual.

After the advent of democracy in India, a special consideration was made of the education of the Scheduled Tribes, which witnessed massive social change. It is due to it that the Constitution has given safeties and securities to the tribal. The philosophy behind these constitutional privileges is that the tribal in the past had been exploited by the non-tribal society. For fulfilling the constitutional commitment and for ameliorating the condition of the deprived sections of the society, particularly the Scheduled Tribes, it was contemplated that extra efforts need be put in to augment the education expansion. An elaborate programme of scholarship, reservation of seats in educational institutions along with various other ancillary facilities in operation. Therefore, the problems of education among the tribals have received a good deal of attention in recent years, the education of the tribal people is a major programme of equalization of the spirit of social and national integration.

Education in Andaman and Nicobar

The Andaman and Nicobar Islands, a Union Territory is a classic homeland of indigenous tribes. There are six different types of tribes inhabited in the chain of islands. First four tribes belongs to negrito race. They are called Great Andamanese, Sentinelese, Onges, Jarawas who are living in Andaman Group of Islands. Rest two tribes are Mongoloid who are Nicobarese and Shompens living in Nicobar Group of Islands. The total tribal population of the State is 29,469 (2001 Census), which constitute about 8.45 per cent of the total population of U.T. (3,56,152).

Table 17.1: Demographic Situation in UT's Tribals

	1951	*1961*	*1971*	*1981*	*1991*	*2001*
G.A	23	19	24	26	—	49
Onges	(150)	129	112	97	—	95
Jarawas	50	500	Nil	31	—	(266)
Sentineles	50	50	—	—	—	(100)
Nicobari	11902	13903	17874	21984	26206	28769
Shompen	(20)	71	92	223	—	—
Total UT population	30971	63548	115133	188741	280661	356152
% of Tribal population	38.14	23.01	15.75	11.84	9.47	8.45

* In bracket are estimated figures.
Source: Basic Statistics, 2006, pp. 16-17.

The British unfolded that door of Virgin Islands in Bay of Bengal before the world viewers in 1858. An unsuccessful attempt was made by the British rulers in 1789 for starting penal settlement, but it could not last for a long time. The First War of Independence of 1857 brought the islands into prominence again and the islands were considered to be the best place for deportation of Anti-British's people. Hence, since 1858, British started second penal settlement in Andaman Islands with the help of Indian convicted prisoners, prisoners of war (Sepoy Mutiny in 1857), and political Prisoners. Over time British explored each and every part of the islands and came into contact with indigenous tribes of Great Andamanese, Jarawas and Onges in Andamans and Nicobarese, Shompen tribes in Nicobar Islands.

The post-independent era had opened the islands for free Indian people to immigrate to these islands, now it is the home of multi-ethnic, multi-lingual people. Of approximately 500 islands, only 38 islands have been inhabited by the people, of which 12 islands of Nicobar district are inhabited by the Shompen and Nicobar tribes. Apart from Nicobar tribes, population of other tribes is negligible. Nicobarese constitute a major part of the tribal population who are considered to be marching towards modern lives and mainstream.

To identify the educational status of tribals of the UTs other than Nicobar tribes, four Nigrito tribes and one Mongoloid are primitives. Their number of population is in extinct conditions. Except Onge and Andamanese, other three tribes are not coming in the mainstream. Few children are available among Onges and Andamanese as school going stages. Therefore, Nicobari, a major tribe is in the stage of modernization and development going to count in the present study.

Earlier Education System

The educational facilities in the Union Territory started in 1870, when the British felt the need to communicate with the Indian convicts to make them work as labourers in the penal settlement. On experiment basis, an educated British soldier was thus given the responsibility of teaching English to some workers. With the success of this experiment, a regular primary school was started in 1881-82. Later on six primary schools were opened in and around Port Blair, on the other hand to make friendly relations with primitive tribes. In May 1861, 3 Great Andamanese were sent to Maulemein (Burma) for education. Further in 1863 "Andaman Home" was established to civilize and educate the Great Andamanese. By the end of 1870, an orphanage-cum-school was started; where Andamanese children were taught English. The Annual Report of Penal Settlement authority states that in 1873-74 a nursery school for small children was also established at Viper Island. Similarly an isolated and irregular attempt had been made to give education to the Onges and the Jarawa by the British authorities.

Before British approached the Nicobar Group of Islands, foreign invaders like Portuguese, French Jesuit Missionaries visited the Nicobars in 15th, 16th and 17th centuries with the mission of prorogating Christianity. The father of Modern Nicobari society, Bishop John Richardson stated in his diary that in 1896 Vedappan Soloman landed on Car Nicobar from Port Blair. He started a school to teach modern education to Nicobarese. He went Burma to take Higher Education in theology. Many students were sent to Rangoon for further education by British authorities. There were five schools for imparting education to Nicobari children till World War-II broke out in 1939.

Post-Independence Education

Country's independence had opened a new chapter in the history of education in these islands specially among Nicobari society. For accelerating modern education among Nicobari children, the missionary schools were taken over by the Government According to 1955 Education Survey, in Nicobar, there were five primaries and one middle school with a total of 621 students. Within five years, a Higher Secondary Multi-purpose school with 58 students on roll was started. Since early sixties a handful of meritorious students have availed higher education in mainland institutions. For obtaining technical and professional education, the Government of India has reserved 20 per cent of seats for tribal students, out of total seats available for U.T. students in various institutions in the mainland.

As per the 1991 Census, the tribal literacy rate was 56.62 per cent of which female literacy was 48.74 per cent whereas, the literacy rate of Union Territory was 73.02 per cent.

The post-independence education for Onges and Great Andamanese is not encouragable. Since early seventies, *Bharatiya Adimjati Sevak Sangh* had taken the initiative to start schools for these two tribes. Later in 1976, Andaman *Adim Janjati Vikash Samiti* (AAJVS) look forward with the same mission by opening two primary schools, one at Strait Island, the settlement area of Great Andamanese and another at Dugong Creek, (Little Andaman) Onge settlement area.

Educational Infrastructure

As far as infrastructure for schooling in tribal areas is concerned, there are 59 schools of which 25 are primary, 10 middle level, 10 secondary and 5 senior secondary level and two Ashram schools. The local administration and the Union Government are very serious about the education of the tribals of this Union Territory. A number of schemes and programmes have been undertaken to give best and favourable education atmosphere to these tribal students. Centrally sponsored schemes for accelerating education facilities among tribal students are:

- Free higher education to tribal girl students on special central assistance at Banasthali Vidyapith, Rajasthan.
- Free uniform.
- Mid-day meal to students of Class I to VIII.
- Free note books and text books.
- Free coaching classes.
- Free boarding and lodging facilities for studies in Port Blair and mainland educational institutions.

Since early eighties, more than ten girl tribal students have been obtaining education from class V to P.G. level at Banasthali Vidyapith, Rajasthan. Boarding, lodging and education expenditure has been borne by the Government of India. An amount of Rs. 2,67,000 have been sanctioned (for the 2005-06) against 8 girls, who are now studying in this institution. Since 2004-05; an additional scholarship at the rate of Rs. 500 per month to 30 tribal students have been sanctioned against them who have been pursuing higher or professional education in the mainland. In addition to that all tribal students are getting free fooding and lodging during their studies in mainland (*Educational Report*, 2007).

Moreover, all the tribal students have been exempted from payment of fees in respect of examinations conducted by recognized universities/Boards. The administration is making necessary payment under these schemes to the concerned institutions. A special study centre has been opened at JNRM Degree College campus for providing free coaching to tribal students for degree education as well as competitive examinations.

The enrolment of tribal students for three academic sessions reveals that the number of primary level students has been increasing. But the number of enrolment at middle level has been reduced to just half of the total strength at primary level. Further the number has been falling down in secondary level. Only 10 per cent to 15 per cent students are appearing in the XII Board out of the total enrolment of middle school students. At degree level their number is further decreasing. In teacher training and technical education, the number of enrolment is very less. The dropout rate is very high among tribal students.

Higher Education Status

In the latter half of the seventies, few students from Nicobari tribes had enrolled in Degree College at Port Blair. The number of students at degree level has been increasing over the years. For accelerating higher education at the door step to Nicobari students, the local administration had decided to open one more degree college in 1989 at Car Nicobar, the headquarters of Nicobar District. The idea behind the opening of new degree level institution in tribal area was to access higher education atmosphere and facilities to them and to encourage tribal students for further education at their own choiceful subjects. But this initiative failed within a short period of time. The tribal leader and parents too were not in favour of this degree college at their place. Their thinking was, their children should be sent to Port Blair and elsewhere for getting proper knowledge, modern academic atmosphere, which need to enlighten their tribal lives and education.

JNRM Degree College is the pioneer institution for higher education in the UT. Eighty per cent tribal students are obtaining higher education from this college. The enrolment figures of last two academic sessions say that more than two thousand students are enrolled of which only (6.25%) 125 are tribal students (See Tables 17.2 and 17.3). The number of girl tribal students is more than boys. In science and management faculties the strength of tribal students is only 2 per cent. Similarly in P.G. courses only 3 per cent of tribal students are studying. Hence, the strength of tribal students was very poor. As per reservation policy, 7.5 per cent seats are reserved for tribal students. Therefore, due to non-availability of tribal students for further education, the reservation policy could not become effective for island's tribal students.

The performance of the tribal students in degree course examination is also very poor. The final year results of 2003 academic session shows that in Arts facilities 26.08 per cent of tribal students succeeded in the examination but the overall pass percentage of the college was 65 per cent. The performance of the tribal students has further improved in 2004 final examination. In 2004 only 41.68 per cent tribal students succeeded in the final examination against the overall result 69.50 per cent in the college. In science 2003 examination, only 2 students appeared but none of them succeeded in the examination. Whereas, in 2004, only two students appeared but both of them succeeded. Except two students in management for the year 2004 no tribal student appeared in P.G. Examination for two sessions (2003 and 2004) (Table 17.4).

Reservation of seats for S.T. candidates for major technical and professional courses for last five years has stated that Central Government has been allotting 20 per cent seats for them out of total seats allotted for Islander's students for higher institutions. Except medical course, in B. Engineering courses and National Technology Institution seats reserved against S.T. candidates were not being utilized. Similarly in other professional and non-technical seats reserved against the tribal students were not utilized properly. Only 10 per cent to 18 per cent seats were utilized for tribal candidates against the seat reserved for them. Hence, due to unavailability of tribal candidates for filling up these seats, the unutilized seats were transferred to non-tribal candidates. As a good number of students are not found in science stream at school level, so the major seats are being unutilized so far (Table 17.5).

Table 17.2 : Enrolment of Tribal Pupils in Andaman and Nicobar Education

State of education	*Boys*			*Girls*			*Total*		
	2002-03	*2003-04*	*2004-05*	*2002-03*	*2003-04*	*2004-05*	*2002-03*	*2003-04*	*2004-05*
Primary	1625	1868	1964	1507	1675	1786	3132	3543	3950
Middle	920	1002	1052	812	845	831	1732	1847	1883
Secondary	398	436	482	436	486	477	834	922	959
Sr. Secondary	89	108	123	121	158	169	210	266	292
TTI and B.Ed	7	1	3	23	21	26	30	22	29
Polytechnics	—	2	2	2	5	5	2	7	7
Colleges	60	69	67	49	57	89	109	126	156
ITI	6	2	5	11	6	4	17	8	9
Ashram	60	60	60	—	—	—	60	60	60
Total	3165	3548	3758	2961	3253	3387	6126	6801	7145

Source: Basic Statistics, 2004-05.

Table 17.3 : Enrolment Statement of S.T. (Nicobari) Students in JNRM, 2004-05 and 2005-06

Courses	*Year*	*ST 2004-05*			*ST 2005-06*			*Total enrolment 2004-05*	*Total enrolment 2005-06*	*% of S.T. 2004-05*	*% of S.T. 2005-06*
		B	*G*	*T*	*B*	*G*	*T*				
B.A	I	16	37	53	24	10	34	471	447	—	—
	II	19	14	33	10	34	44	380	411	—	—
	III	8	16	24	15	12	27	368	328	—	—
	Total	43	67	110	59	56	105	1219	1186	9.89	8.90
B.Sc	I	—	6	6	1	4	5	139	162	—	—
	II	—	2	2	—	3	3	94	109	—	—
	III	—	1	1	—	—	—	100	75	—	—
	Total	—	9	9	1	7	8	343	346	2.60	2.31
B. Com. Other	I	—	—	—	2	—	2	108	120	—	—
	II	—	1	2	5	—	5	103	108	—	—
	III	—	1	1	1	1	2	94	93	—	—
	Total	1	2	3	8	1	9	305	321	0.90	2.79
P.G. all subjects	I	1	2	3	—	4	4	88	87	—	—
	II	—	1	1	1	1	2	84	82	—	—
	Total	1	3	4	1	5	6	172	169	2.32	3.57
Grand Total		45	81	126	59	69	128	2039	2022	6.18	6.32

Source: Office of the Principal, (Statistical Bureau), JNRM, Port Blair.

Table 17.4 : Degree Level Final Year Results (2003, 2004) of S.T.

Courses	*Total Students appeared*		*Total ST students appeared*		*Total ST students passed*		*Passed % of ST students*	
	2003	*2004*	*2003*	*2004*	*2003*	*2004*	*2003*	*2004*
B.A	317	345	23	24	6	10	26.08	41.68
B.Sc	81	98	2	2	–	2	0.00	100.00
B. Com and Management	89	104	–	2	–	–	–	–
P.G.	77	87	–	–	–	–	–	–
Grand Total	564	634	25	28	06	12	24.00	42.78

Source: Office of the Principal, JNRM, Port Blair.

Table 17.5 : Allocation of Seats for Tribal Students in Mainland Institutions

Discip-line	2001-2002		2002-2003		2003-2004		2004-2005		2005-2006	
	Seats Reserved	Seats utilized in %	Reserved	Seats utilized in %	Reserved	Seats utilized in %	Reserved	Seats utilized in %	Reserved	Seats utilized in %
B.E %	18	Nil	18	2 11.11%	18	2 11.11%	19	1 5.26%	19	1 5.26%
MBBS	3	2 67%	2	2 100%	3	3 100%	4	4 100%	4	4 100%
NIT	5	Nil	5	Nil	5	Nil	5	Nil	5	Nil
Other*	18	3 16.67%	21	4 19.04%	23	1 4.34%	24	4 16.67%	23	3 13.04%
Total Seats	44	5 (11.38%)	46	8 (17.39%)	49	6 (12.24%)	52	9 (17.30%)	51	8 (15.68%)

* Other Courses: Diploma, General Nursing, Hotel Management, Craft Courses, PG Courses, B.Ed, Para Medical, BHMS, etc.

Source: Educational Reports, 2006-07.

Observations

- The Literacy rate of island's tribal is 47.02 per cent (1991) as compared to Mizoram (88.8%) and Nagaland (66.60%) tribal dominated States. Though as compared to all-India level, the literacy rate of island's tribes was very high (India 24.60%).
- Educational infrastructure facilities available in tribal areas are very poor when compared to educational facilities available in non-tribal areas of UTs.
- Adequate number of tribal eligible candidates is not found for filling up the seats reserved in medical, engineering and other professional courses in mainland institutions.
- The administration is committed towards the reservation of 20 per cent seats for island's Tribal in higher technical and professional educational level in mainland bound institutions, but on the other hand, the number of eligible tribal students is not available for this quota seats. It is observed that while the schools in the tribal areas have been upgraded, science has not been promoted, along with the promotion of English as medium of instructions (State Development reports: 2005).
- The prevalent practice of compulsory passing up to the eighth standard results in a drastic increase of failures (up to 50%) in standard IX and only 20 per cent make it through to standard X and less than 5 per cent enrol for the higher secondary level.
- Shortage of qualitative (in many cases) teachers leave the students (National Commission for Women) and tribal areas generally are not devoted towards their profession.
- The far flung Islands in tribal areas are not well communicated (only sea transport) with education networks at headquarters. Therefore, teaching materials/ aids are delayed.
- The total education system had collapsed in Nicobar district due to earthquake followed by Tsunami in December 25, 2004. The school buildings, infrastructures of entire tribal dominated islands have been badly effected, more than fifty teaching staff were killed or missing during natural disasters on that day. The local administration and education department have been facing a tough challenge

in reviving the education system in right track. The work progress is very slow.

- Reservation policy in higher education (both technical and professional) for UTs tribal students has not been much success. Last five years data shows that only 15 per cent of seats (out of total seats reserved for tribals) have been utilized by the tribal candidates against the quota seats reserved for them.
- A special coaching centre was opened at JNRM degree college campus at Port Blair which was closed down.
- The Nicobari vernacular (dialect) is not followed as medium of instruction in school teaching. As a result, the children of Nocobari community face problems to follow Hindi or English taught in schools.

Conclusion

The reservation policy in higher education institutions in mainland would be meaningless for tribal communities, unless quota seats are being utilized by them. The administration's Education Department needs to be serious about the policy and initiatives by increasing the number of tribal students in science stream at school level. A good number of tribal students need to be identified at primary level and give them proper education facilities. In this direction the responsibilities can be entrusted upon schools like Carmel School, Vivekananda School, Kamraj, Naval Public School, with a fixed quota for them. Similarly, in mainland standard schools for some tribal students can be accommodated for better education. From class XII extra coaching and tuition has to be provided to them for good results in Board examinations.

A proper network facility has to be maintained between the remote and isolated island's schools and Directorate of education for providing best infrastructure and dedicated teaching staff. Voluntary organizations or institutions like *Bharatiya Jain Sangathan* (BJS), *Rama Krishna Mission,* and Christian charitable institutions can be asked to run schools in the tribal areas of Nicobar districts.

A good number of tribal girls were admitted in Banasthali Vidyapith, Rajasthan in the early eighties, but now-a-days only few (8 students are studying at present) girls are pursuing education in this institution. The matter should be taken into account and try to find out, why the parents are losing interest to send their children is such facility oriented education institutions. In this direction village captain and church priest should take initiative to convince the villagers for availing good education facilities for their children.

NOTES

Government of India letter No. 5-4/95-UT-I Ministry of HRD (Department of Secondary and Higher Education) issued ordered by Under Secretary GoI, dt. 01.03.2006 subject contained-exemption of SC and ST students from payment of examination fees. The ordered stated that UT tribal students are exempted from payment of fees in respect of examination conducted by recognized universities/Board in all the UT's for a further period of five years 2004-05 to 2008-09. The administration concerned may make necessary payment direct to the Universities/Board concerned on the basis of the students belonging to SC and ST appearing in the examination.

Directorate of Tribal Welfare, Andaman and Nicobar Administration letter No. 1-116/2001-TW/603 dt. 21.09.2004 issued by Research Officer as intimation to Director of Education subject contained that a grant of additional scholarship at the rate of Rs. 500 p.m. should be given to 30 ST students pursuing high/professional education in the mainland.

REFERENCES

Andaman and Nicobar Administration (2005): *Draft Development Report on Andaman and Nicobar Islands-2005*, Port Blair.

Directorate of Economics and Statistics (2004-05): *Basic Statistics*, Port Blair: Andaman and Nicobar Islands.

Biswas S.K. (2008): 'Political Administration of Tribal: Post Tsunami Scenario', *Oriental Anthropologist*, 9 (2).

_____, (1992): *Andaman and Nicobar Island's Same Problems and their Modernization—Special Reference to Two Ethnic Groups.* (unpublished) Thesis in Political Science, (Calcutta) Rabindra Bharati, University.

Department of Social Welfare (1969): *Report of the Study Team on Negrito Tribes of the Andaman*, Port Blair: ASI., pp. 3-4.

ICSSR, (1971): *Education of the Scheduled* Tribes, New Delhi.

Justin, Austice (1990): *The Nicobarese*, Kolkata: Seagull Books.

Kloss, Bolen C. (1908): *Andaman and Nicobar Island* London, Reprint in India in 1971.

Malhotra, O.P. (1980): *Tribal Education in Andaman and Nicobar Islands*, New Delhi: S. Chand.

Mathur, N.N.G. (1994): *Problems of Tribal Education: Past, Present and Future*, Udaipur: Siva Publishers and Distributors.

Mazumder R.C. (1975): *Penal Settlement in Andaman*, Ministry of Information and Broadcasting, New Delhi: Government of India.

Naik, T.B. (1969): *Tribal Education*, Bombay: Bombay Publication.

National Commission for Women (2005): *A Situational Analysis of Women and Children of A & N Islands*, New Delhi: NCW.

Sachchidananda (1964): *Cultural Change in Tribal Bihar—Munda and Oraon*, Calcutta: Bookland.

Shah, Dilip (2003): "Tribal Development: Planning and Performance", *Kurukshetra*, 51 (8), pp. 34-36.

Superintendent of A & N Islands (1931): *Census Report 1921, 1931*, Calcatta.

Verma, R.C. (1990): *Indian Tribes through the Ages*, Ministry of Information and Broadcasting, New Delhi: Govt. of India.

Office of the Secretary Education Development III, A & N Administration.

Office of the Principal JNRM, Port Blair.

18

Mainstreaming the Marginalised : Status of Tribal Education and Development in Gujarat

Ratnawali Sinha

Introduction

Education is central to the development of human societies and is instrumental in bringing about new ideas, knowledge, norms and values that augment the survival of society by making them adept to the changing need and aspiration of its members. It shapes human personality and enhances their capabilities to realise the goal of worthy life. Apart from socialising the individual, education helps instilling democratic ideals, bringing equalities and results in the formation of human capital which are essential to power the engine of economic growth.

Communities that are deprived of this enabling tool remain underdeveloped for want of adequate human capital to invest in their growth potentials. Historically in India, the social stratification excluded many communities to avail the resources necessary for their development. Such exclusions fostered backwardness and poverty in these social groups and pushed them at the margin of the development. With the independence, the ideals of democracy called for equality of opportunity to let these deprived people grow with the mainstream population. Constitutional provisions were made to protect their rights and take care of specific needs of these groups.

Realising the role of education in bringing down social

disparity and in improving the socioeconomic condition of marginalised group. Constitution provides for universal approach to educating the mass in the Directive Principal of State Policy under Article 45 it calls for "Right of children to free and compulsory education" followed by the recognition of the need of weaker section in Article 46 where it directs the state "To promote educational and economic interests of weaker sections to protect them from social injustice." In the 83rd constitutional amendment "Righ to Education" is accepted as a fundamental right where it reads as "The State shall provide free and compulsory education to all children of the age of six to fourteen years in such manner as the State may, by law, determine". Looking into the above provisions, and a passage of six decades after Independence, it is pertinent to assess the educational achievements among the tribal. Since one of the goals of the education is to improve the economic status and facilitate the upward social mobility of the community, an attempt has been made in this chapter to present the educational status of tribes of Gujarat and the role of education in attaining productive and gainful employment helpful to improve their economic status.

Education Scenario among Scheduled Tribes

India is an abode to 4,693 communities (Singh, 2002), comprising of scheduled castes, scheduled tribes, other backward communities and upper castes in varying proportion. Tribal communities constitute around 8 per cent of the total population and are one among the most underdeveloped social groups. Efforts to uplift the socio-economic condition of this group remained one of the biggest challenges to the Government of India.

As the tribal communities were at the farthest end of development, special attention was paid to the needs of tribal population to bring them at par with other communities. In the Fifth Plan period, Tribal Sub-Plan was introduced to focus on the all-round development of tribal people. A host of welfare measures along with educational requirement were introduced to make community capable to take charge of its destiny. National policy on Education 1986 also outlined specific attention to tribal education which is as follows:

- Priority will be accorded to opening primary schools in tribal areas.
- Need to develop curricula and devise instructional material in tribal language at the initial stages with switchover to regional languages.
- Encouragement to tribal youths for taking up teaching in tribal areas.
- Establishment of residential schools in the tribal areas.
- Incentive schemes to recognise the special needs of tribal communities.

In addition to these, consideration was also accorded to the flexibility in norms for opening of schools to improve the access to the education. Though the policy and plans adopted so far has yielded considerable improvement in the literacy status of the population, the difference between the population groups is yet to bridge. Literacy status of the various social groups are presented through Table 18.1.

Table 18.1 : Literacy Rate among Social Groups in India

Items	*Literacy rate among social groups*			*% Literacy gap of SC and ST to others*	
	SC	*ST*	*Other than SC/ST*	*SC*	*ST*
			Year 1991		
Male	49.91	40.65	69.53	19.62	28.88
Female	23.76	18.19	44.81	21.05	26.62
All	37.41	29.60	57.69	20.28	28.09
			Year 2001		
Male	66.64	59.17	78.7	12.06	19.53
Female	41.90	34.76	58.17	16.27	23.41
All	54.69	47.10	68.81	14.12	21.71

Source: Report of the Task Group, 2005, Planning Commission.

It is evident from the figure that more than half of the tribal population is still illiterate though the gap between the others and ST population has reduced to seven points from the previous decade. Female literacy among scheduled tribes show even poorer deceleration when compared with the other population group. The gap has reduced to 3 points only reflecting poorer environment for the girl's education. According to an estimate 37 per cent of girls aged 7-14 belonging to the lowest castes or tribes do not attend school, compared with 26 per cent of majority of girls population group of the same age (Lewis and Lockheed, 2007).

The literacy rate among the tribal population has reported wide variation across the States. In the States where they are in the majority population, the literacy rate has been exceptionally higher reaching 60 to 80 per cent (North East States, Anadman and Lakshadweep etc.) whereas the State where they are in minority (Orissa, MP, AP, Gujarat, Maharashtra, etc.) their literacy rate is nearly 15-25 points lower than the general population; unfortunately these States cumulatively holds a total of 80 per cent of tribal people (Sujatha, 2002). Thus a low priority or subtle discrimination in providing schooling facilities to Scheduled Tribes in these States cannot be ruled out.

Literacy among Tribal in Gujarat

Gujarat is one among the major States that have substantial tribal population. The State has 15 per cent tribal people in its total population and is home to 29 tribal communities spread across twelve districts in the eastern and southern belt of the State.

Historically, the systematic attempt to tribal education started after 1882 with the effort of Government, Princely states and religious organisation. Before that sporadic effort by individuals, some officers and the state in Khandesh and Rewakantha areas have been reported (Joshi, 1985). With the establishment of *ashramshalas* during independence movement, tribal participation in education increased. It is probably because of this reason the literacy rate in the Scheduled Tribe of the State was little higher as compared to general tribal population of the country even in the early decades after Independence (Figure 18.1).

However, the pace could not be maintained and it came at par with the national average in 2001. Comparing the figures (Figure 18.1) from 1961 to 2001, it is seen that while tribal literacy has improved 5.5 times at the national level, it is slower in case of Gujarat. It is little over 4 per cent over the decades.

The State though a front runner in economic development, the social indicators have not been equally good as disparity between various social groups have widened over the years. As in other States of the country Scheduled Tribes are the most

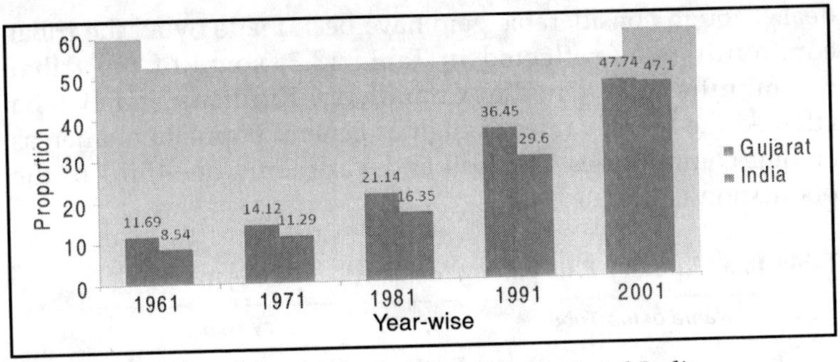

Fig. 18.1 : Literacy Rate among Tribals in Gujarat and India

marginalised and deprived section of the population with the highest proportion of people living below the poverty line. In rural areas nearly a third of the ST population and in urban areas 36.66 per cent people live below poverty line (Kachhap and Kachhap, 2008). The economic disparity is also reflected in the social indicators. A look at the literacy rate reveals this difference. As shown in the Table 18.2, literacy rate of the State is better than the country but the gap between general and ST population is wider than the situation at the national level. It is 22 points lower in Gujarat while it is 17 points at the national level (Census, 2001). Illiteracy is the highest in Scheduled Tribes where 53 per cent are returned as Illiterate.

Table 18.2 : Literacy Rate in Gujarat

Social Groups	*Male*	*Female*	*All*
1991			
General	73.13	48.64	61.29
Scheduled Castes	75.47	45.54	61.07
Scheduled Tribes	36.45	24.20	36.45
2001			
General	79.7	57.8	69.1
Scheduled Castes	82.6	57.6	70.5
Scheduled Tribes	59.2	36.0	47.7
2011			
Gujarat—General	87.23	70.73	79.31
India—General	82.14	65.46	74.04

Source: Census Report of 1991, 2001 and 2011.

Within tribal population also, the literacy rate varies a great deal. Though considerable gain have been made by all the tribal communities as reflected in Table 18.3, some of the tribal communities like Dhodia, Chaudhary, Kunkana and Patelia attained the literacy rates as high as general population whereas among communities like Koli and Varli, only one-third of the population is literate.

Table 18.3 : Literacy Rate among Major Tribes of Gujarat

Sl. No.	Name of the Tribe	Literacy Rate			
		Total (1971)	Total (2001)	Male	Female
1.	Bhil	11.7	44.3	59.2	36.0
2.	Chaudhary	20.7	62.4	71.3	53.4
3.	Dhanka	17.0	52.9	66.7	38.1
4.	Dhodia	31.2	75.9	85.3	66.5
5.	Dubla	13.8	47.8	56.8	38.7
6.	Gamit	14.9	52.9	61.7	44.2
7.	Kokna	12.3	51.5	62.6	40.3
8.	Koli	—	26.3	38.4	12.8
9.	Naikda	9.5	35.6	45.6	25.2
10.	Patelia	18.9	62.5	78.5	49.5
11.	Rathwa	5.7	36.8	50.2	22.8
12.	Varli	5.0	32.1	42.1	22.2
	All Scheduled Tribes	14.12	47.7	59.2	36.0

Source: Census 1971 and 2001.

It is important to note that while there is a spectacular increase in the literacy, the spatial distribution of tribes still influences their literacy status. Thus tribes who are more remotely located like Varli, Rathwa, Bhil are not only at the lowest end of development but are also at a greater risk of having more illiterate people. Further, gender gap among the tribal is high as female literacy is 23 points lower than the male literacy. Among tribes like Dhanka, Rathwa and Patelia the gap is even higher.

Disaggregated data by age group in overall tribal population show that in the age group of 5-14 years, 56.9 per cent of tribal children were attending school, whereas in 15-19 age group 31 per cent were attending educational institution. In the higher age groups of 20-24 and 25-29 years less than 7 per cent of the people were enrolled in any educational institution (Census 2001).

Preschool and Elementary Education in Tribal Areas

With the implementation of ICDS programme and establishment of Anganwadis/Balwadis, children are introduced to their culture and environment through informal learning by way of reciting the poems, song, dance and other educative materials. Similarly, they are introduced to formal education in the primary school. Status of these institutions are presented below:

Anganwadis

Under the ICDS scheme, along with the nutritional support, pre-school education is expected to be imparted to the children in the 3-6 years age group to accustom them to the schooling environment. In a study of forty *anganwadis* located in the scheduled areas, it was found that nearly half of the *anganwadis* were not involved in any kind of educational activities. Poor attendance of children which is just one-fourth of the enrolled children further stays many kids away from receiving any kind of education which would have enabled them to adjust to the formal schooling (Ratnawali, 2010). It also impacts their nutritional status as nearly half of the tribal children are underweight. Poor nutritional support undermines the cognitive development in children. In areas where *anganwadis* are poorly functioning, the pre-school children accompanying their older siblings in primary schools are not uncommon. It thus increases the chances of dropping out of children from the school to care for the younger siblings. Since first six years of life has a deciding and lasting influence on the life of the child (*Focus*, 2006), sincere attention is required to improve the reach of the *anganwadis* for the proper nutritional support and development of the child.

Schooling in the Tribal Areas

Rise in the literacy of the State reflects upon the better access of education to the children. In the predominantly tribal habitats, 85.6 per cent had a primary school within their areas. Overall 96.66 per cent of such habitats have a primary school within 1 km distance. The upper primary schools are relatively less accessible. 66.24 per cent of the upper primary schools are located within the habitation whereas a total of 95.96 per cent were situated up to a distance of 3 km. Habitations having secondary school within are just 15.5 per cent which increase to 78 per cent for distance up to 5 km. Availability of higher secondary school is still farther. Only 7 per cent habitations had one school within whereas 65.2 per cent are found up to a distance of 8 km (NCERT, 2007). Schooling facility in the villages with varied proportion of tribal community is given in Table 18.4.

In terms of availability of school it thus shows that primary schools are fairly accessible to tribal communities. Yet, the existence of school within areas with high concentration of tribal is relatively low. Compared to non-tribal villages; proportion of these schools are two-third in upper primary, one-third in secondary and one-fourth in higher secondary schooling facilities. The proportion of primary to upper primary school as per SSA (Sarva Siksha Abhiyan) norms is 2 : 1. In case of Gujarat this ratio is 1.5 : 1, much lower to all-India figure which is 2.5 (NUEPA, 2008). In view of the Table 18.4, this ratio is expected to be much lower in the scheduled areas.

Table 18.4 : Percentage Availability of Schools with respect to Tribal Concentration

Proportion of ST Population	*No. of Villages*	*Percentage of villages having schooling facility for*			
		Primary	*Upper Primary*	*Secondary*	*Higher Secondary*
0 Tribal population	7,642	97.68	93.8	22.3	4.9
1-25%	5,117	98.8	94.9	29.3	8.6
26-50%	1,396	98.2	98.2	17.7	6.8
51-75%	953	96.7	80.37	14.5	4.5
> 75%	3,120	93.2	63.1	7.56	1.85
Total	18,228	97.3	87.57	21.0	5.5

Source: Computed from NCERT, 2007

For the teacher-pupil ratio, schools in the tribal areas are within the norm laid by the government. In a study of ten villages in the Bharuch district (Ratnawali, 2007), the ratio was 30-35 children per teacher. However, as most of the schools were 1-7 grades, strength of teachers in some of the schools was found to be just 3. As a result teachers had to engage more than two classes at a time.

Further no school had supporting staff like peon and clerk. Hence all the administrative work along with the regular teaching often constraints the quality of teaching. Visit of principal to district/ Block office many a time reduces the teaching strength significantly, not to mention the leaves taken by the teachers. Besides, engagement of teachers for surveys, Census, election duty and other such work stresses them further, impacting their teaching. Absence of residential facility in remote villages causes a lot of problem and often teachers have to take up daily commuting. This is particularly difficult for the women teachers and is likely to result in absenteeism by the teachers.

Enrolment and Dropouts among School-going Children

Enrolment and dropouts present the status of schooling in the children. According to the Table 18.5, considerable improvement is seen in the enrolment and dropout situation in the State. It has registered more than 90 per cent enrolment in the primary grade.

Though a general increase in enrolment is reported, the difference between various groups reveal that ST population still lags much behind other population groups. Gender-wise substantial increase in girl's enrolment is evident in all social groups. Among tribal the increase is double to the boy's enrolment which will help improve the literacy rate among females substantially.

The overall dropout rate among the children of primary and upper primary has also declined for all groups since last decade. As indicated in Table 18.6, the dropout rate among school going children has declined to 2 per cent from 21 per cent in the primary grades. Substantial deceleration is also evident from 1-7 grade but it also points to the fact that more children are still dropping out after Grade 5.

Though a general improvement is seen by the figures given in Table 18.6; data released in Rajya Sabha says that between grade I to X, 58.84 children dropout of studies in the State. The figures for boys and girls dropout are 55.88 per cent and 62.25 per cent respectively (Kaushik, H., 2011). The situation for tribal children would have been much more alarming. As seen in Table 18.7, data for enrolment and dropout rates among ST in the State reveal a far poorer statistics.

Table 18.5 : Enrolment of Children among Different Social Groups

Year	*All Students*			*SC*			*ST*		
	Boys	*Girls*	*Total*	*Boys*	*Girls*	*Total*	*Boys*	*Girls*	*Total*
2001-02	306201	252561	558762	31245	27707	58952	43474	34748	78222
2004-05	340365	293292	633657	34936	31288	66224	45605	37950	83555
% increase in enrolment	11.16	16.13	13.40	11.81	12.92	12.34	4.90	9.21	6.82

Source : SSA Project, District Primary Education Programme IV, Education Department of Gujarat.

Table 18.6 : Proportion of Dropouts in Gujarat among School-going Children

Year	*Grade I-V*			*Grade I-VII*		
	Boys	*Girls*	*All*	*Boys*	*Girls*	*All*
2001-02	21.5	20.81	20.93	39.16	35.28	37.22
2010-2011	2.08	2.11	2.09	7.87	8.12	7.45
Improvement	18.97	18.7	18.84	31.29	27.16	29.77

Source : District Information System for Education, GoG.

Table 18.7 : Enrolment and Dropout Rate in Scheduled Tribe in Gujarat

Grades	*Enrolment*			*Dropout*		
	Boys	*Girls*	*All*	*Boys*	*Girls*	*All*
Grade I-V	92.5	100.48	95.90	I-V 6.18	43.10	39.35
Grade VI-VIII	77.74	67.58	72.90	I-VIII 66.45	68.66	67.41
Grade I-VIII	87.88	90.33	89.01	I-X 80.20	82.93	81.45

Source : Selected education statistics 2003-2004, GoI cited in Kachhap and Kachhap, 2008.

The figures show the deficit in enrolment and increase in the dropouts particularly in the upper primary and later grades. While 40 per cent leave study in the primary grades, it is two-third for the primary and upper primary and four-fifth for the schooling up to Class X. The mid-term appraisal of Eleventh Plan Document (2010) observed that at the national level, GER for STs have went up from 85.6 per cent in 2001-02 to 109.6 per cent in 2007, but the dropout rate appears to be widening between the social groups as nearly 52.6 per cent of SC children and 63.30 per cent of ST children are still dropping out at the elementary level.

A look into the Table 18.8 for primary and upper primary schooling in some of the tribal dominated districts of the State, reveals the status of elementary education.

The enrolment in primary classes is more than 90 per cent but the same in upper primary is declined to the half of primary enrolment. Thus more than half of the school-going children drops-outs of study after primary schooling. Even in the primary schools the retention rates are not more than 90 per cent with substantial low figures for Dang and Dohad, one among the highest tribal populated districts of the State. These are also the districts where repetition rate seems to be the highest. Considering the poor

Table 18.8 : Status of Education in Districts with High Tribal Population

Indicators	*Districts with respective proportion of tribal population*									
	Dohad (72.3%)		Dang (93.8%)		Narmada (78.1%)		Navsari (48.1%)		Valsad (54.8%)	
	P	UP	P	UP	P	UP	P	UP	P	UP
NER	100	52.2	100	9.5	97.2	3.7	71.8	37.5	91.0	41.6
DOR*	6.2	7.7	7.8	9.0	3.6	5.2	2.1	7.0	4.0	3.0
RR*	11.7	10.1	18.9	14.4	2.4	2.2	8.1	4.5	6.4	3.9
Rt R	75.2	—	56.8	—	91.0	—	90.9	—	87.3	—
GDI	0.95	—	0.97	—	0.94	—	0.90	—	0.90	—
Pupil Teacher Ratio	39	29	27	0	27	33	25	36	28	42
	40 (P+UP)		34 (P+UP)		34 (P+UP)		29 (P+UP)		31 (P+UP)	

P-Primary, UP—Upper Primary, NER—Net enrolment rate, DOR—Dropout rate, RR—Repetition rate, Rt R—Retention Rate, GDI—Gender Development Index,

*Figures under UP are for Class VI.

Source: Compiled from NUEPA 2009.

qualitative and quantitative schooling in the rural areas in general and tribal in particular the above figures seem to justify the situation in these two districts. It should be noted that Dang is all rural whereas Dohad holds 91 per cent rural population. In the study mentioned earlier, among the total dropouts in the age group 6-20 years, nearly one-third belonged to tribal community followed by Scheduled Castes (15%). It was highest among the Muslim community. Further, girls were more likely to be withdrawn in the secondary grades for reason to avoid sending them to other village.

Household Expenditure on Schooling

Most of the dropouts were reported from the households having monthly income of Rs. 3,000. Nearly 80 per cent of total children belonging to this income group had left their study mid-way. Tribal apparently were the foremost in bearing this burnt as 80 per cent of them had income less than Rs. 3,000 per month. Despite the policy of free elementary education, studies have found significant expenditure by the households in educating their child. Nearly one third of tribal household was found to spend on an average Rs. 900 annually per child in the State (Ratnawali, 2007). Expenditure on elementary education was also observed in States like Tamil Nadu, Kerala, HP and North East Region (Tilak, J.B.G., 2002).

Some of the reasons mentioned for the dropping out of school were mentioned in Table 18.9.

Table 18.9 : Reasons for Dropping Out of School

Reasons	*No. of Respondents*	*Proportion*
Failed in examinations	19	14.28
Disinterest in the studies	42	31.57
Fear of corporal punishment	6	4.51
Economic hardship	39	29.32
Illness, poor facility	4	3.0
Transportation problem	5	3.7
Did not want children to send away from the village	9	6.8
Prefer Madarsa education (Muslims)	9	6.8
All	133	100.00

Source : Ratnawali, 2007.

One can thus find that apart from poor interest in study, economic hardship lead one-third of the children to dropout of school. It thus points to a strong association between schooling and economic status of the household. In addition to dropping out, nearly 11 per cent of the schooling age (6-15) children were never been to school.

Quality of Education

Though the schooling scenario shows considerable improvement in the provisioning of educational facilities, it was not found commensurate with the quality of learning achievement. Objective of the literacy is to read and write with understanding. Just being in the school or passing out of school serves no purpose if children fail to read and write in accordance to their grade attainment.

Survey revealed that more than half of the children studying in Class IV to VIII were having substantial difficulty in reading and writing the text of the class two years junior to them. Only one-third of the students could read and write without difficulty while 6-8 per cent were unable to read and write (Ratnawali, *ibid.*). Similar observation was reported in a recent survey by Partaham (2010). It found that half of the children in class V attending school in rural areas are not able to read a Class III text book. In Gujarat too the same situation is met, as 40-50 per cent was unable to read class II text and less than 30 per cent could do division in mathematics. Comparing the situation in 2010 with 2001, the survey did not found much difference in educational achievement for the children entering Class I in 2001 with the children entering the same class in 2005. The impact of five years of schooling then and now has resulted in just little improvement in the ability of the children to read and write. Government school were worst offender as 50 per cent of the children studying in Government school cannot read, write and do basic mathematics despite being in school for 4-5 years (Pratham-ASER 2005 and 06). An upper primary private school principal reported that they had to do extra coaching for the students coming from the primary schools run by the government bodies (Ratnawali, *ibid.*). The sorrow state of affair has a bearing upon the attainment of level of education. It is pertinent to quote the UNESCO statement in this regard that reads "how well students are taught and how much they learn can have a crucial impact on the how long they stay in school" (UNESCO, 2005). This is also evident in the level of education attained by Scheduled Tribe.

Attainment of Educational Level among the Tribes of Gujarat

Attainment of education by the tribe shows a progressive decline with gradual increase in the level of education, a fact that corroborates with the dropout figures for the tribal. From the Table 18.10, it is apparent that among various social groups, attainment of education in the ST has the lowest proportion in all categories except the illiterates. While it does not differ much with SC and OBC, it fares poorly when compared with others population category.

Table 18.10 : Level of Education (%) by Social Groups in Gujarat

Social Groups	*Illiterate*	*Literate below Primary*	*Middle*	*Secondary*	*Higher Secondary*	*Diploma/ Certificate*	*Graduate and above*
ST	48.9	22.7	13.6	6.3	4.2	1.6	2.7
SC	38.5	21.0	22.4	8.8	4.8	1.3	3.3
OBC	38.6	25.4	18.3	9.8	3.9	1.0	2.5
Others	16.5	20.6	20.4	18.4	9.9	2.3	11.9
All	31.8	22.8	18.9	12.4	6.3	1.6	6.1

Source: Report No. 518, NSSO, 2005-06.

The proportion of ST is 66.6 per cent to the others proportion in middle school which plummeted to 22.7 per cent for graduation and above category. At the all-India level the enrolment in higher education is 6.52 per cent, 6.57 per cent and 8.77 per cent by ST, SC and OBC respectively, whereas it is 17.22 per cent for others (Eleventh Five Year Plan 2007-2012, Planning Commission of India).

The above scenario thus points to two propositions—first, either secondary or higher education is not a priority for the marginalised group as poverty is much more compelling to take on earning early; and second, even after attaining the higher education the employment opportunity/income prospect is not promising, hence there is a lack of motivation that translates in the poor attainment of higher education.

For the first observation the poverty scenario among the tribal population lends support. As we have mentioned earlier, proportion below poverty line is the highest among the tribal. According to NSSO (2004-05), nearly 37 per cent of rural tribal population lives below Rs. 455 per capita/month expenditure while one-forth spends less than equal to Rs. 580 in the urban areas[1]. For general population the proportions are 24 and 11.7 per cent respectively. Environmental degradation and poor agricultural output in the rural areas push substantial proportion of people to migrate to urban areas to secure livelihood. Such migration also impact children's education as many of the parents are forced to discontinue their schooling. Though, the measures have been taken to provide boarding facility to these children but these are few and far between. Many school going children had to take up work to support the family. Figures from the Census (2001) are illustrative. A total of 3,57,536 (19.2%) children in 5-14 years age groups are reported main worker while 1,80,796 (9.7%) were marginal worker. From among the school attending (50%) children of 5-19 years age group, 7,463 (0.6%) were main worker and 22,799 (1.8%) were marginal worker. Besides other work, employing children in cotton fields is a well documented fact (Kothari, 2007). The economic compulsions thus hardly give children the opportunity to continue with their study which adversely impacts the prospect of higher educational attainment among the tribal.

Education and Occupational Placement among Tribes

Attainment of education and economic achievement reinforce each other. One of the important roles of education is its ability to improve the productive potential of individual which help him attain better economic condition and improve the social status. Occupational placement thus provides an opportunity to attain this goal. The occupational structure in the tribal population with respect to their educational attainment is presented in Table 18.11

One can thus find that a large proportion (over 67%) of literates are engaged in cultivation and agriculture labour. Among the total main worker, literates above secondary education occupy only 2.5 per cent of the total. It also reveals that even among the graduates and above, nearly one-third is cultivators and 7 per cent are engaged in agriculture labour. For those who have acquired

Table 18.11 : Occupational Category by Level of Literacy (%)

Level of literacy (% of total main worker)	*Occupational Categories of Main Worker (as against total proportion of respective level of literacy)*				*Seeking or available for work (% to total level of literacy)*	
	Cultivator	*Agri. Labour*	*HHI*	*Others*	*Marginal worker*	*Non-worker*
Illiterates (57.6)	44.4	41.1	0.7	13.7	4.5	1.02
Literates (41.4)	38.4	29.13	0.9	31.5	4.0	3.17
Below Matric (30.49)	38.8	34.3	0.9	25.8	3.5	2.2
Matric/Secondary (8.3)	41.6	17.1	0.78	40.45	9.0	9.8
Tech dip or certificate not equal to degree (0.92)	8.8	1.75	0.2	89.2	3.4	6.1
Graduate and above (1.33)	29.2	6.3	0.55	63.95	5.6	9.2
Technical degree or diploma equal to Post-Graduate (0.26)	12.8	2.1	0.3	84.7	—	—

Source: Computed from Census, 2001.

technical degree 13 per cent are cultivators while 2 per cent are agricultural labour. Among the job seekers 14.5 per cent are literates who have attained education beyond secondary level. Another feature is the rise in proportion of other workers category with the commensurate improvement in the level of education. Though this means diversification in occupational structure, it may not be construed as economically more gainful activity pursued by the population. A micro level study about employment scenario among 18-35 years above primary literate youth in 7 tribal dominated districts of the State reveal that overall 45.5 per cent are in farming, 4.7 per cent have government jobs, 40.3 per cent are casual labours, 6.4 per cent have private jobs, 1.8 per cent are engaged in business, while 1.2 per cent are unemployed (Behavioural Science Centre, 2008). It further observed that even among the persons with vocational training 62.7 per cent are engaged in farming and 25.5 per cent are casual labours. It seems thus plausible that underemployment is common in the tribal areas and skill development training has not been qualitatively good enough, rendering them unemployable. Underemployment leads to poor economic gain. Thus more than 96 per cent has monthly income less than Rs. 5,000. Those in government jobs are only engaged in class 3 and 4 category. Employment for post-graduate, graduate and trained also could not fetch high income as nearly 94 per cent of them earned less than Rs. 5,000. Only 7 per cent of the post graduates are earning 5,000-10,000 while 13 per cent of diploma holders had an income more than Rs. 10,000. Tribal are more often contracted for manual work which does not fetch high remuneration. In the perception of educated tribal youths, the employing agencies also discriminate them against the general population group. It, therefore, seems that higher education may not be as gainful as to change quality of life especially after investing substantial years in study. The anxiety of a tribal teacher is thus expressed as *"How can we create job opportunities in villages? Can this be achieved via the medium of education"* (Bagai and Nandi, 2009). Besides, bribery and other corrupt means in getting certificate and job are not uncommon.

1. While the literacy rate of the State is better than the country for all population, it is at par in case of tribal. Thus there seems to be a lack of adequate effort towards education of

tribals. However, recent efforts by the government is likely to pay dividends in tribal education.

2. Though the enrolment in primary grades have seen significant rise, enrolment beyond this grade is yet to pick up.
3. Only 8 per cent go for higher secondary and above while just 3 per cent study up to graduation and above.
4. More than 60 per cent of children leave their study mid way either because of economic compulsion or poor motivation to continue with the study.
5. Learning achievement among the children is poor. Little over 50 per cent are poor achiever as are not able to read and write and do numerical calculation without any difficulty for the standards two grade below theirs. Thus even those who have attained 5-7 years of schooling can hardly be called literate in practical terms and this too is more likely to be wiped out with the discontinuity in schooling.
6. While few go for study in higher classes, employment opportunity in accordance to educational achievement is little.
7. Only 30 per cent of literate with education beyond higher secondary comes under main worker status. Thus a substantial proportion of educated persons are either marginal worker or unemployed/non-worker.
8. Underemployment and low wages further dampen their motivation for higher studies. Only 7 per cent P.G. holders and 17 per cent of technical degree holder earn Rs. 10,000 and above.
9. Even those with vocational training are not able to get good job opportunity as most of them are engaged in agriculture and work as casual labour. Thus the quality of training could also be substandard that lowers their employability.

The Way Forward

Education cannot be seen in isolation of cultural context. The role of family, community and government are interlinked. Notwithstanding the infrastructure need for the easy access of education by the government, family and community also need to be engaged in making education a reality. Children require adequate environment to play out their potential. While role of *anganwadis* in preschool education is important to shed away initial inhibition of children and making them receptive to the formal education later, the primary schools too need to create an environment where education does not seem to be thrust upon the child. Role of teachers in this regard is important. Children imbibe learning when taught with concern. This is the reason that emphasis is being placed on appointing teachers from the community. However, study have found that this may not be the only solution to the vexed problem of dropout as even tribal teachers may not be very receptive to the requirements of teaching (Dsara). It is not uncommon to find teacher sitting outside or engaged in other work when classes are going on. The responsibility of improving learning among children must be a goal inculcated into teachers while training them. Also, rather than the number of trainings that a teacher undergoes, far more important is the innovative ideas he/she develops in teaching that can impact better learning outcome in children. Encouragements to teachers in sharing their ideas/experience with the peers and evaluating the pupils by them may develop their stake in teaching. Such involvements could make children/parents to take their studies seriously thereby creating a viable environment for sustained learning.

Apart from the role of teachers, community participation in the schooling is also very significant especially after the formation of village education council (VEC). In many of these councils' meetings either members do not attend them or it is mainly focussed on the infrastructure development. Improving quality of education and experimenting with ideas hardly come in the discussion. The workshop conducted by NCERT (2008) in the Baroda (Gujarat) to strengthen the monitoring mechanism of school education observed that though the Sarpanch is the president of VEC, many of them remain absent or seldom participate in the meeting. It also observed that *"the analysis of school data is important but what is more important at each level is the implementation of the corrective measures taken after the analysis"* (Indian Express, 2008).

Similarly, economic productivity by the learning is an important factor that creates people's faith in the ability of education. As we have seen, those who have attained the higher education are not much fortunate in getting employment. While jobs may not be created for all hands, every hand must be capable of creating economically viable alternatives to improve their living. Role of government machinery is important in this regard. Linkages with industries and trained people could be strengthened with standard training or help people to set up their own production unit. Adequate direction to orient youth towards such activity will be useful in enhancing their living conditions. Economic improvement thus will lead to social mobility which is essential in creating confidence and environment for future learners of the family.

Conclusion

Literacy among tribes is a complex issue. It needs to be seen in the overall perspective of tribal situation. Providing infrastructure may increase the access but this cannot be the only factor for improving the educational status of tribals. Access of schooling should also be followed by quality education that can retain children in school by creating their interest in the study. Innovative pedagogic material and adequate environment is essential to engage children in education. Besides these critical inputs in the education, livelihood issues also need to be tackled at the priority basis. There is a strong association between education and economic condition of people. Linkages between education and productive employment have to be strengthened to facilitate the upward mobility of the community and bringing them to the mainstream.

NOTE

1. Official poverty line specification for rural India is Rs. 438/capita/ month and for urban population is Rs. 578/capita/month based on above report (Planning Commission). However, it is much contested.

REFERENCES

Behavioural Science Centre (2008): *Status of Employment among Adivasi Youths of South Gujarat*, Ahmedabad: Behavioural Science Centre.

Census (2001): Government of Gujarat.

District Information System for Education, GoG www.gujarat_education.gov.in/primary).

Focus (2006): *Focus on Children Under Six—Abridged Report*, December, New Delhi.

Joshi, Vidyut (1985): "A Century of Tribal Education in Gujarat" in Ghanshyam Shah *et al.* edited *Tribal Education in Gujarat*, Surat: Centre for Social Studies.

Kachhap, A. and Suvashi Kachhap (2008): *Tribal at a Glance. A Statistical Profile.* New Delhi: Manak Publication.

Kaushik, Himanshu, (2011): "58 of every 100 school kids dropout in Gujarat", *Times of India,* dated 20/4.

Lewis, M.A. and M.E. Lockheed. (2007): "Getting all girls into school". *Finance and Development*. International Monetary Fund, VII. II. Number 2.

Mid Term Appraisal of Eleventh Plan Document (2010): New Delhi: Government of India.

National Sample Survey Organisation (NSSO) (2006): *Employment and Unemployment Situation among Social Groups in India*. Report No. 518, NSSO, 61st Round. New Delhi.

NUEPA (2009): *Elementary Education in India. District Report Cards 2007-08.* Vol I, National University of Educational Planning and Administration, New Delhi

NUEPA, (2008). *Elementary Education in India Progress towards UEE.* NUEPA, New Delhi.

Planning Commission: *Eleventh Five Year 2007-2012, Vol II, Social Sector.* Planning Commission of India, New Delhi.

Planning Commission: "Report of the Task Group, 2005, Planning Commission", New Delhi. Cited in *Tribal at a Glance,* pp 123 by A. Kachhap and S. Kachhap 2008.

Pratham (2006): Annual Status of Education Report 2005 and 06, ASER (2010): *Annual Status of Education Report,* ASER.

Ratnawali (2007): *Education and Health Need Assessment of Some of the Villages of Bharuch District,* (Mimeograph), Surat: Centre for Social Studies, Surat.

Ratnawali (2010): "Supplementary Nutrition to Women and Children: A Situational Analysis of Anganwadis in the Tribal Areas of Gujarat", *Social Change,* 40(3), pp. 319-343.

Singh, K.S. (2002): *People of India, Gujarat,* Part I, Vol. XXII. Mumbai: Anthropological Survey of India, Mumbai.

Sujatha, K. (2002): "Education among Scheduled Tribes", In Govinda, R. (ed.), *India Education Report: A Profile of Basic Education*. New Delhi: Oxford University Press.

Sweta Bagai and Neera Nandi (2009): *Tribal Education in Fine Balance.* Mumbai: Dasara.

Tilak, J.B.G. (2002): *Determinants of Household Expenditure on Education in Rural India.* National Council of Applied Economic Research Working Paper Series No. 88. Delhi: NCAER.

UNESCO (2005): "Education for All: The Quality Imperative", *EFA Global Monitoring Report,* Paris.

19

Status of Primary Education with Special Reference to Tribal Child Literacy : A Micro Level Study of West Bengal

Swapan Kumar Kolay

Introduction

After sixty-three years of Independence, the goal of tribal education has not been achieved so far. In spite of the remarkable expansion of the elementary education in the last two decades, a very large number of tribal children and more among tribal girls who are deprived sections of the society in India continue to remain out of school. Out of all the children enrolled at primary stage, a very high percentage dropouts. Nearly 160 million children of 6-14 age group, do not enrol in school (based on sixth education survey data and available statistics on 5-14 age group children in India, NCERT (2002)) and among those who are enrolled, nearly half drop out before completing the primary education. About 10 million children of school-going age are not attending elementary schooling even today (Aggarwal, 2002: Vol. 2). Elementary education is a priority area in the *Tribal Sub-Plans* from the Fifth Five Year Plan. Education of ST children is considered important, not only because of the Constitutional obligation but also as a crucial input for total development of tribal communities. Another important development in the policy towards education of tribals is the National Policy on Education (NPE), 1986 which specified among other things the following: (i) Priority will be accorded to opening primary schools in tribal areas; (ii) There is need to develop curricula and devise instructional material in tribal language at the initial stages with arrangements for switchover to regional languages; (iii) ST youths will be encouraged to take up teaching in tribal areas; (iv) Ashram schools/residential schools will be established on a large scale in tribal areas; and (v) Incentive schemes will be formulated for the STs, keeping in view their special needs and lifestyle. The main causes of the non-implementation of this basic objective of our national policy are well known, viz., (a) financial inadequacy; (b) non-availability of a sufficient number of suitable teachers; (c) lack of motivation; and (d) poverty (Aggarwal, 2002).

Education has still to play a significant role in the overall development of the poor people and especially among the poor tribal population of India where there is high dropout and low participation rates which is again gender sensitive. The impact of tribal education policy after independence can neither be said to be much satisfactory nor can it be taken to be very disappointing (Thakur, 1995). Studying the shortcomings of the tribal education policy is the need of the hour as tribal people are the most backward communities in India. Russel (1932) in his divergent theories of education noted that "education is to be considered rather in relation to the community than in relation to the individual". Education is not only imparting theoretical knowledge, but a process of enculturation and socialization. Education must be associated with the cultural pattern and way of life of specific communities. "One of the avenues to speedy development is education" (Sachchidananda, 1992). Education leads to overall development of an individual and in turn it influences on development of a whole society.

But it has been observed throughout these years that the extent of benefits of these schemes varies from one district to another and from one region to another within the State. It has also been observed that the number of tribal children of deriving benefits of these schemes is far less than of others. The efforts were made by the Government and the Missionaries to educate tribal people. But the pace of development was slow for them. Venkataiah (2001) noted that tribal education is not a different kind of education, but it is to suit the special needs and aspirations of the tribal groups who are in the different stages of development. It is, therefore, necessary within the circumstances contributing to the differential success of the schemes in three districts with special reference to Santal, Mahali and Lodha/Savar groups.

The tribal got opportunities of education through Missionaries and NGOs in West Bengal. They experienced different socio-political upheavals in their life which affected their education. An increasing number of researchers strongly advocate the use of the mother tongue or home language as medium of instruction in early stages of education. This assumes greater significance in the context of education of tribal children because their mother tongue is often quite distinct from the prominent languages in the State or regional languages. ST children face problems wherever teachers do not speak their dialect at all. From the perspective of language, it is desirable to have a local teacher from the same tribal community (Jha & Jhingran, 2002).This chapter aims at understanding the gaps in education among these tribals of Midnapur, Bankura and Purulia districts of West Bengal.

Population Distribution in West Bengal

The total population of West Bengal at 2001 Census has been 80,176,197. Of this 4,406,794 persons are Scheduled Tribes (STs) constituting 5.5 per cent of the total population of the State. There are total 38 notified STs in the State.

Table 19.1: Population and Proportion of Ten Major STs in West Bengal

Sl. No.	*Name of the Scheduled Tribe*	*Total Population*	*Proportion to the total ST Population (%)*
1.	Santal	2,280,540	51.8
2.	Oraon	617,138	14.0
3.	Munda	341,542	7.8
4.	Bhumij	336,436	7.6
5.	Kora	142,789	3.2
6.	Lodha	84,966	1.9
7.	Mahali	76,102	1.7
8.	Bhutia	60,091	1.4
9.	Bedia	55,979	1.3
10.	Savar	43,599	1.0
	All Scheduled Tribes	4,406,794	100.0

Source : Census of India, 2001.

The Santal represents more than half of the total ST population of the State (51.8%). Oraon (14%), Munda (7.8%), Bhumij (7.6%) and Kora (3.2%) are the other major STs having sizeable population. Along with Santal, they constitute nearly 85 per cent of the State's total ST population. The Lodha, Mahali, Bhutia, Bedia, and Savar are the remaining STs, and having population of one per cent or more (Table 19.1). The rest of the STs are very small in population size.

Literacy and Educational Level in West Bengal

Among all STs, 43.4 per cent of the population has been returned as literate, which is lower than the national average (47.1 per cent). The male literacy rate of 57.4 per cent and female of 29.2 per cent, show a gender disparity in literacy. Of the ten major STs, Bhutia with 72.6 per cent overall literacy, 80.2 per cent male and 65.2 per cent female literacy respectively, is well ahead of others. Savar are at the other extreme having 26.3 per cent overall literacy and 16 per cent female literacy rate (Table 19.2).

Of 51.7 per cent of the STs in the age group 5-14 years have been attending any educational institutions. Of the ten major STs, Bhutia has recorded the highest 77 per cent and Savar the lowest 35.5 per cent of their respective population attending educational institutions. Merely 8.4 per cent of total literates among STs are having educational level above matriculation.

Table 19.2 : Literacy Rate among Ten Major STs in West Bengal

S.No.	*Name of the Scheduled Tribe*	*Literacy Rate (above 7+ years)*		
		Male	*Female*	*Total*
1.	Santal	57.3	27.0	42.2
2.	Oraon	55.4	31.0	43.4
3.	Munda	54.0	27.7	41.0
4.	Bhumij	61.6	29.1	45.6
5.	Kora	58.4	28.2	43.4
6.	Lodha	46.8	22.5	34.8
7.	Mahali	55.6	26.3	41.1
8.	Bhutia	80.2	65.2	72.6
9.	Bedia	61.7	34.6	48.4
10.	Savar	36.4	16.0	26.3
	All Scheduled Tribes	57.4	29.2	43.4

Source : Census of India, 2001.

Methodology

Universe of the Study

To achieve the above objective the following methodologies are being followed. Researchers used both quantitative and qualitative methods. Creswell (2003) and Bernard (2000) recommend qualitative method of inquiry to achieve such type of purposes when the task is to investigate the behaviours rather than count down. Data has been collected from major two level of sources, i.e., Primary and Secondary.

Primary informations with reference to selected parents of tribal communities and primary school teachers were collected with the help of structured questionnaire and schedule followed by personal interview, participant and non-participant observation. To have views from various government and non-government officials the second type of structured questionnaire was also designed.

Secondary information pertaining to relevant government records and other facts have been collected from various government records and bulletin. Various types of related government journals and research monographs are also being consulted for the present study.

The gathered information from primary and secondary level sources are being analysed and tabulated with the help of simple method of statistical tools and techniques for writing the final report.

Sampling and Procedure

Purposive sampling design has been adopted to decide the size of sample by taking into consideration the following criteria. Keeping in view the two Blocks from Midnapur and Bankura districts and three Blocks from Purulia district have been selected for in-depth study. Selection of the sample Blocks was done on the basis of the following criteria :

(a) Concentration of tribal population in the selected ITDPs.
(b) Communities have been selected from the villages which was close to urban areas and far away from urban areas

by taking into consideration the existing available infrastructure facilities.

(c) Communities also have been selected on the basis of who are residing near to the forest and plain areas.

(d) The population of the Blocks belongs to different socio-cultural categories. The sample Blocks will have a sizable section of these populations.

(e) Performance level of these communities relating to primary education is likely to differ from one Block to another within district. It is also unlikely that the level of performance of these have been the same in any one Block. Hence, enrolment of children of tribals in class I in primary schools in a given/available year have been considered for assessing the level of overall performance of primary education in the Blocks. Matching with the criterion of socio-cultural diversity, one best and one worst performed Block from three different districts have been selected.

Study Area

For the present study the researcher carried out the field work in 18 villages of the related three districts considered namely (i) Midnapur; (ii) Bankura; and (iii) Purulia of West Bengal.

Result and Discussion

A study has been conducted among the Santal-settled agriculturists, Mahali-basket makers and Lodha/Savar still dependent on forest to a great extent. Keeping these three tribal communities, three tribal dominated districts namely Midnapur, Bankura and Purulia selected bordering the State of Bihar and Orissa. From each district two villages from each community were identified on the basis of population of the concentration of the respective community. Further from each village 25 families were selected on random sampling method. In case of Mahali, only 18 families were found in one village, all of which are covered under the study. Lodha village was selected from Midnapur district whereas in Purulia and Bankura districts Savar villages were selected and here Lodha population is very insignificant. At the same time it is difficult to locate the Lodha villages in these two districts.

It is also to be mentioned here that in Bankura district the total families of Savar in one selected village were 19 instead of 25, which were taken as a whole for the study. In this regard, Table 19.3 described in details may be seen.

Table 19.3 : Villages with Major Tribal Groups

State	*District*	*Block*	*Village*	*Tribal Group*				
				Santal	*Mahali*	*Lodha*	*Savar*	
West Bengal	Midnapur	Narayangarh	Bahurupa	25	-	-	-	
			Kotaigarh	-	25	-	-	
			Birkarh	-	-	25	-	
		Nayagram	Benachui	25	-	-	-	
			Chowkapathra	-	25	-	-	
			Ghoratoria	-	-	25	-	
	Bankura	Ranibandh	Madalbhanga	25	-	-	-	
			Rajakata	-	25	-	-	
			Katium	-	-	-	25	
		Khatra	Lucaicanali	25	-	-	-	
			Amdiha	-	18	-	-	
			Jalhari	-	-	-	25	
	Purulia	Hura	Sukunibasa	25	-	-	-	
			Magurai	-	-	-	25	
		Manbazer	Barkadam	-	25	-	-	
			Boro	-	-	-	25	
		Kashipur	Keliathol	25	-	-	-	
			Majura	-	25	-	-	
Total				150	143	50	100	443

Source : Primary Field Survey Data.

Education and Literacy in Three Districts of West Bengal

Education is one of the essential factors for bringing any positive change or development. The persons even engaged in any traditional occupations need education so as to adopt the new technology which has been developed in every sphere of occupations, be it agriculture, animal husbandry, pisciculture or even any type of handicraft. To make from these types of occupations, it is necessary to understand not only the modern technology but also the management and marketing of the same and for this process, education is the only answer. In view of this, the position of educational status rather rate of literate persons among the three tribal communities of three different districts have been examined and shown in Table 19.4. Here it may be mentioned

Table 19.4 : Community-wise Distribution of Literacy Level of Three Districts of West Bengal

Community	*District*	*Population*	*Illiterate*	*Literate*					
				Total	*R+W*	*Primary*	*Secondary*	*H.S.*	*Graduate and above*
Santal	Midnapur	252	55.96	44.04	23.42	41.45	31.53	2.70	0.90
	Bankura	206	37.38	62.62	17.82	29.45	50.39	1.56	0.78
	Purulia	272	52.94	47.06	8.60	47.66	37.50	3.12	3.12
Mahali	Midnapur	200	54.00	46.00	26.09	47.82	21.73	3.27	1.09
	Bankura	149	54.37	45.63	10.30	42.64	42.64	2.94	1.48
	Purulia	192	69.80	30.20	3.45	36.20	53.45	5.18	1.72
Lodha/Savar	Midnapur	198	59.10	40.90	16.04	62.97	20.99	–	–
	Bankura	158	81.64	18.36	41.38	44.82	13.80	–	–
	Purulia	188	80.31	19.69	8.10	78.38	13.52	–	–

Source : Primary Field Survey Data.

that the Census calculate the rate of literates by excluding the population of below 7 years, but in this study population below 5 years have been excluded as it has been observed during the field study that children at the age of 5 years are attending primary school. It has been observed that 50.41 per cent of the Santal are literates. Among the Mahali the said percentage is 40.30 and it is lowest among the Lodha/Savar with 27.02 per cent. By analyzing the district-wise literacy rate it is found that the Santals of Bankura district have achieved the highest literacy rate in comparison to two other districts. The Santal of Purulia has the highest number of persons read up to primary level whereas the minimum number of Santals of Bankura district continued their study up to secondary level of education. Here, it may be mentioned that about 56 per cent of the Santals are literate in the districts of Midnapur and Purulia respectively.

In case of Mahali the highest number of persons with primary level of education have been recorded in the district of Midnapur followed by those inhabiting in Bankura district. Among the Mahalis who have read or reading in secondary stage of education, highest number has been recorded in Purulia district followed by Bankura district. In this connection, it may also be noted that the percentage of illiterate is highest among the Mahalis of Purulia district and the said percentages are 54 and above in two other districts.

Of the Lodha/Savar, the literacy rate is more in Midnapur district, more or less similar literacy rate have been noted in two other districts. About 78.38 per cent Savaras of Purulia district have read or continuing study at primary level, on the contrary the said percentage is 69.97 and 44.82 among the Lodha and Savaras of Midnapur and Bankura districts respectively. In secondary level Midnapur have highest position both the districts of Bankura and Purulia have sent almost equal number of students at secondary level of education. From the field survey it has been observed that among the Lodhas of Midnapur the percentage of illiterate is about 59, which is as high as 80 per cent among the Savaras of Purulia and Bankura districts. By examining this fact it may be clearly stated that except the Santals of Bankura, more than half of the population of these tribal groups are illiterate. This is more prominent among the Lodha/Savar and Mahalis.

Some of the common problems observed in course of popularization of education among tribal children are as under:

1. *Physical Location of Tribal Village :* Maximum number of tribal villages are in a scattered manner specially in Purulia followed by Bankura and Midnapur districts respectively. Most of the villages have low population. So, it becomes impossible to open separate schools in each village where the required students strength is not available. On the other hand, Lodha/Savar habitations remain segregated from each other by some physical barriers like rivers, *nalas* and forests. So these physical barriers create a hindrance for the children to attend the school in a neighbouring village.
2. *Economic Condition :* The sole income of tribals depends on forests for maximum months and on agriculture for rest of the months. The children of 4 to 7 age group are found to be helping their parents in collection of forest products. In this situation, parents do not desire to spare their children or their labour power and allow them to attend schools. In many tribal areas in three different districts of West Bengal where community development programme have embarked on ambitious programmes of economic development but the majority of the people do not come forward to take advantage of the schemes. In cases where they do take up such schemes, they have come to grief or have been cheated out of their well earned income by middlemen. Thus even through economic development puts more money in their hands, their standard of living does not show any appreciable improvement. Money-lenders, petty government employees and contractors exploit them as before.
3. *Parents Attitude :* Majority of tribal parents are basically illiterate. Their illiteracy does not permit them to understand the long term values of education. As education does not yield them any immediate economic return, they prefer to engage their children in remunerative employment which supplement the family income and strengthens the family economy. Further, a few parents who have become aware of the values of education, fail to accord education to their children as they cannot afford finances for it.
4. *Village Education Committee :* In remote tribal villages of West Bengal, VECs have been constituted to preserve and

monitor the functioning of the schools. Till now people are not aware of the role of the VECs. Neither the villagers nor the members of the VECs take any active interest to enhance enrolment and attendance of children in primary school.

5. *Teachers Problem :* There is near absence of relationship between school teachers and the villagers. Maximum tribal parents have virtually no relationship with the teachers. Teachers do not get any accommodation facility in the village, which makes them irregular which hampers the normal routine of a school. Further, the apathetic attitude among these tribal communities, and their simplicity provide ample scope to the teachers to act accordingly. Untrained appointment of teachers in tribal areas diminishes the values of education. However, recently the Government has started posting trained teachers in tribal schools. The lack of special incentives for the teachers in tribal areas serve as a demotivating factors for the teachers and degrades their efficiency. Teachers do not feel that their own children would be illiterate in tribal areas. Most of the teachers have a preconception that tribal children are average students; also they don't take special care in promoting their education. The pre-conceived notions of the teachers that the tribal children cannot grasp anything beyond nature, forest and agriculture create barriers in expanding primary education among these tribal villages. The non-tribal teachers adopt an attitude of indifference to tribal languages, traditions, cultures and life-styles. They fail to perceive the human values ingrained in these folk cultures. When they try to impart an education which neglects these human values and culture, they fail to make it interesting for the tribal children. The idea of the non-tribal teachers about tribal environment and culture is narrow and hollow. For this they fail to cite examples from the surroundings and make the concepts complicated for the tribal students. The in-built creativity of tribal children remains unknown to the teachers. Teachers face wide gulf between the language used in the books and the native uses while teaching the tribal students. They simply opine that the content of the text books is beyond the

comprehension of the students, so teaching becomes futile. No special training on tribal languages, cultures or current problems is being imparted to the teachers serving in tribal areas. Children's engagement in household works, agriculture coupled with parent's indifference towards their children's studies deprive the teachers to render their services in the classroom. No effort is made on the part of the higher authorities and the tribal masses to curb the frequent absenteeism among the teachers. The lack of a frequent and recurrent inspection mechanism no doubt aggravates the situation.

6. *Tribal Students* : The survey conducted in three different districts of West Bengal shows that only 20 per cent Savar children attend the school. The reasons for this mass non-attendance are as follows: (a) helping parents at home, (b) discharging sibling care responsibilities, (c) no positive environment or inspiration for students at home, (d) school environment is uncomfortable and horrifying, (e) teachers inflict heavy punishment and do not help in studies, (f) No regular supply of study materials, (g) Parents have migrated from the village to earn their livelihood because of drought or other natural calamities, (h) teachers do not bother whether the child comprehends the teaching or not, (i) the content and language of the primers are beyond the comprehensive ability of the tribal children, They don't find any example or experience of their environment in the books, (j) no health care facilities for the children suffering from malaria, skin diseases and anaemia, (k) tribal children contribute their physical power to supplement the family income, and (l) the school timings hamper the routine household work of the tribal children.
7. *Girls Education* : The extent of education among tribal women is low. In all the three different districts of West Bengal it has been found that most tribal societies, men and women enjoy equal status and work shoulder to shoulder in the home, field and the forest. Women are not segregated or confined behind the *pardah.* If men alone are educated, it creates an imbalance, among couples (Sachchidananda, 1992). With the husband educated and

the wife unlettered, there is emotional maladjustment. Educated young men move for educated wives and if they are not available in their own religious fold they are even prepared to change their faiths.

8. *Teaching Learning Materials (TLM)* : Even if cultural differences are marked on regional basis in the three different districts of West Bengal, the Government has prescribed uniform primers at primary school stage. Among the 38 tribes found in the State, most of them have their own language and for them Bengali language appears to be an alien language.

   Even though the National Education Policy has insisted on teaching the children in their mother tongues at the primary level, this has not been implemented for the tribal. The educationists have thoroughly neglected the tribal language and culture and have ignored the problems of tribal children while framing books for them. So far as study materials are concerned, the following problems came to light: (a) the language used in the books are beyond understanding of the tribal children; (b) sometimes the local teachers also get swayed way by the bookish language and don't try to communicate in the tribal languages. As a result teaching seems to be artificial for the tribal children; (c) the contents of the primary school books are less practice oriented and are more factual and abstract; (d) teaching at primary schools ignore the local nature, culture and environment; (e) there is dearth of study materials and kits in the class rooms; (f) the kits that have been provided to the schools under the Operation Black Board Scheme are not properly utilized by the teachers; (g) books are not supplied to the schools at the session beginning by the Tribal Welfare Department and the Text Book Press. This irregularity found in the supply of books creates problems both for the teachers and students. Further, stipends are not given in due time; and (h) Also, school fails to work out the idea of utilizing the services of the local architects, painters and artists at a low cost to prepare some of the educational kits for the children.

9. *Condition of Primary Schools* : Maximum primary school

buildings in most of the study villages are in broken condition and hence not attractive. Lack of care and repair makes it difficult to sit in the collapsing class rooms. Children of 2/3 classes are accommodated in a single class room. Neither the villagers nor the Village Education Committee (VEC) take any active interest to preserve and protect the school building. They preserve the impression that it is the Government outlook and not theirs. No accommodation arrangement is being made for teachers either in the school or in the village. The tribal habitations remain in scattered forms. So, they don't fulfil the needs of the required amount of child population to open a school within 1 km. radius. So, in the tribal areas schools remain far away from the habitations. The number of *Ashram* schools is scanty. *Ashram* schools are best fitted for the tribal children. In the primary schools, no effort is made to provide incentives and scope to music, dance, games, paintings, etc., which remain as latent potentialities with a child. In a school, a tribal child undergoes mental stress and strain. A fear free environment is required for their proper development. Physical barriers and communication difficulties also keep the tribal children away from the schools.

10. *Condition of Ashram and Residential School:* The *Ashram* schools are run by Government as well as the non-official agencies. *Ashram* type schools should also do well for the children of the ex criminal tribes or denotified communities like Lodhas of Midnapur district, who need segregation from their parents so that they may not pick up criminal habits. However, it is imperative that they do not breathe in an atmosphere of fear, shame and guilt. The attendance in *Ashram* schools depends upon the locality in which the schools are situated and the tribes for whom they cater. Among the Lodha and Savars, admissions are generally few, and desertions from the school within the first-six months of admission to the school are considerable. But among Santal and Mahalis comparatively better accultured tribes predominate, such desertions are fewer. Desertions also depend upon the atmosphere prevailing inside the school. Some schools do

not permit non-vegetarian food. Most tribal are non-vegetarians and they do not like such restrictions. Unsympathetic behaviour of the teachers may also lead to desertions. It is necessary to examine, at the outset, whether or not, the teachers being appointed to these *Ashram* schools belong to the right type, have sincerely and a missionary spirit and take due interest in their work. Being cut off from the main centres of educational enlightenment, the methods used by the teachers in these schools are apt to become stale.

11. *Hostels* : The Tribal population in three different districts is very much scattered, a number of hostels have been started for housing school. All the boarders are given a hostel allowance, but this is barely sufficient to meet the cost of living. It is desirable that the vegetable and lighting allowance should be suitably increased to relieve the difficulties of students. Most of the boarders bring foodgrains from home and pool their resources together. These hostels are maintained by the Government as well as the voluntary agencies. The comforts in these hostels are the same as those provided in other hostels. Boys sleep on mats in big dormitories or in smaller rooms in groups of 4 or 6. In many areas, only hostels for schedule tribes accommodate the tribals. This is bad in as much as it creates social distance between them and the other communities. It is desirable that all communities live together. Seats for Scheduled Tribes must be reserved in all hostels of educational institutions in tribal areas, in proportion to the tribal population in that area. The State should meet the cost of the maintenance of tribal students in such hostels. This would do away with the idea of exclusiveness or segregation.
12. *Scholarships:* Serious complaints are constantly made about the irregularity and delay in the payment of scholarships at every stage and the State government have admitted this to be true. Because of this delays, students are compelled to borrow money for their sustenance at heavy rates of interest., They have little effort for their studies. The scholarships reaches the students at a time when his needs have been satisfied or he has already given up his

studies in despair. He receives a large sum which he spends in bying articles of luxary such as a cycle or wrist watch. Thus the purpose for which scholarship is meant is defeated and the poor parents who bear all the burden of expenditure for their children's education do not get any relief. It is, therefore, necessary that scholarships be paid every month by the authorities. Delay in the receipt of scholarships amounts in a large measure, to their denial. Regarding pre-Matric scholarships, committees of representative of non-officials have been formed for deciding upon the award. At the time of disbursement a number of malpractices have been discovered. In many cases, the full amount of the scholarship does not reach the student or his guardian. Young students and their illiterate parents have no idea of the actual amount they are entitled to receive. Local authorities must take extra care to see that the full amount reaches the person concerned.

13. *Technical Education* : In many tribal areas of Midnapur, Bankura and Purulia districts of West Bengal, new industries are being established. These require skill technicians. In the absence of skilled workers in the local population, such workers have to be imported from outside. Thus, the local population does not derive much benefit by the opening of industries. It is, therefore, desirable that technical training institutes should be established in such areas to enable the tribals to secure skilled employment. This will not only improve their economy but solve the problem of unemployment and underemployment. This is all the more necessary as the tribals in the neighbourhood of huge industrial complexes had to leave their hearths and homes so that the factory and its township could be built. The uprooted populations would, in this way, get some succour.
14. *Lack of Inspection* : School inspectors (at the Block and district level) are not active in solving problems associated with the primary schools in the tribal areas. The surveys bring to notice that the Block level inspectors have not inspected all the schools in their areas. Inspectors do not provide equal importance to the schools of hill areas as they give to the

schools of plain areas. The tribal teachers remain indifferent to tribal education. They are also marked with some mental stress. The non-tribal teachers adopt an apathetic attitude towards tribal school management.

15. *Social and Cultural Problems* : The community life, the economy, the life style, the traditions of the tribals and their outlook of the world is totally unique. All these have got their humanitarian values and cultural significance. But they have not found recognition in the ideas of local inspectors, teachers, parents and policy planners. The root cause of this can be attributed to the stratification system and the tribal and non-tribal attitude. Thus, a strong consciousness and pro-tribal attitude have not been built up among the people. The NGOs have no doubt taken some steps in this area. But how far the efforts of the NGOs will be successful in changing the institutionalized practices of society is still doubtful. The greatest problem is, the tribals have come to recognize the modernization and the demands of time. But they are not coming forward to bring reforms in the educational status and economic standards. Now a strong campaign is needed for this. The voluntary agencies should try to launch this campaign on a long term basis with constructive ideas.

Suggestions and Recommendations

Suggestions and recommendations have been devoted to the analysis of different educational facilities, problems and their impact on the tribal communities, with special reference to the Santal, Mahali, Lodha and Savar tribes for their overall socio-economic upliftment. The analysis has also been made to ascertain their capabilities and constraints with regard to educational development programmes causing dissatisfaction among the tribal communities. In spite of various plans, programmes and projects taken up of the government machinery, the result has been far from satisfactory. The reason as far as can be ascertained, is due to faulty scheme and lukewarm support of the people in these educational development programme. It is an established fact that there is necessity for development of the tribal communities, in general. Constitutional provisions and various educational development strategies adopted during the different plan periods clearly indicate the action pattern of the Welfare State of India. The following points are important in this respects:

(i) Policy Interventions

- Minimizing the barrier to literacy and education related services for the tribals, physically, financially and culturally;
- Improving basic literacy and educational services, particularly for the tribal girl child, including formal and non-formal education;
- Orientation towards basic literacy and education for the tribal girl child by improved outreach activities, formally as well as non-formally;
- Providing competency based training to teachers and others involved in imparting education and literacy;
- Collaboration between public and private sector for management and delivery of services for education and literacy: (i) To supplement the logistic, finance and educational expertise of the private sector with that of the public sector so as to develop the required synergy to deal with the low level of tribal child education in the Midnapur, Bankura and Purulia districts of West Bengal, and (ii) Building managerial capacity to address service delivery provision;
- Benefits should be taken from the frontier areas of technology, e.g., information and communication technologies;
- Policy development, financing, regulation, monitoring and evaluation of tribal educational programmes.

(ii) Awareness Campaign

- Promote tribal education campaigns aimed at improving knowledge, skills and attitudes. This training can augment future earning potential for these girls who will benefit from dual utility of basic education along with an initiation into some basic vocational practices (Chattopadhyay *et al.*, 2005);
- Professional groups should be involved like teaching

communities, community groups, religious and philanthropic bodies in the promotion of tribal education and literacy related issues. Media, both electronic and print, play a vital role in the awareness campaigns which need to be channelized in the areas having a bearing on the tribal education.

(iii) Community Mobilization

The issues like enrolment, education of girl children, retention of children in schools and school involvement should be carried out in tribal areas. The specific features of such mobilization are :

- Use of tribal/folk art forms;
- Meetings of mothers and family meetings and involvement of tribal youth volunteers;
- Leaflets posters, Kalajathas, and videocassettes in tribal languages;
- Organization of meetings in tribal *haats*/bazaars and use of tribal fairs and festive occasions to discuss primary education issues;
- Involvement of traditional tribal organizations in the mobilization effort; and
- Involvement of the community including VECs members in documentation of local folklore, history, traditional medicine, agricultural practices.

(iv) Community Partnership

- It not only encourages but also facilitate for the involvement of community and non-governmental organizations for the tribal child education and literacy. These organizations have some experience and operate at the field level and can be involved in an interactive mode of relationships with family and government and private educational initiatives within the national educational policy framework.

Conclusion

There is a need to make attempt to prepare district-specific and tribal-specific plans for primary education within the broad strategy frame of micro planning through people's participation. The strides made by our government for tribal education needs proper implementation. As hunger is more dangerous than illiteracy, the policy makers need to sort out and prioritize area specific problems. First and foremost there is a need to implement programmes for a stable earning through land reform, extension of irrigation, small scale industrialization and provision of basic amenities for mere survival of the poor tribal. Public-private partnership in innovative entrepreneurship is necessary to improve the demand as well as the supply side. Provision of transportation and basic amenities in schools need to be guaranteed to attract and retain these indigenous tribals.

REFERENCES

Aggarwal, D.D. (2002): *History and Development of Elementary Education in India,* New Delhi: Sarup & Sons, Vol. 2.

Bernard, H.R. (2000): *Social Research Methods: Qualitative and Quantitative Approaches,* Thousand Oaks, New Delhi: Sage Publications.

Census of India (2001): Ministry of Home Affairs, Government of India, New Delhi.

Chattopadhyay, A.; Papiya G; Vijaya D. (2005) "Scenario of Primary School Attendance: A Study of Less Developed States in India," J. *Educ. Plann. Adm.* 19(1): 111-130.

Creswell, J.W. (2003): *Research Design: Qualitative, Quantitative, and Mix Method Approaches* (2nd ed.), Thousand Oaks, New Delhi: Sage Publications.

Jha, J. and Jhingran, D. (2002): *"Elementary Education for the Poorest and Other Deprived Groups: The Real Challenge of Universalisation"* Delhi: Centre for Policy Research.

NCERT (2002): *Sixth All India Education Survey,* New Delhi, Vol. 1.

Russel, B. (1932): *Education and Social Order,* London: Unwin Paperbacks.

Sachchidananda (1992): "Structural Constraints in the Education of Scheduled Tribes and Scheduled Castes," *Tribal Transformation in India,* Vol. IV (ed. By Chaudhuri, B.), New Delhi: Inter India Publication.

_____(1992): *Tribal India: Past and Present,* Calcutta: Institute of Social Research and Applied Anthropology.

Thakur, D. (1995): *Tribal Education,* Delhi: Deep and Deep Publications.

Venkataiah, S. (2001): *Modern Tribal Education,* New Delhi: Anmol Publications Pvt. Ltd.

20

Enhancing Education among Tribes of Orissa : Issues and Concerns

Soubhagya Ranjan Padhi

Introduction

The term 'Development', in a value-free understanding, would mean as a process of maximizing human potential. Similarly, education is also commonly defined as a realization of human potential. While education is considered as an important factor in the process of development, progress of educational status is considered as an important indicator of development itself. However, education in a broader sense would involve the process of acquiring the knowledge and skills, appropriate in a particular situation and cultural context, in order to put into its maximum use for productive and creative purposes, in the progress of a particular individual and society. On the other hand, development always implies the progressive expansion of the existing potentialities towards higher outcome. Thus, development and education have common grounds in the process of making human existence worthy and meaningful.

Education is not only an instrument of enhancing efficiency but also an effective tool of augmenting and widening democratic participation and upgrading the overall quality of individual and society. India has a vast population and to capture the potential demographic dividend, to remove the acute regional, social and gender imbalances, the Government is committed to make concerted efforts for improving the quality of education.The process of development and participation are inherently associated. Participation of tribal people in the development process can be enhanced only through a proper educational system. The underdevelopment and backwardness of rural population in general and of the tribal population in particular has been attributed to their low level of participation in the developmental plans and programmes. Changes, though have taken place in tribal areas; the pace of change is very slow and discouraging. Culturally, socially and economically, tribals stand apart from the mainstream culture, for which they cannot keep pace with the development achieved by the latter. Education has been considered as a critical input for economic and social development. It empowers disadvantaged groups with increased efficiency and ability to protect their interest, raise voice against oppression and make them politically conscious. Literacy is the first step of empowerment of an individual; it opens the door to acquire knowledge. It is the pre-requisite factor, which improves human capabilities, enhance increased participation of people in production and thus, establish synergic relationship between human development and social development. The most urgent priority is to ensure access to, and improve the quality of education for tribals to remove every obstacle that hampers their active participation in developmental processes. In recent days "Inclusion" is the progress *mantra* for policy-makers of our country. In this context of inclusive growth, "education" is the best input that can open up opportunity, empower marginalized section, ignite social change and catalyze economic growth.

This chapter presents a framework of analysing the relationship between development interventions and the process of exclusion of various sections of people in an inter-disciplinary perspective. Theoretically, what follows is not the article's attempt at a generalisation, but at providing a structure with which development interventions can be better understood and, therefore, more effectively promoted or opposed, depending on the objectives of each group of stakeholder, planners, bureaucrats, academics, etc.

The long road to self-actualization is interspersed with encounters and experiences with a series of social processes, products and with dynamics of human interaction. With the passage of time, physical prowess, occult power and wealth have steadily been replaced by knowledge as the powerful determinant of human capability, hence, the most valued of all possession. However, the access to knowledge is severely limited if we take into account of marginalized communities across India in general and Orissa in particular. A vast majority of Orissa's poor and marginalized communities are categorized as Scheduled Castes and Scheduled Tribes. In spite of Government support, these communities, especially Scheduled Tribes suffer from series of discriminations and inequalities. As educational development is a stepping-stone to economic and social development, and the most effective instrument for empowering the tribals, maximum efforts were made to improve their educational status. The planned approach to socio-economic development has laid considerable focus on the access and outreach of education at all the three levels—elementary, secondary and higher education. The emphasis has not been merely restricted to literacy, school enrolment and expansion of network of schools and spread of institutions of higher education. A great deal of effort has also been carried out to ensure and improve the quality of education in India. The Eleventh Plan's strategy on education is directed towards achieving inclusive growth. This strategy envisages bridging regional, social and gender gaps at all levels of education by eliciting a participatory development process. The Scheduled Tribes are among the most socio-economically backward community. Thus, the objective of inclusive growth would be fulfilled only if the education and economic status of STs are improved at par with other communities. Nevertheless, it is observed that in terms of access, utilization, and equity in education, the tribal India lags far behind than the other communities. Despite a sharp increase in the share of tribals who enrol in, attend, and complete various levels of schooling, an educational gap remains. Education enlightens mankind and one of the prominent objectives of nation becomes complete when it reaches to remote areas such as tribal peripheries. However, it is well observed that it is not evenly and equally distributed amongst all. Discrimination in the availability of education has created inequality in our society. The tribes of Orissa are confronted today with an extremely complex situation. Lack of education is definitely one of the major problems of tribals in contemporary period.

Nature and Extent of Education among STs in Orissa

The educational development of Scheduled Tribes has been initiated dates back to pre-independence period. Yet it has not yielded satisfactory result. In spite of several constitutional provisions and efforts put in the successive Five Year Plan period by Government, the educational level of tribals in Orissa has not increased significantly. It seems that people belonging to STs, still have to go a long way to come up to the average level in the field of education.

The literacy rates of the general population and ST population from 1991 to 2001 are presented in Table 20.1. The overall literacy rate of the STs has increased from 22.3 per cent in 1991 to 37.4 per cent in 2001. Despite this improvement, the literacy rate among the tribals is considerably below the national average (47.1 per cent). Among ST males, literacy increased from 34.4 per cent in 1991 to 51.48 per cent in 2001 and ST female literacy has increased from 10.2 per cent to 23.37 per cent during the same period. The ST female literacy is lower by approximately 28 percentage point as compared to the overall female literacy of the general population in 2001. Likewise the ST male literacy is lower by approximately 25 percentage point as compared to the overall male literacy of the general population in 2001. Further, the gap between the literacy rates of the general population and STs in 1991 was 26.8. But it has not appreciably decreased in 2001. Still the gap between the literacy rates of the general population and STs is 25.71in 2001.It

Table 20.1 : Literacy Rate of General Population and ST Population in Orissa during 1991-2001

Year	General			ST			GAP*
	Male	Female	Total	Male	Female	Total	
1	2	3	4	5	6	7	8
1991	63.09	34.68	49.09	34.4	10.2	22.3	26.8
2001	75.95	50.97	63.61	51.48	23.37	37.37	25.71

* Shows the gap between the total literacy rates of STs and of the general population

Source : Government of India, Census of India, Orissa, 1991 and 2001, Office of the Registrar General, Bhubaneswar.

is indicating that the literacy drives of the government have not equitably benefited all citizens of the country.

Male-female gap in literacy rate increased from 22.2 percentage points in 1991 to 28.11 percentage points in 2001 for STs while it declined from 28.41 percentage points in 1991 to 24.98 percentage points in 2001 for total population. Nevertheless, the increase in total as well as female literacy among STs is healthy sign for tribal society.

Table 20.2, shows that still all the districts have the ST literacy rate less than the general literacy rate. The Table 20.2 shows that the literacy rate of most of the tribal dominated districts in the State is less than the literacy rate of tribes of State (37.37%) and country (47.10%). per cent. The Malkangiri district has the lowest tribal literacy, i.e., only 14.69 percentage.

The percentage of literacy gap between STs and all population varies from 8.21 to 46.42 percentage points in different districts during 2001. In case of eight districts like Balasore, Bhadrak, Cuttack, Dhenkanal, Jagatsingpur, Jajpur, Kendrapara and Khurda, the percentage of literacy gap between STs and all population is more than the State averages, i.e., 25.71 during 2001.

The Case Study of Koraput

As per the Scheduled Area Order 1977, Orissa is one of the scheduled areas. The order again specifies that Koraput district is one of the major scheduled areas of the State. Koraput was the largest district of Orissa till 1992 (undivided districts of Koraput), and was divided into four districts—Koraput, Nabarangpur, Rayagada and Malkangiri on 2nd October, 1992. The district is located between 18°-13′ and 19°-10′ North latitude and 82°-23′ east longitude in extreme south part of Orissa. It is bounded by Rayagada district of Orissa and Vizianagaram and Srikakulam districts of Andhra Pradesh in the east, Malkangiri district of Orissa and Bastar district of Chhattisgarh in west, Nabarangpur and Kalahandi district of Orissa in the north and Vizianagaram and Visakhapatnam district of Andhra Pradesh, in the south. According to the 2001 Census, the total population of Koraput district is 11,77,954. (5,89,438 males and 5,85,516 females). The sex ratio of the district is 998 females for 1000 males. The density of population is 134 per sq. km. The district ranks 15th among the districts in

Table 20.2 : District-wise Literacy Rates (2001 Census)

Sl. No	*District*	*All Communities*			*Scheduled Tribe*			*Gap in Literacy Rate*
		Total	*Male*	*Female*	*Total*	*Male*	*Female*	
1	2	3	4	5	6	7	8	9
1.	Angul	68.79	81.43	55.37	45.35	60.25	30.05	23.44
2.	Balasore	70.56	81.69	58.90	31.88	45.63	17.69	38.68
3.	Bargarh	63.99	77.41	50.26	50.20	65.87	34.44	13.79
4.	Bhadrak	73.86	84.65	62.85	27.44	38.00	16.43	46.42
5.	Bolangir	55.71	71.67	39.51	43.64	61.96	25.52	12.07
6.	Boudh	57.73	76.23	39.02	46.65	68.29	25.81	11.08
7.	Cuttack	76.66	85.82	66.90	35.75	50.49	20.14	40.91
8.	Deogarh	60.36	73.33	47.18	45.26	59.41	31.23	15.10
9.	Dhenkanal	69.42	80.57	57.89	39.41	53.69	24.66	30.01
10.	Gajapati	41.26	54.71	28.42	27.77	41.60	14.83	13.49
11.	Ganjam	60.77	75.22	46.44	35.54	50.22	20.65	25.23
12.	Jagatsingpur	79.08	88.55	69.28	48.62	59.87	35.91	30.46
13.	Jajpur	71.44	81.89	60.76	31.41	45.48	16.93	40.03
14.	Jharsuguda	70.65	82.16	58.48	57.23	71.86	42.27	13.42
15.	Kalahandi	45.94	62.66	29.28	34.17	51.70	17.15	11.77
16.	Kandhamal	52.68	69.79	35.86	44.47	62.72	26.87	8.21
17.	Kendrapara	76.81	87.11	66.76	40.07	53.52	25.21	36.74
18.	Keonjhar	59.24	71.99	46.22	40.30	54.63	25.97	18.94
19.	Khurda	79.59	87.90	70.36	49.91	65.43	33.07	29.68
20.	Koraput	35.72	47.20	24.26	18.68	29.25	8.38	17.04
21.	Malkangiri	30.53	40.14	20.91	14.69	22.05	7.50	15.84
22.	Mayurbhanj	51.91	65.76	37.84	38.80	54.11	23.51	13.11
23.	Nawapara	42.00	58.46	25.79	33.12	50.69	16.18	8.88
24.	Nawarangpur	33.93	47.04	20.67	24.00	36.86	11.12	9.93
25.	Nayagarh	70.52	82.66	57.64	47.09	64.81	28.83	23.43
26.	Puri	77.96	88.08	67.57	58.72	73.37	42.11	19.24
27.	Rayagada	36.15	48.18	24.56	20.23	31.16	10.07	15.92
28.	Sambalpur	67.25	78.99	55.16	52.67	66.92	38.40	14.58
29.	Sonepur	62.84	78.94	46.17	52.16	69.53	34.29	10.68
30.	Sundargarh	64.86	75.34	53.88	52.75	64.66	40.90	12.11
	Orissa	63.08	75.35	50.51	37.37	51.48	23.37	25.71

Source: Government of India, Census of India, Orissa, 1991 and 2001, Office of the Registrar General, Bhubaneswar.

Orissa in terms of population and contains in it 3.21 per cent of the total population of the State in 2001 Census. The district ranks third in the State and 86th among the district of India in terms of geographical area. It has 8,807 sq. km. total geographical area, which covers 5.66 per cent of the total geographical area of the State. According to 2001 Census, 83.18 per cent of the total population of Koraput district live in rural areas.

The tribal communities are living throughout the length and breadth of the district. 62 types of tribal inhabit the Koraput district. Majority of the people speak the local language of Kuvi, Gadava, and Paraja. However, Oriya language of the State, act as a link language for the people. The major types of the primitive tribes are Paraja, Kondha, Soura, Gadaba, Halva, Bhumia, Koya, Kotia, Pentia, Santala and Bhatada. According to 2001 Census the total tribal population of the district is 5,85,830 which constitute almost 50 per cent of the total population of the district.

The tribes of Koraput have a miserable educational status. Poor socio-economic condition and lack of interest with school education are major reasons for the low enrolment and high dropout rates in the rural and tribal areas. Access to education is denied more often to the girl child, reflected in the female literacy rate. The literacy rates in respect of Scheduled Tribes are still low. The undivided Koraput districts in terms of literacy still occupy the lowest position in Orissa. According to 2001 Census, Koraput district ranks 28th among the total districts (30) in Orissa. The tribal literacy rate is only 8.34 per cent. It is 14.61 for male but just 2.14 for the tribal female, which indicates that tribal female well lag behind their male counterparts (1991 Census). In 2001 Census, the tribal male literacy rate is 29.20 per cent but tribal female literacy is only 8.40 per cent (see Table 20.3).

Table 20.3 : Educational Status of Tribal Women in the District

Year	*All classes*			*Scheduled Tribe*		
	Male	*Female*	*Total*	*Male*	*Female*	*Total*
1991	39.99	15.15	24.64	14.61	02.14	08.34
2001	47.20	24.26	35.73	29.20	08.40	18.90

There are problems relating to high dropout rates also. Various issues like inadequate school infrastructure, high teacher absenteeism, large-scale teachers vacancies, inadequate teaching and learning materials, unsuitable timing of schools, unsuitable school atmosphere are some of the factors responsible for the low educational status of tribal women. The dropout rates in respect of ST total was 63.92 per cent. Among tribal boys it is 59.13 per cent but for ST girls it is very high, i.e., 70.55 per cent.

The Sample Study

This chapter is well supported by a micro empirical study. The attempt is made to study the educational status of tribal people in Ranikona village of Koraput district. The village is located in the Daleiguda Gram Panchayat of Semiliguda Block. Majority of the households of this village belong to the Paraja tribal community. The village has 78 households out of which 70 households belongs to tribal community. The study has covered all 70 tribal households for sample study.

The study was conducted using a combination of qualitative and quantitative methods. Participatory Rural Appraisal is adopted to collect wide ranging information from the tribals regarding their educational status. In view of the present study the researcher has used the interview schedule technique to collect the general information regarding their educational status from field. Data has also been collected on various constraints for educational advancement by using interview schedule. Besides interview schedule, observation has been used in this study as a method in the field to scrutinize the responsibility of various complex social institutions and to understand the socio-economic conditions which play a major role in determining educational status of these people. The information collected in this manner is supplemented with data from other relevant secondary sources like official records of Census, District Statistical Handbook, Official records of Gram Panchayat and Block.

Education is the most important social input for the development of any society. Literacy enhances the awareness level of people and augments the health status of any community. However, this is the most neglected aspect in tribal society. In Koraput district the tribal literary rate is only 18.7 per cent. It is 29.2 per cent for male but just 8.4 per cent (2001 Census) for the tribal female, which indicates that female literacy, is very poor in tribal society. The total literacy rate of the sample village is only 18.12 per cent. The female literacy rates among STs continue to remain a serious cause of concern. Low educational status of tribal community has adversely affected the socio-economic condition of the tribal people (Table 20.4).

Table 20.4 : Literacy Rate of Family Members of Sample Households

Name of village	*Total Literates*			*Total Illiterates*			**Total eligible popul-ation*
	Male	*Female*	*Total*	*Male*	*Female*	*Total*	
Ranikana	16 (9.35%)	15 (8.77%)	31 (18.12%)	63 (36.85%)	77 (45.03%)	140 (81.88%)	171 (100%)

* The total eligible population for the calculation of literates is total population—the population found in the age group of 0-6. Out of the total sample population of 276, 171 are eligible (above 6 years) for the calculation of literacy rate.

Source: Field study.

Barrier in Tribal Education

Despites many steps taken by the government to enhance the educational status of tribes, the Gross Enrolment Ratio (GER), and Dropout rate amongst SC and ST population continue to remain a serious cause of concern. Notwithstanding the fact that there has been an increase in the literacy rates of SCs/STs since independence, the present position is still far from satisfactory. The dropout rates for ST students are much higher than the SC students across the years and sexes.

Lack of education often leads to alienation among tribals which denotes the estrangement of these people from themselves and others. This sometimes include the feeling of separation from other educated mass, discontent with society, dimension of 'powerlessness'—which forces the tribal people to feel that they cannot influence their social surroundings. 'Self-estrangement' occurs when they realize their inability to find activities that are psychologically rewarding.

Some of the major barriers of tribal education are discussed below :

- Teachers absenteeism.
- Heavy dropout.
- School is not an attractive place.
- Curriculum not attractive for tribal students.
- School timing is not suitable to tribal students.
- Language barrier.

- Poverty and backwardness.
- School is at a distant place.
- Lack of awareness of parents.
- Teachers attitude and behaviour.
- Lack of teaching/learning materials.
- Absence of vocational education.
- Social discrimination and exploitation.
- Lack of aspiration and awareness.
- Marginalization in the society.
- Lack of political will.
- Insufficient teaching staff.
- Absence of a balanced, sensible and realist approach.

Suggestions to enhance Tribal Education

The following steps need to be taken to ensure universalisation of primary education among tribal children.

Proper Incentive to Teachers working in Tribal Areas

For addressing the teacher's absenteeism, government should open teacher's hostel in every Panchayat headquarters. Teachers should be appointed where there is a requirement. Proper incentives should be provided to the teachers working in tribal areas. Besides this the higher authorities of education department must supervise and monitor the teacher's work on regular basis.

Reduction of Dropout Rates

Empowerment and regular involvement of Village Educational Committee such as Mother Teachers Association (M.T.A.) and Parent Teachers Association (P.T.A.) are necessary for persuading the parents to send the children to school. The livelihood problems of tribal people must immediately address through various government programmes. Education Guarantee Scheme (EGS) should be reintroduced to facilitate the children of small hamlet for education. Residential schools must be introduced in every village Panchayat. ICDS Centres in every village should properly work to facilitate pre-school learning. The school should have the proper infrastructure like boundary, lavatory, play ground, drinking water facility which will attract the students for education. Awareness campaigning for the parents is vital to reduce the dropout rate in tribal areas. Besides this, mid day meal and health check-up should continue on regular basis. Timely supply of text books, learning materials and school uniforms is also very necessary to reduce the dropout rate in tribal areas.

Joyful Learning in the School

Learning in the schools in tribal areas must be joyful, meaningful and interesting, so that children will develop a desire to go to school. These may include sending students of primary level on a local tour to parks, historic sites, temples, etc., using some techniques like theatre, music, song, dance, skit, puzzles, etc., and promoting sports and games in the school. In tribal areas education must include culture friendly and child friendly materials like the folk stories, tribal dance and festivals, stories of successful tribal leaders, hunting techniques in the course curriculum to make learning enjoyable and to create interest among the tribal children for education. Every school in tribal area should include a period for local games. They must paste the photographs of the local tribal leaders along with national leaders in the school and adopt various joyful methods of teaching to enhance the attendance in the school.

Growing Consciousness

While there is a lot that the government needs to do to provide quality education to its tribal people, an equal responsibility rests with society to do its bit. Various civil societies must work practically to provide education to these backward communities. Apart from teaching community, every now and then—the politicians, bureaucrats, social workers, youth and others should take the responsibility to literate the needy. This growing social consciousness need to be promoted and sustained.

Skill Development

Skill development is a significant mechanism of a nation's knowledge initiative. There is a growing concern today that the education system is not fulfilling its role of building a bunch of skilled manpower, resulting in mismatch between the skill requirement of market and skill base of the employment seekers. As a result many educated people also suffer from unemployment. To address this problem we need to refurbish the system of vocational education and training especially in tribal areas of the country.

Capacity Building Programmes for Teachers

There is a greater need to provide capacity building programmes to upgrade the professional skills of teachers. It can be done through providing motivational and leadership training to teachers. Vocational training programmes should be mandatory for teachers who are serving in tribal areas. As far as practicable the teachers should be trained in local tribal language or dialect to amplify intensive interaction with tribal students.

Mobile School Facilities for Out of School Children

There are some children in tribal areas who cannot afford school education. Due to economic backwardness they are forced to remain in homes or go outside the homes to earn certain livelihood. But they also need education for a better life. Mobile school facilities should be launched to provide education for these out of school tribal children. The training of these children should be fixed by considering their leisure hours.

Greater Decentralization

Management of tribal education needs to build in greater decentralization, accountability and professionalism, so that it is able to deliver good quality of education to all and ensure optimal utilization of available resources.

Conclusion

In one of his early interviews, after resuming office in the Ministry of Human Resource Development, Mr. Kapil Sibal remarked "certainly, I am looking at three issues. One is the issue of access, which means the expansion. The other is the issue of equality, which means inclusion. And the third is the issue of quality, which means excellence. I think I'm going to combine all three to take this country forward". Truly the future roadmap of tribal education has to follow these three issues. Making tribal education a socially inclusive activity is the call of the day. This dimension is important as too many students from ST community are still excluded from education of all levels, due to their low background and other barriers. These disparities foster alienation among them. The blue print to reach the final goal of creating an educated community that is inclusive, firmly based on fairness of access and quality—is to be drawn, the sooner it is the better. As the nation waits with high expectations for legislative formalities to complete, a relook into certain areas of potential threat, particularly with regard to access and equality are relevant. India is actively pushing forward with its agenda for revamping and restructuring education. To move towards a new century of growth and innovation, we need overall progress on all fronts. Education policies should be context specific to enhance access and remove barriers. In this circumstance the introduction of Right to Education Bill is a significant catalyst. We need mindsets with innovative and practical ideas to make delivery of services easier and to create opportunities where they did not exist.

Index